INFORMATION, PLEASE

INFORMATION, PLEASE

By Martin Grams, Jr.

BearManor Media
2003

Information, Please
© 2003 by Martin Grams, Jr.
All rights reserved

Published in the USA by

BearManor Media
P. O. Box 71426
Albany, GA 31708

bearmanormedia.com

Cover design by Joel Bogart
Typesetting and layout by John Teehan

ISBN—0-97145-707-7
978-0-97145-707-2

Library of Congress Control No. 2003101694

TABLE OF CONTENTS

Introduction 1
Standard Opening 3
Dan Golenpaul: The Early Programs 4
Raising Your Parents 6
The Education of Hyman Kaplan 12
A History of *Information, Please* 14
The Canadian Connection 24
Biographies 33
How To Fool the Experts: Bloopers and True Stumpers 39
The Errors of Their Ways 43
The *Informaion, Please* Card Game 45
The First (Two) of Many Lawsuits 47
And The Winner Is... 49
Minority Report: The Quizzers Had Their Say 51
The Lucky Strike Years 54
How The Questions Were Chosen 67
The War Bond Tours 69
The "Lucky Strike Goes To War" Lawsuit 72
The Heinz Seasons 78
The Mobil Season 86
The 1945 *Information, Please* European Tour 90
The Parker Pen Season 93
A Mutual Understanding Gone Bad 97
The Taft-Hartley Lawsuit 100
The Mutual Lawsuit 103
The Final Seasons 106
The Thirteen *Information, Please* Short Films 108
History of the *Information, Please Almanac* 118
The Television Series 128
Television Episode Guide 136
Parting Is Sweet Sorrow 141
Broadcast Log 149
Appendix A: About the Guest Expert 198
Appendix B: Celebrity Letters Received By the Stumpers 201
Appendix C: The Contracts 208
Select Bibliography 238
About the Author 241
Index 242

INTRODUCTION

"Walking Encyclopedia" is the term that had become associated with Clifton Fadiman's board of experts. A literary editor of *The New Yorker* magazine, Fadiman queried three of the country's best-informed people: Franklin P. Adams, better known as F.P.A., noted author and columnist whose "Conning Tower" was a feature of the *New York Post*; John Kieran, Sports Editor of the *The New York Times*, but whose interests were widespread judging by the steady stream of knowledge, which poured from him like tap water. Lastly, Oscar Levant, who shined at the questions devoted to music, but was an authority on other subjects as well being an outstanding composer, arranger and director.

Dan Golenpaul was the genius behind the program's success, an idea man who shared a wealth of knowledge with radio listeners. When he first conceived the idea of the *Information, Please* radio program, he was very down on his luck. He hunted up the wittiest, most literate men he could find for his "experts" and quizzer—a revolutionary notion for radio. At that time, none of the four he found were known outside the small circle of New York's Literati. But three years after the program premiered, Fadiman, Adams, Kieran and Levant were regarded as the smartest people in the country, and Golenpaul was the proud owner of several cars, two homes and all the impedimenta of a radio magnate.

At its peak, *Information, Please* had an estimated audience of fifteen million listeners a week. In the opening scene of the 1941 movie, *Woman of the Year*, Spencer Tracy, playing the role of Sam, sat in a bar listening to *Information, Please* over the radio. Just a year earlier, RKO began releasing a series of movie shorts based on the popular radio program and movie audiences flocked to see their favorite experts answer questions about topics ranging from elements on the periodic chart to the moons of Saturn.

But the radio industry smelled "commercialism" with Golenpaul's intellectual program, and one legal battle after another branded Golenpaul a public hero for attempting to keep his program "honest." Yet he was regarded as a trouble maker to the giants in the broadcasting industry. Eventually Golenpaul's multiple lawsuits and threats to create bad publicity for both the networks and the sponsors ultimately led to the demise of *Information, Please.*

This is the true story behind *Information, Please*, through the eyes and ears of those who participated in the program, and through extensive research (not to mention listening to over 200 recorded broadcasts on audio cassette). A work of this size, obviously, could not have been accomplished without the grateful assistance of many friends: Bhob Stewart, Peter Greco, Ted Davenport, Terry Salomonson, Harvey, Derek Tague, Ben Ohmart of BearManor Media, Jay Hickerson, and a big kudos to Maggie Thompson and Arlene Osborne. I especially have to thank William Abbott who spent a good deal of time and patience gathering material needed for my book; this volume wouldn't be so extensive if it weren't for his generosity.

The purpose of this compilation is to give both the fans of the program and the people who have admired the broadcasts for its valued knowledge, wit and charm, a compilation of information designed to give knowledge and insight behind the legacy of *Information, Please.* Through a series of Almanacs, movie shorts, card games, quiz books and an assortment of recordings that still entertain listeners today, *Information, Please* has held its own for more than half a century. I predict it will continue to hold its own for another half-century.

Martin Grams, Jr.
May 2003

STANDARD OPENING

"Here's how it goes. For every question used, whether or not it's been answered correctly, the sender gets five dollars. If your question stumps our board of experts, you not only get $10.00 more, but in addition you'll receive a current 24-volume set of Encyclopedia Brittanica. Mind you, this is only if your question stumps our board of experts. Our editorial staff may reword your question a trifle; don't worry about it. Whenever there is a duplication of questions, *Information, Please* uses the one that was received first. All questions become the property of *Information, Please*, and should be addressed to Canada Dry, 1 Pershing Square, New York City."

DAN GOLENPAUL:
THE EARLY PROGRAMS

Before the success of *Information, Please*, Dan Golenpaul had been very active in radio as a program builder. He was singularly successful in developing discussion-type programs for major networks. Fully understanding the rewards for both creating and producing successful radio programs, Golenpaul drafted audition scripts, mailed samples and examples to both networks and potential sponsors, and composed a large number of letters. He created and produced the *Magazine of the Air*, one of the first variety shows of its kind with Heywood Broun delivering his own columns, Sigmund Spaeth discussing music, Alice Hughes discussing fashions and Gilbert Seldes as master of ceremonies. *Magazine of the Air* originated from the studios of WOR in New York as early as January of 1934. Two years later in 1936, the Heinz Company began sponsoring the program and it was then that the series took off. But by the time Heinz

came into the picture, Golenpaul had left the series for other ventures.

In 1942, Dan Golenpaul commissioned an audition script in hopes of reviving the program, with Russel Crouse as emcee, Franklin P. Adams as the columnist, Bob Considine as the sports editor (Joe Louis was the guest), Deems Taylor discussing music, and John Mason Brown as the drama editor. The pilot never went any further than the transcription.)

The Forum of the Air was a special program Dan Golenpaul created and produced during his term as Special Events Director at Station WHN (1934 to 1936). The program was broadcast over WHN and originated from the New School of Social Research. A different topic was discussed each week, i.e. Theater, Literature, etc. Golenpaul created and directed this well-received program. Aaron Stein, radio editor of the *New York Post* wrote in his column of March 23, 1936: "Quite apart from our special interest in what was said, we were impressed with the proficient and seemingly effortless staging of a difficult broadcast, and within our hearing it is radio's most marked success to date in the field of free discussion." It is apparent from what little is documented, that *The Forum of the Air* made important contributions in the technique and stylizing of radio rallies, round tables and symposia.

Of course, Golenpaul had created radio programs that never went anywhere, such the odd-ball *Humans and Animals*. But his next creation, *Raising Your Parents*, was an instant success.

RAISING YOUR PARENTS

Raising Your Parents *was a juvenile forum program produced by Paul Wing and Alice White Benson, and presented over the Blue Network as part of the Sunday morning* Children's Hour *program for only one year beginning October 17, 1936 and ending October 16, 1937.* The Children's Hour *was broadcast from 1924 to 1948 under various titles including* The White Rabbit Line *and* Coast to Coast on a Bus.

The idea of the program was to make child-parent relationships a two-way proposition. The material for the program was prepared thusly: children throughout the country were invited to submit their problems with their parents, friends and relatives. (Complaints of parents were also considered.) Each week a number of these letters, representing basic problems, were submitted for discussion in a conference under the supervision of a child psychologist. The conference was attended by a group of children who appeared in the broadcast. Notes of the discussion were taken down by an attending stenographer and formed the basis of the script prepared for the broadcast.

The idea of children discussing problems concerning their relationships with parents was considered an original approach in child study and the method was enthusiastically approved by child psychologists and parent-teacher organizations. The idea was also well received by the press, and an article appeared in the *Parent-Teachers Magazine* which was the official magazine of their organization of two million members. *Billboard* magazine featured a review of the program in their July 24, 1937 issue which said:

"With the exception of one glaring fault this is a swell show. It's humorous, serious, interesting at all times and chock-full of human interest to boot. Title should convey the program's thought, but if it doesn't, it consists of discussions, by kinds, of problems arising from their upbringing and treatment by their parents. It's dramatized by Angelo Patri, but of course, in reverse.

"Milton Cross, the announcer who conducts the show, was an ideal choice, his basso voice exactly the proper contrast to the younger treble. One of the kids reads the question or problem submitted, as a mother to refusing to let her kids go on a camping trip because older boys in the trip drink, or a parent insisting on certain musical studies. Then the various opinions are given by the juvenile counselors from the script.

"The one fault consists of having every one of the juve actors in the studio holler at the same time every time a question is read or every time a telling point is scored. This happens frequently, too frequently, with annoying reactions. Scripting, acting and direction tops."

ANNOUNCER: Well, boys and girls just look what we have here. More mail than I ever saw at one time before on our White Rabbit Bus!

CHILDREN: (ad lib)

DRIVER: Where did all that come from, Mr. Conductor? Are those letters from Santa Claus?

ANNOUNCER: No, they're all directed to *Raising Your Parents*, remember?

DRIVER & OTHERS: Oh yes, etc.

PEGGY: What's *Raising Your Parents* ,Mr. Cross?

ANNOUNCER: Weren't you here last Sunday, Peggy?

PEGGY: No.

CROSS: Well, last Sunday we read some letters from girls and boys who had questions and problems concerning their parents, and our own girls and boys here on the bus tried to answer these problems. And then we invited everybody to let us know whether or not they agreed with our answers. Today we have some replies to our answers last week and some more complaints and problems. And I think we'll try to answer some of them right now.

8 Information, Please

PEGGY: Oh that'll be fun...

CROSS: Of course we realize that some of you parents out there will disagree with the replies given. If you do, write in to us, telling us where you think we're wrong and we'll read your letters, too, and perhaps hear an argument or two of them right here in the studio. But here we go. Here's today's first letter. It's from a boy. "My mother is so careful about the movies. She'll only let me go once a week and then she has to know just what's playing at the theater and what it's about and everything and lots of times she won't let me see something that I want to see. I don't see why I can't pick out my own pictures. Other fellows do and they go more than once a week, too." Has anyone anything to say about that?

GIRL: I have.

CROSS: All right _____(girl)_____ has the floor.

GIRL: Well, my mother always picks out the pictures she wants me to see and she goes to the movies with me, too. I always see good pictures, so I guess my mother knows best.

BOY: Yeah, but how can you tell when you haven't seen the ones—well, the ones you haven't seen?

GIRL: I don't have to see them because I see enough of them that I do like.

ANNOUNCER: This all sounds like double talk. How about being allowed to go more than once a week to the movies?

GIRL: Well, I think maybe that's because this little boy's mother doesn't want him to fail in school. She wants him to have a lot of time to study his lessons.

BOY: Lessons in vacation time? That's a good one!

GIRL: Well, now wait a minute! If you don't learn to save some time for your lessons when you haven't got any, you won't know how to when school starts. You have to practice saving time, my mother says.

The end of each broadcast closed with a similar signature from Milton Cross:

CROSS: And I think this is a good place to stop for today. We'll bring you some more problems next Sunday at this time. In the meantime we'd like to hear from you. If you disagree with the opinions of those whom you've heard this morning, tell us about it. We'll discuss your letters during this period. And if any of you young people out there have a little problem you'd like to air, write it in to us: "*Raising Your Parents* care of the White Rabbit Bus" and we'll have your friends on this program try to answer it.

These sketches originated from the studios at WJZ in New York (NBC Network), and were sustained, which meant there was no sponsor. They were broadcast on Saturday evenings from 10:15 to 10:45 p.m. EST. If the format sounds much like the *Information, Please* broadcasts that would premiere months later in 1938, that's not far from the truth. Milton Cross, who was the host of the program, would become the announcer for *Information*. The idea of having listeners write in was also used (obviously, for a different purpose).

The October 17, 1936 broadcast concerned such topics as...
"Why can't I go out nights?"
"My mother won't give me a bicycle."
"Why doesn't my little sister play with her own friends?"
"I ought to be able to read whatever I like."
And the ever important "I don't think Mothers and Fathers want to talk to you."

The November 7, 1936 broadcast...
"I don't want to go to bed at eight o'clock!"
"I still can't live on my allowance."
"Why can't I go out with older fellows?"

The February 6, 1937 broadcast...
"Why can't a girl play a saxophone?"

"I want to invite boys to my Valentine's party!"
"My friend's a dictator—I want to be a dictator."

The May 22, 1937 broadcast...
"I can't help using slang sometimes."

The June 12, 1937 broadcast...
"Family feuds belong to the past."
"I don't know much about skirts and dresses."
"A promise should be kept."

Reprinted below are letters that represent a cross-section of the youthful *Raising Your Parents* audience, but they all agree on two fundamental points. One, even the youngest child has problems that are serious and sometimes tragic to him which he yearns to confide to someone outside his family. Two, children recognize the cast of *Raising Your Parents* as friends who can help them.

Raising Your Parents,
    I have a little girl nine years old who just can't stop biting her fingernails. Whenever I put bitter or ugly tasting things on her nails she picks them down to the flesh. Does anyone have a suggestion for us? If so, please give it over the air on Saturday, March 20. Her name is Phyllis.

                              Mrs. E.L. Lightner, Springfield, Mass.

P.S. We listen to your programs and think you give some good advice.

Dear Sponsor,
    I am 13 years of age, and in need of advice. My mother sends me to bed at eight o'clock. What time do you think I should go to bed?
                              Yours Truly,
                              Wyndham Morton,
                              Parkersburg, West Virginia

Dear Nancy,

    I like to play G-Men with the members of my club, "The Secret Four." We also have two divisions of it in different parts of the city for those who cannot reach our clubhouse. We are going to give a parade on June 10, 1937. My brother doesn't want me to take trumpet lessons, but I am going to. I play his saxophone and he doesn't like it because when he wants it he can never find it. I also play the violin, piano and clarinet. I am twelve years old. I know that I am a tomboy in every way, but I don't like to play girl's games. Please help me with my problem. Should I give up my idea to become a G-Man?

Your friend,
Mary Heaton

Dear Friends,

    We are a club of eight girls and would like to make a suggestion. We thought it would be nice to have a pin for each of the members of all the clubs. Each club would send in the amount of money required and also the number of pins.

P.S. We like Tommy very much and would appreciate it very much if he would read this letter.

Yours sincerely,
Club No. 30, York, PA

    During the summer of 1937, Dan Golenpaul showed what appears to be his first notion of creating radio programs other than *Raising Your Parents*. A letter dated July 14, 1937, addressed to Bertha Brainard, the Commercial Program Manager of NBC, was typed by Golenpaul, requesting a brief conference to discuss certain activities that he planned to undertake with the agencies in behalf of *Raising Your Parents*. "Aside from *Raising Your Parents* I would like to discuss two additional program ideas that I have been working on that may be saleable. One of these ideas involves the participation of a group of national magazines. I already have acceptances from such publications as *Red Book, Pictorial Review, McCalls, Harpers Bazaar, Cosmopolitan,* etc." Could Golenpaul's other program idea have involved a panel of experts who answered questions from faithful listeners?

THE EDUCATION OF HYMAN KAPLAN

Another of Golenpaul's successful works before *Information, Please* was *The Education of Hyman Kaplan*, based on the book of the same name by Leonard Q. Ross, which originally appeared as short stories in the *New Yorker*. The *Kaplan* series never made it on the air as a regular weekly program – rather as a series of short sketches on Rudy Vallee's *The Royal Gelatin Hour*, one of the top-rated radio programs at that time.

Very little is known about this series, but this excerpt from the December 23, 1937 issue of the *World-Telegram* helps reveal a few facts: "Reading those sketches all these weeks, a lot of us have been wondering why some radio show hadn't wanted to try at least one of them. Arrangements to make them available for radio were made shortly after the skits started a year or so ago. The Vallee hour has been planning this for a month, but delayed because it was difficult to find exactly the right actors. Louis Sorin, who does dialect roles for several radio programs, has been cast as Mr. Kaplan. No plans for Kaplan beyond tonight's skit have been made, but if this one is successful the Vallee hour is sure to use more of them – possibly even as a weekly feature." (Sorin would later play the role of Pancho on radio's *The Cisco Kid*.)

As broadcast over the Rudy Vallee program, the announcer introduced the sketch: "Tonight it is our great privilege to introduce to our audience the amazing person of Mr. Hyman Kaplan, an imaginary character created by Leonard Q. Ross. Some of you may have had the pleasure of meeting this gentleman and his teacher, Mr. Parkhill, through the pages of the *New Yorker*, or through Mr. Ross's recent book, *The Education of Hyman Kaplan*. For the benefit of those who have never met our hero before, let us tell you a few things about him. Hyman Kaplan, a loveable, plump, blonde, middle-aged gentleman is an ardent pupil in Mr. Parkhill's English class in the American Night Preparatory School where he is preparing himself for American citizenship. His unbelievable distortions of the language which he offers in a completely innocent manner have never been equaled."

Apparently four (if not five) scripts exist for this series, but whether all of them were dramatized over the Rudy Vallee program, or just the premiere sketch of December 23, remains unknown. According to internal evidence, the character of Hyman Kaplan was played by radio's character comedian Teddy Bergman, who would later change his name to Alan Reed and voice numerous characters on both radio and television, including that of Fred Flintstone.

This sketch alone—and the fact that Alan Reed was the lead actor – suggests the basis for a later radio program, *Life with Luigi* which starred J. Carroll Naish. Luigi was an Italian immigrant with a sweet and loving disposition, consumed with the hope of someday becoming an American citizen. Luigi also attended night school to learn about America and the proper use of the English language. Alan Reed played the role of Pasquale, owner of the Spaghetti Palace in the Little Italy section of Chicago.

Among Golenpaul's correspondence was the suggestion that the Rudy Vallee program stop presenting the *Hyman Kaplan* sketches after a few weeks. Frank J. Roehrenbeck at the station WHN wrote to Dan Golenpaul on February 24, 1938 explaining, "I read the radio scripts of the *Education of Hyman Kaplan* and liked them very much. Naturally, the possibilities for the use of this material are unlimited. Personally, I feel that rather than use this material on the MGM show [*Good News of 1938*] or some other network show as a part of the program would not do the subject justice, and I would rather see the material developed into a 'Life of the Goldbergs' program, which, as you know, is probably the most successful play of its kind. I may be wrong in my assumption, having read only the attached radio scripts on the subject. However, I feel the possibilities for developing Kaplan into a natural character like Molly Goldberg is a natural, if properly handled. Despite my feeling in the matter, I shall be only too glad to submit the material to the coast if and when you have completed your extension of the option negotiations."

A HISTORY OF *INFORMATION, PLEASE*

The familiar format of *Information, Please* was a far cry from the original concept of its creator and producer, Dan Golenpaul, who confessed that about all that remained of his idea as it had first existed in his mind was the title. For some time prior to the introduction of the program, Golenpaul had been toying with the notion of a quiz program based upon the experiences of people engaged in the business of dispensing information, but finally abandoned it because of a lack of material to sustain public interest for any extended period.

About that time he tuned in to one of the more routine quiz programs and was annoyed to find the smug director toying with a confused contestant, in much the way a cat plays with a mouse. The director's self-satisfied chuckle when the contender fell down completely furnished Golenpaul with the germ of an idea that resulted in *Information, Please* as it is now popularly known, which its producer described as "a quiz program with reverse English applied."

The original notion was to conduct a series of interviews over the air with telephone operators, information clerks and other persons whose duty it was to answer questions of an inquisitive public. Needless to say, emphasis was to be laid on funny questions rather than on funny answers. Although the concept remained intact, the format of the program evolved, even during the first dozen broadcasts.

"It occurred to me while listening," Golenpaul explained, "that perhaps the experts could not hold their own either if placed in the same question spot. This angle suggested the idea of a quiz program in reverse in which the public would present questions and the experts would be required to answer or else. Convinced that this idea would have tremendous psychological appeal, because of every student's hope to 'stump' the teacher or professor with a surprise question, I went about organizing such a program."

It was rather slow work at first. Golenpaul first approached the so-called "mental wizards," but it didn't take him long to realize that their responses, while perhaps accurate, were practically mechanical and that as personalities they offered very little hope from an entertainment standpoint. The search was then linked to authorities in particular fields who had achieved some standing as popular educators or as nimble wits.

Trading bon mots with the likes of Dorothy Parker and Robert Benchley over lunch sharpened Franklin P. Adams' wit and led him to entertain frequent guests, many of whom were convinced to appear on *Information, Please* courtesy of Adams. When his pal Groucho Marx had an entry accepted for an F.P.A. column, Groucho said, "I thought I was Shakespeare."

Franklin P. Adams initially rejected Golenpaul's offer to sign on as a member of the "board of experts." The concept of answering questions from members of an audience did not appeal to him. But Adams was unemployed and needed the money to support his family. So for financial reasons, on June 27, 1938, Adams signed a contract agreeing to pay him $150.00 per weekly broadcast—more if the program became commercially sponsored.

Clifton Fadiman, then a book critic and reviewer for the *New Yorker*, was approached by Golenpaul to be the master of ceremonies for the program, at an agreed $100.00 per weekly broadcast, and more if the program was to stretch beyond the initial summer season, and even more if the program acquired a sponsor.

In April of 1938, Golenpaul produced a demo recording of the program, which included Clifton Fadiman, Franklin P. Adams, Marcus Duffield of the *New York Herald-Tribune*, and Louis M. Hacker, economics teacher at New York's Columbia University. The audition was recorded in the backyard of Gordon Kahn, a high school teacher selected by Golenpaul as the "editor-in-chief" charged with creating the questions. Bill Karlin, then head of programming for WJZ in New York, listened to the record and agreed to give Golenpaul an eight-week schedule during the summer on a short-run basis to determine if the program would be a success or not.

16 Information, Please

With the official go-ahead from Bill Karlin, Golenpaul starting making all the necessary arrangements, including handing Fadiman a contract dated May 10, 1938. (Franklin P. Adams verbally agreed to become the first regular panelist on the program, but didn't officially sign the contract until June 27, days after the second broadcast!) NBC gave a weekly budget of $400 to start, and Golenpaul stretched it out as best he could, even using some of his own funds to cover expenses for the first few weeks.

The arrangement to distribute the prize money came from a $100.00 kitty, established at the beginning of each broadcast. For every question that stumped the experts, $5.00 was rewarded to the person who submitted the question, which came out of the kitty. At the end of the broadcast, the remainder of the kitty went to provide refreshments for the board members. In order to get a variety of questions, Golenpaul placed an advertisement in a New York newspaper, asking readers to submit as many questions as they wanted, with the stipulation that if their question was used on the program, they received $2.00. The prize money was another incentive, thus offering $7.00 total for anyone who stumped the experts.

The questions, for the most part of the first few broadcasts, were actually read by members of the audience in the studio, who were notified in advance that their question(s) were going to be featured on the program. Those unable to make it to the studio (such as a woman in Philadelphia in the premiere broadcast), had their question read by Clifton Fadiman. Allowing audience members to read their questions proved to be a disaster. Many didn't have a loud enough voice to carry over the portable microphone so quite often, Fadiman had to repeat the question for the experts. This policy was dropped very quickly, allowing Fadiman to read all of the questions, regardless of who submitted them.

Golenpaul admitted that the program showed promise, but was a work-in-progress. Initially, the invitation was for listeners to submit as many questions as they wanted to the WJZ NBC studio in New York, but when people started sending in 10- and 12-page questionnaires, Golenpaul had to limit each submission to three questions, which would become the format for the remainder of the program.

This, however, only solved half of Golenpaul's problems; he was still faced with the riddle of how to overcome the handicap of subjecting these experts to manifestly unfair questions such as, "What was the population of Chicago at the turn of the century?" An editorial board was established to check all the questions that would be presented. At the outset, it agreed to eliminate questions of a purely academic nature or of little general interest, and use only subjects that would enlist the interest of average literate persons. Routine treatment of the questions was also avoided. This explains why so many whose suggestions were accepted were sometimes surprised to hear them rephrased in order to offer greater originality and to give the experts more chance for by-play. Current politics, controversies, affairs, etc. were generally taboo. Biblical questions, for the most part, were out too, ever since John Kieran attributed a bit of scripture to "the Bronx version," which brought on a flood of sanctimonious protest.

The important as well as the astounding fact about *Information, Please* was that it was truly unrehearsed and spontaneous. An average of three or four pages of script was used in total for each broadcast, and featured only the announcer opening and closing each broadcast, the sponsor (if any) making its usual spiel, and Fadiman's opening remarks to introduce the evening's board which usually spread across a page or page-and-a-half. Once the preliminaries were completed, and the question cards were brought out, the entire formalities remained unscripted, unrehearsed and completely spontaneous.

In order to achieve the desired results, every effort was made to put the board at ease, so that its members were able to strike the proper note of informality. For this reason, a fifteen-minute "workout" preceded the program, during which a different set of fairly easy questions was run through, to give the "boys" a chance to warm up and evoke a feeling of confidence, a result devoutly wished for but not always realized. This relieved pre-broadcast tension and created a friendly feeling among the panel of experts. It also sent fans in the audience home with the impression of having watched a complete show.

Richard K. Bellamy, columnist for the *Milwaukee Journal*, described the "warm-up" period: "Fadiman kept on asking questions and cracking jokes right up to [a minute before they were on the air], when he suddenly turned to the audience and said, 'We'll be on the air in a few seconds, ladies and gentlemen: just sit on your hands.' Almost before the board of experts had time to start fidgeting, there came the familiar 'Cock-a-doodle-doo' signature—and *Information, Please* was on its way again."

The only one with knowledge of the questions prior to the broadcast was master of ceremonies, Clifton Fadiman, who was presented with a list several hours earlier. On the pages he made marginal notes that guided him, spicing the questions up here and there with salty wisecracks. The other participants were completely in the dark when the cock crowed at the beginning of the program each week.

The star pupils were so far ahead with their witty remarks that the listening audience took to the 'brain trust' as if they were members of their own family. Franklin P. Adams might be described as the "sassy" boy of the class; he had an answer for everything, even though it may not have been the right one, and he argued with the "teacher" at the drop of a hat. Fadiman's chief task was to keep the irrepressible John Kieran confined to the immediate question; he had a way of rambling on and appeared able and willing, if given any encouragement at all, to give the history, scores, birthdays and batting averages of all ball players in the big league since the concept of the World Series began. But Fadiman proved his mettle, for he seemed to take decided glee in dampening the ardor of the brighter pupils, as well as pooh-poohing the more obvious sallies and quips in which the less serious-minded ones so often indulged.

"For me the charm of *Information, Please* lies in this kind of banter," quoted writer Harriet Van Horne. "That a program can be consistently and intelligently entertaining without the services of a comedian, a set of stooges, a band and a girl singer pleases me every time I think of it. If anything, radio suffers from standardization. A good idea is born and imitations take root immediately, most of them festered lilies right from the start. *Information, Please* actually has no imitators, because there are no substitutes for wit and wisdom."

Foreign Correspondent John Gunther knew immediately that Riza Pahlevi was Shah of Persia:

"Are you shah?" quipped Clifton Fadiman.
"Sultanly," answered Gunther.

Fadiman: Mr. Kieran, was that a look of intelligence on your face?
Kieran: Not a bit.

Levant: I like to play with about five million people behind me—on orchestra I mean.
Political Guest: How would you like to have Congress behind you?
Fadiman: Depends on how far behind.

Fadiman: Who traveled in the air for seven hours, 28 minutes, 25 seconds?

Levant: Well, I've been in the air that long.

Fadiman: You've been in the air for longer than that.

By way of refreshing the program and avoiding dullness, guest artists were introduced from week to week: political figures, musicians, columnists, actors and authors. Three considerations were the chief factors in their selection: guests had to have a definite contribution to make to the program, had to have a facile wit or a likable personality, and must be well known.

In spite of all the precautions that were taken to make the board feel at home before the microphone, the usual reaction of most guests was that of extreme nervousness. There were a few exceptions, according to Golenpaul, who pointed out that even such seasoned performers as Basil Rathbone and Lillian Gish found it difficult to feel at home when on the air.

Radio reviewers and news columnists listened with fascination as the weeks passed, and added their own opinions, most of them favorable. The second broadcast of the series was reviewed by *Variety* magazine in May of 1938: "Thanks to the lively scripting, the saucy emceeing of Clifton Fadiman and the droll situations that spontaneously result from the inability of erudite gentlemen to answer questions that presumably they ought to know, this stands out as a pip novelty. Some doubt might arise among the merchandisers of soap as whether the radio audience's I.Q. is equal to the intellectual strain. Probably the program couldn't sell linoleum polish. One the other hand, it should make plenty of friends in families where the bookcase isn't innocent of all finger marks. Fadiman had Franklin P. Adams, Marcus Duffield, Prof. Lewis Hacker and Dr. Paul de Kruif. Every time one of the gents flops, the cash register sounds and $5 is extracted from an NBC kitty of $100 and goes to the propounder of the question. Fadiman sounds like a personality who will click on the air. He's nimble witted, glib and quite a fellah."

In the fourth broadcast, June 7, 1938, John Kieran made his first appearance, billed as the "special guest" of the week, a billing even Hollywood actors didn't receive on the program. Kieran so impressed the audience – not to mention Dan Golenpaul—that he was approached after the broadcast with the offer of becoming the second permanent expert on the board. Kieran accepted and the week after, June 14, Kieran became a permanent fixture on the board (although he didn't sign a contract until July 8, 1938). His fee? The same as Franklin P. Adams: $50 per weekly broadcast, with the stipulation that if the program became commercially sponsored, he would receive $150 per weekly broadcast.

Other guests during the first few months left an impression on the listeners. Howard Dietz, publicity director of MGM Studios received questions about movies. Alice Duer Miller, novelist, impressed the members of the panel by knowing that a batter may reach first base without hitting a ball if he walked, was hit by a pitched ball, stole after a dropped third strike, or was interfered with by a catcher. Howard Brubacker, paragrapher for the *New Yorker* magazine, knew that Olive Oyl was the object of Popeye's affections. (Brubacker, incidentally, appeared on the program despite suffering from a bad cold.) Carmel Snow, editor of *Harper's Bazaar*, became the first woman to appear in *Information, Please*. When Ben Hecht was guest one week, after stumping the experts with a question, Fadiman answered. "An 'alderman' is a humorous name for a turkey. Mr. Hecht, you are the author of many plays. You ought to know what a turkey is." In one of these early broadcasts, after Fadiman gave the final score and total loss from the kitty, one of the guests asked on the air "So what do we get?" and was answered with "not a thing."

The boys felt cheated at one time when Fadiman asked, "What young trio gave promise at best of becoming hams, despite all expectations, by dancing and singing their way to fame?" The answer was the three little pigs. The experts were not amused.

On July 5, 1938, Oscar Levant made his first appearance on the program. As he recalled in his 1965 autobiography, *Memoirs of an Amnesiac*:

"I was approached to go on *Information, Please* after an interview I'd given to Michael Mok appeared in the *New York Post*, in which he called me 'the wag of Broadway.' I'd never listened to the show, but I'd heard about it from Leonore Gershwin's sister Emily. They were talking about F.P.A. and, not having heard the show, I thought that John Kieran must be an interloper, because F.P.A. was then the ultimate in judgment about everything.

"I had met Frank Adams at a luncheon of many celebrities in Bucks County and had talked so incessantly during the entire lunch that F.P.A. finally asked incredulously, 'Is he reading?' I'd still never heard the show the first time I went on it. One of the question concerned Moussorgsky's 'Pictures at an Exhibition.' I happened to know the answer and I unwittingly said some funny things and was hired as a permanent panel member."

On the program, Levant was an expert on music and sports. One reason he got to know so much about music before the program was that John Totten, then the superintendent of Carnegie Hall, used to let Levant attend any performance free of charge. "I've never publicly acknowledged his great gift of freedom of access to those performances," said Levant. "I owe part of my education to his generosity. Because of *Information, Please*, I became pretty well known as a statistician on baseball players and fighters. I had been reading the sports pages since I was six."

With the incentive of prize money, listeners began writing in. Within the first two weeks, a staff member at NBC reported that *Information, Please* was receiving more letters each week than any other radio program. The ratings were growing steadfast, not just because of the fascination of the question and answer discussions, but because listeners had high hopes of hearing their own question read over the air. Even famous people were submitting questions in an attempt to stump the experts. Carloyn Wells, Herbert Bayard Swope and Patricia Collinge were just a few of the celebrities.

On the broadcast of August 23, 1938, Professor Morris Cohen, a formidable name as professor of Philosophy at New York's City College, and one of America's leading philosophers and thinkers, submitted a question to the panel of intellectuals in hopes of publicly stumping them. Fadiman discussed his reputation at great length, emphasized his many achievements, thus making the panel of experts more nervous. What intellectual Gibraltar was this great brain asking them to conquer? Finally, after getting the boys all adither, Fadiman popped the question. "What National League baseball team won the pennant only once?" John Kieran fielded the answer.

John Cecil Holms, co-author of *Three Men on a Horse*, submitted questions about sporting events. Dr. Frank Black of Radio City, orchestra conductor of the air, sent in a musical question, in hopes of stumping Levant. The boys of the Sports Department of the *Daily Mirror* submitted a question identifying the names of athletes. One question was submitted by writer Upton Sinclair, who won $10.00 for his trivia about the New Testament.

Frederic Dannay and Manfred Lee submitted questions every few months (always under the authorship of Ellery Queen) asking who the authors were for a list of specific mystery detectives. Even with at least three attempts, the board proved smarter than Queen. The entire freshman English class of a high school in Bridgeport, Connecticut submitted a series of questions. Ring Lardner, Jr., son of playwright Ring Lardner, submitted questions about the fictional characters in Sherlock Holmes stories.

Hollywood actor Sidney Blackmer submitted questions twice. The first time they were rejected because as Golenpaul explained in a courtesy letter, "they were far too difficult for any expert to answer." On the broadcast of September 17, 1940, Blackmer's second submission made it to the program: "Of the three main bodies of water on which [the U.S.] borders, which forms the longest general coast line and which the shortest?" Someone on the board answered incorrectly the first time, and Blackmer won $15.00 and a set of encyclopedias! Lou Gehrig won the same prize when he asked "Give the order of the first four teams in the American League as of noon today and the order of the first four teams at the close of last season."

"Must you call me an intellectual?" asked Clifton Fadiman with a pained expression. This, itself, was a poser. Fadiman preferred to be billed as a businessman during his occasional appearances on *The Magic Key* program (August 21 and September 11, 1938). Milton Cross was the announcer for both *The Magic Key* and *Information, Please*. On Tuesday evenings Fadiman sat to one side of the studio with his quartet of experts up on a platform with a low table in front of them. Fadiman threw the questions to the lions, usually with a good natured jeer, and then indulged in a bit of heckling. The September 11 broadcast featured Fadiman as master of ceremonies and teamed in a skit with Franklin P. Adams.

Reviewer Leonard Carlton remarked in the September 13, 1938 issue of the *New York Post*: "A major controversy has raged about *Information, Please* since its first broadcast. To date no sponsor has been courageous enough to take on this menagerie of untamed and uncageable intellects. It's a new idea and new ideas are to be regarded with profound suspicion. Fadiman, however, isn't particularly worried about that phase of it."

"They'll come around," Fadiman commented when asked why the program had yet to gain a sponsor. "Sooner or later everyone will realize how badly they've been underestimating the intelligence of the radio audience." Fadiman knew that it was not enough for his quartet to be just learned, smart and witty. "We've got to compete with radio comedians, particularly in showmanship. And that doesn't mean just individual showmanship. *Information, Please* is a team program. I'd be lost without the support of the others and their entertainment sense."

Dan Golenpaul, Clifton Fadiman. Franklin P. Adams, H.V. Kaltenborn, John Kieron, Oscar Levant. November 1940. Courtesy of Photofest.

THE CANADIAN CONNECTION

Before the end of the year, *Information, Please* gained their first of five sponsors. The November 23, 1938 issue of *Variety* reviewed the program's premiere under the new sponsorship:

"Fadiman and his troupe have made a quick claim for attention. And they'll continue to get it. Canada Dry is now paying the bills, in return for which the maker of mixers allows himself a few brief plugs in Milton Cross' best diction. Also a little kidding from the hirelings who saucily

'guessed' that they were now being sponsored. Granted that informality and human embarrassment form the backbone of quiz programs, this one has something else by way of wallop. Fadiman's troupe isn't milk-shy or wilting. They are all extroverts, fresh, crafty and sometimes impertinent. That's a new twist—and hard enough to keep imitation at a minimum. Listeners send in the queries, and if the gang cannot answer, a prize is awarded. This gag is okay. Consumer products depending on big turnover generally cram their stanzas so full of plugging and contests that the listener gets slap-happy enough to buy something. Maybe Canada Dry is trying to accomplish the same end by reverse methods."

With the introduction of their first sponsor, Golenpaul was able to balance the books with a larger budget of $10,000 a week, and a larger incentive. As of the broadcast of November 15, 1938, the prize money changed to $5.00 if submitted to the experts, and $10.00 more if the question stumped the experts. Another noticeable change occurred under the Canada Dry sponsorship. Months after the first Canada-Dry sponsored programs were heard, the policy of announcing the complete address of the submitter changed to the city and state. This policy was enforced when one of the prize winners became "harassed" by a company in the area, who heard their neighbor had won the prize money. A formal complaint was registered against the producer Dan Golenpaul, the sponsor Canada Dry and the National Broadcasting Company.

Whenever questions were submitted to Canada Dry Ginger Ale, Inc., a courtesy letter in the form of a two-page spread was mailed to the submitters.

CANADA DRY GINGER ALE, INCORPORATED
"World Famous for Quality Beverages"
One Pershing Square
New York City

      Thank you for your question,
      We want you to know that it has been forwarded to the Editorial Board upon whose decision depends its possible use on *Information, Please*. As you know, we receive many thousands of questions each week. We deeply appreciate the interest and effort that yours represents...and assure you that every question receives careful consideration.

If yours is chosen for use on *Information, Please* you will be notified immediately after the program on which it is used. Winners, of course, receive their checks after their questions are broadcast. On the following pages you will see photographs of the *Information, Please* experts. Now that you know what they look like we sincerely hope that you will become an even more interested listener to our program.

                        Very truly yours,
                        CANADA DRY GINGER ALE, INC.

The flier was mailed to every fan who submitted a question, the back which included a description of Canada Dry products. Inside, the two-page spread featured photos of Clifton Fadiman, John Kieran, Franklin P. Adams, Oscar Levant and Milton Cross.

The quiz "craze" was starting to sweep the airwaves. By December of 1938, a month into the new sponsorship, Levant had become the third regular panelist, appearing on every other broadcast. *Information, Please* was whirled out of the nebula. Without deviating from the original formula, the show would go into its second year by celebrating a renewal of the sponsor's contract, for even the experts found broadcasting much more fascinating than before.

A review in the February 8, 1939 issue of *Variety* observed: "The editorial board of the Canada Dry program had been 'off' on some of its recent question selections. Tendency of experts to over-argue and over-quip slows down program for non-visuals. Many of the guests mean little, despite the deference paid them by Clifton Fadiman."

As entertainment, the broadcast had once or twice slipped a bit, chiefly because the brand of questions was not up to standard or a guest on the board of experts turned out to be a dud. But as a whole the show had maintained the intelligent pace with which it started. It was generally conceded that the questions did not appeal to the minds of the masses. Nevertheless, when it was recalled that the average intelligence of the radio audience was that of a 12-year-old, it was interesting to note that bright 12-year-olds have been known to put this broadcast on their never-miss list of programs.

Evidence of the program's growing popularity during the first few seasons was found in the fact that the *Information, Please* idea was spreading to other fields. By March of 1939, negotiations for motion picture rights were under way and a leading publisher was already selected to bring out a book based on the questions.

The highlights and hilarity grew with popularity. Harpo Marx (who remained silent in the movies) was guest on one particular week, whistling his way through the program. Lillian Gish impressed the board of experts for answering some of the toughest questions. Russel Crouse, Broadway producer of *Arsenic and Old Lace*, lived within blocks of the NBC Studio and often appeared on the program as a last-minute substitute when a regularly-scheduled guest could not (example: August 1, 1939 when Rex Stout had to undergo an appendix operation). Sherlock Holmes expert Christopher Morley answered questions about mystery novels and fictional detectives with almost 100% accuracy.

On the broadcast of January 3, 1939, Irwin Edmund, Professor of Philosophy at Columbia University, was the latest guest panelist. Fadiman admitted at the beginning of the program that he was once a student of Prof. Edmund for four years, and now the tables were turned.

There were rare occasions when Clifton Fadiman was unable to perform the task of moderator, which gave guest moderators the opportunity to fill in. Franklin P. Adams took over the chore once, and with very little personality compared to Fadiman, although Deems Taylor left a very good impression with the audience. John Erskine, novelist, musician and teacher, got so flustered at his only appearance as moderator that he once read the answers instead of the questions!

When George Kaufman acted as moderator, he asked the experts to sing the last line of three old-time tunes. The experts did their best. "You boys did more than answer the question," Kaufman commented. "You just composed three new melodies." Later that same broadcast, the board was asked to identify six birds by their calls. Cracked Kieran: "We work, while they whistle."

Of course, there were trick questions tossed toward the experts, who felt they were cheated by the question. One such example came from a woman in New York. "What sextet sang their way to fame recently?" The boys pondered and pondered, even making a guess at the Marx Brothers, only to discover the answer was the Seven Dwarfs. (Dopey could not sing.) The panel of experts was not amused.

In August of 1938, Walter Winchell had revealed in his column that he was a frequent listener, but his comments were not as favorable. One week later, F.P.A. commented about his appearances on *Information, Please*.

"Franklin P. Adams once wrote an article about *Information, Please*," recalled Levant, "in which he said that as a pair of veteran newspapermen when he and Kieran had nothing to say, they said nothing."

On January 10, 1939, Walter Winchell attempted to make peace with Franklin P. Adams and the rest of the *Information, Please* crew by printing a special column in the day's newspapers. "We are too busy covering plays, doing columns, broadcasts and keeping Stork Club chairs warm to accept the invitation of Clifton Fadiman to 'guest it' on his *Information, Please* program. But one of these Tuesday evenings we intend accepting. And when we do we'd like to stump Mr. Wise Guy Fadiman for a change, by golly. And dare F.P.A., Oscar Levant, John Kieran and all those other dummies, to identify the following people: Simon Neucome, Joseph Henry, Aza Grey, Maria Mitchell, Joseph Story, and Mary Lyon & James Kent." Fadiman attempted to see if the men could overcome Winchell's challenge, by naming the occupations of the respective list. The experts were able to cover five of the seven, despite Mr. Winchell's confidence and reclaimed its reputation if it had ever lost it.

On the February 7, 1939 broadcast, The University of Michigan chose Myron Wallace, a 21-year-old student, to represent the school. Wallace proved he was one of the brighter students of the institution, and answered quite a number of questions accurately. Myron Wallace, incidentally, would years later change his name to Mike Wallace and become a member of the highly-rated television program, *60 Minutes*. (He was also announcer for radio's *The Green Hornet*.)

The March 11, 1939 issue of *The Saturday Review in Literature* actually included a brief mention of the program's new sponsor in their opening editorial: "Speaking of radio, something has been happening to our favorite radio program. We listen every Tuesday night to *Information, Please* but we can't remember having any information on it since about last November. This is no reflection upon Clifton Fadiman, Franklin P. Adams, John Kieran, or their assorted guests, all of whom carry on with spontaneity, liveliness, and resource; they are as entertaining as ever; but their wit is wasted on a succession of questions which have been approaching the level of inanity. The sponsors seem to like trick questions, such as, 'Name a famous blonde who moved in on a family of three and was obliged to scram.' (Answer: Goldilocks) That one is typical. We neither expect nor desire to repair our neglected education by listening to *Information, Please* but it used to appeal to collectors of miscellaneous, useless, and therefore esthetically satisfying knowledge; now it is just a party game. There must be others who feel as we do, and who would like to see the sponsors put some information into *Information, Please.*"

On March 21, 1939, Moe Berg, catcher for the Boston Red Sox, discarded his basic rule of keeping his intellectual life private when he agreed to appear on *Information, Please.* Berg had been induced to go on the show by baseball officials who wanted to erase the general notion that ballplayers were a bunch of "dese" and "dem" guys. Berg startled hundreds of thousands of listeners by his commanding knowledge. More than 10,000 persons called NBC, the program's producer, demanding to know more about Moe Berg.

Among Berg's correct answers were that "loy" was the ancient French word for "law"; Halley's Comet of 1910 is the brightest comet; Venus is the brightest planet we see; and that poi is the Hawaiian substitute for bread. Dan Golenpaul was even more intrigued by Moe Berg away from his program. "I had a nice relationship with Moe but I knew nothing about him," said Golenpaul. "No one else did either. He sort of withdrew – there was an untouchable quality in his makeup. He was the man who wouldn't talk."

Being spontaneous also proved to be a mistake in many cases. On the March 28, 1939 broadcast, John Kiernan's address was given during the broadcast, and before the end of the week, listeners with quick memories were able to write it down and send fan mail!

FADIMAN: You've heard of Bucarest, Mr. Levant, haven't you?

LEVANT: We haven't been close lately.

On the April 18, 1939 broadcast, Levant was asked to play love songs by named composers such as George Gershwin, but he played somber songs that bordered on "love songs" instead. This prompted Adams to remark "I don't think a girl would have much fun with him."

"The famous names of the time paraded through *Information, Please* as guests," recalled Oscar Levant. "The great George M. Cohan was asked a question about *Uncle Tom's Cabin*: 'What happened to Topsy at the end of the drama?' None of us knew. There was a long silence. Then Cohen said, 'She probably went to her dressing room, took off her makeup and went to the hotel.'"

For the May 2, 1939 broadcast, actor George M. Cohan came through with a few snappers on his guest stint, but was hardly an informative goldmine on the straight questions. The actor got away fast with answers to some queries on vaudeville, but thereafter he was mostly silent, with John Kieran and Oscar Levant carrying the brunt of the defense. As usual, Levant came through brilliantly with bafflers about musical composition, but an error made by Kieran about sports went unnoticed. Answering a question about the "hat trick," Kieran was given a 'correct' when he defined it as a cricket term used when a batter scores 32 runs in a one "over." Although Clifton Fadiman and no one else in the studio seemed to know it, his answer was wrong. This "hat trick" may be accomplished by a bowler in taking three "wickets" (scoring three outs) on three successive balls. It corresponds roughly to a pitcher striking out three straight batters in nine consecutive pitches. The correct answer is that three goals in one regulation ice hockey game is known as a "hat trick."

On the June 20, 1939 broadcast, Gracie Allen, wife of comedian George Burns, remained in dipsy character throughout. When Gracie was attempting to answer a question and Fadiman was about to offer assistance, she remarked, "No, no. Don't tell me." Later, when asked what silk underwear had to do with the recent news, Gracie remarked "Macy's basement."

On July 4, 1939, The National Cash Register Company gave the boys a new register for their program, to replace the previous one that was heard every time the producer rang up $10.00 to a listener who stumped the experts. The company received a small "pitch" on a couple programs as a result.

On July 25, 1939, Maury Maverick, Mayor of San Antonio and former Texas Representative in Congress, appeared as guest on the program. A question, directed to Mayor Maverick by Clifton Fadiman was: "What is the Holman Rule in parliamentary procedure and state instances when it may be invoked." Mayor Maverick paused in deep thought and confessed that he was unable to answer the question. As it turned out, New York's Mayor LaGuardia had submitted the question. Maverick then remarked, "Well, now he's taken a dirty advantage of me!" Mr. Fadiman explained that the Holman rule related to limiting appropriation bills.

By September of 1939, it was reported that hard-working Dan Golenpaul went through 5,000 fan letters which came in each week and, out of the approximate 75,000 questions they contained, had to pick twenty for the show. The number of letters submitted each week, obviously, would grow substantially as the months passed. That same month marked the premiere of the first *Information, Please* short, released in movie houses across the country.

Beginning October 24, 1939, *Information, Please* added a new prize. Besides the usual $10.00 in prize money, if the question stumped the expert, the submitter would win a complete 24-volume set of *Encyclopedia Britannica*. This was through a special arrangement between Dan Golenpaul, the producer, and the publishing company. For the company, it was free advertising at the cost of an average of three sets of encyclopedias each week. For Golenpaul, it was a necessary incentive to encourage listeners to submit questions. The first to win a set of *Britannica* on that date was Prisoner Number 12,973 at the Connecticut State Prison. His poser: "This man was an Assemblyman, Assistant Secretary of the Navy, Governor, and President of the United States." The answer was Theodore Roosevelt. Guest Louis Untermeyer and the others incorrectly said Franklin Roosevelt.

The broadcast of November 14, 1939 marked Canada Dry's first anniversary and the broadcast originated from a ballroom in the Waldorf Astoria, with an attendance consisting of many former guests of *Information, Please*. During the sponsor's speech in acknowledgement for the anniversary, he made a mistake by calling Dan Golenpaul "Donald Golenpaul." Milton Cross couldn't make it to the microphone for the middle commercial because he was busy eating cake.

Postmaster General James A. Farley was the guest that last evening, with the result that he was still national chairman of the Democratic party, and possibly an authority on the history of anesthetics. James Farley was asked several questions that dealt with the postal service. All of these drew no response from Farley, but were answered correctly by members of the team. Then Clifton Fadiman, interrogator of the program, asked for the name of the inventor of anesthesia. "Dr. Crawford Long," said Mr. Farley. As a result, the team of question-answerers came through with the first perfect score since the program appeared under commercial sponsorship a year ago.

What even the most faithful of the *Information, Please* audience didn't know was that after the broadcast was over, Clifton Fadiman undid another sheaf of questions, some new, some missed at previous sessions. This time, physicist Bernard Jaffee knew what kind of fathead (a type of fish) might properly be boiled in oil. Deems Taylor remembered of what musical composition a baby's cry reminded him (Richard Staruss's *Domestic Symphony*). Moe Berg identified Garibaldi's *Carbonari*. Russel Crouse still thought the football team suggested by the ocean was C.C.N.Y. (book answer: Tulane's Green Wave). Lillian Gish remembered her Browning better. Clifton Fadiman even asked a new question: "Identify the contemporary ruler or political bigwig who is a bastard's son." Oscar Levant's candidate was Adolf Schickelgruber. A woman in the audience disagreed, and she was right. Hitler's father was legitimized before Adolf was born. "Wasn't he really?" queried Fadiman, glancing owlishly around.

On the January 2, 1940 broadcast, *Radio Guide* magazine presented an award on the air to *Information, Please* for being voted as "the best program of 1939." Martin Lewis, Associate Editor announced: "I am here tonight to present to *Information, Please*, the Radio Guide Award for the Outstanding Program of 1939. Mr. Fadiman, I am happy to have this opportunity to express the appreciation and thanks from the millions of listeners who each week are delighted by the graciousness with which you handle your experts. Marvel at the vast font of knowledge contributed by John Kieran. Welcome the puns and charm of Franklin P. Adams. Enjoy the remarkable musical ability and wit of Oscar Levant. And appreciate the opportunity of meeting outstanding personalities from week to week. *Radio Guide* also desires to give recognition at this time to Dan Golenpaul, who created *Information, Please*, a program which has set a high standard for all radio entertainment. We wish particularly to give credit to Canada Dry, which respected these high standards and has done everything to maintain them. Mr. Fadiman, will you therefore accept this plague on behalf of everyone who has contributed to the success of *Information, Please*, Radio Guide's selection as the outstanding program of 1939."

Later that same evening, John Kieran predicted that the New York Yankees would win the World Series for 1940, a noble prediction since the Yankees won the last four years (1936 to 1939), but would be proven wrong later that year when the Yankees failed to make it to the Series.

On July 16, 1940, actor Monte Woolley was guest. Woolley was in New York at the time starring in the Broadway smash hit, *The Man Who Came to Dinner*, at the Music Box Theater. As soon as the questions stopped, Woolley had to rush off to the theater, where his waiting audience had been listening to him prove he was just as much a wit on the program as in the play itself via a loud speaker.

BIOGRAPHIES

CLIFTON FADIMAN was nicknamed Kip because once as a youngster he had the hiccups for several days and a syllable sounding like that was his sole conversation. On *Information, Please* he enjoyed ribbing author-guest stars whose books he had panned as the *New Yorker*'s critic. When George Kaufman guested, Fadiman asked: "What was outstanding about your play, *Deep Tangled Wildwood*?" Kaufman didn't know. "It flopped," said Fadiman.

"When I opened and read the first page of a book for the first time, I felt this was remarkable," recalled Fadiman years later, "that I could learn something very quickly that I could not have learned any other way." His quick deliveries and compliments toward the members of the board were sharp and to the point. On the rare occasion that he was unable to perform his duties as master of ceremonies, the position was substituted by another. George S. Kaufman substituted twice, John Erskine once and even Marc Connelly was master of ceremonies for one broadcast. Franklin P. Adams was a last-minute replacement and failed so miserably that Golenpaul insisted Adams remain with the brain trust. Deems Taylor was perhaps the best of the substitutes, occasionally making a jest here and there, and was the closest to Fadiman's personality.

Years after *Encyclopedia Britannica* made an agreement with the producer of the program, Dan Golenpaul, to literally give one complete set of the Britannica to any listener who was able to stump the experts, Fadiman was approached by the editorial board to become a consultant and contributor to the Britannica. He wrote informal essays for *Holiday* magazine for ten years, abandoning the column when he discovered to his horror that "I had written more essays than Charles Lamb."

"Cheese – milk's leap toward immortality."
—Clifton Fadiman

"When you travel, remember that a foreign country is not designed to make you comfortable. It is designated to make its own people comfortable."
—Clifton Fadiman

"For most men, life is a search for the proper manila envelope in which to get themselves filed."
—Clifton Fadiman

FRANKLIN P. ADAMS, best known as Frank to his closest friends, was known as "F.P.A." under the byline of the *New York Post*'s popular "Conning Tower" column. He had top writers vying to contribute to his "Conning Tower" where he also supplied his own crisp, humorous verse and wide-ranging commentary. On a regular basis he substituted a diary of his doings on the New York literary scene, in a style parodying 17th-century English diarist Samuel Pepys. Well-remembered for his 1910 verse "Tinker to Evers to Chance," Adams could recite classical works of poetry, Latin poets and nursery rhymes so well that frequently guest experts would comment over the air how impressed they were with his intelligence.

In one particular broadcast, however, Fadiman asked Adams to name the author of a quip so famous as to have become a byword. "Who wrote this?" "I haven't the faintest idea," puzzled Adams. "Who did?" "You did," said Fadiman. The audience roared.

When reporters were not taking pictures, Adams handled cigars with ease, even during the broadcasts on stage, regardless of the studio policies. He was an expert at tennis and pocket billiards, though his favorite game was poker. Adams played the harmonica, was a fan of the Gilbert and Sullivan operettas, and said he never went to the movies. In one of the early broadcasts, Adams claimed that his favorite film was *Soldier Arms*, a silent comedy starring Charlie Chaplin—which became the subject of a recurring joke on the air for many years.

When asked how he came to have so much knowledge, Adams explained, "I find that a great part of the information I have was acquired by looking up something and finding something else on the way."

"To err is human. To forgive, infrequent."
—Franklin P. Adams

"When the political columnists say 'every thinking man' they mean themselves, and when candidates appeal to 'every intelligent voter,' they mean everybody who is going to vote for them."
—Franklin P. Adams

JOHN KIERAN was termed a living encyclopedia and by 1947, became involved in editing and writing the *Information, Please Almanac*. An expert on sports, Greek mythology and birds, he was able to answer questions that would normally have taken the average listener five minutes to look up in a book. He loved nature so much that his enjoyment of the scenery continually interrupted his golf game. Finally one day, he threw away all his clubs except for his midiron, playing the entire course with it, which took 95 strokes. Kieran was the encyclopedic brain of the "expert" battery, and claimed he had only seen two movies in his life, as reported twice over during the broadcasts: *The Gold Rush* and *Goodbye, Mr. Chips*. One critic commented "his camera and radio performances are reminiscent of Mickey Rooney."

John Kieran knew his Shakespeare and listeners often wrote in trying to see if they could stump him on a quote from one of the Bard's plays. Always making sure that he knew the answer before speaking out, Kieran never answered unless he was coached into it by Fadiman, or if no one else on the panel wanted to give it a shot. Kieran concealed his talents from the radio audience by denying he could play the piano or organ, even stating that he never took lessons. While it was true that he never took lessons, when he was alone with his closest friends Kieran played the piano and sang tunes. Off-stage Kieran was a humorist, literary critic and an authority of social, political and economic questions.

OSCAR LEVANT was superstitious. Someone gave him a shirt which he wore to the broadcast of July 5, 1938 (his first appearance on the program); it gave him the confidence to be a success. He wore the same shirt to every broadcast thereafter. Fadiman once suggested that Levant insure the clothing because if Levant lost his shirt, there would be no telling what would happen.

Levant was attracted by bookies, showgirls, gangsters, and Gershwin. While rapidly ascending on wings of talent and wit into the highest circles of New York popular music, Levant seemed nonetheless to have made time to attend concerts, recitals and opera, hearing the leading artists of the day. The only member of the board of experts to attend the movies every week – and quite often – he was able to answer the majority of the questions relating to Hollywood films and movie stars. Levant publicly admitted the reason he attended the movie houses every week was because he could deduct the costs from his taxes!

FADIMAN: Who actually said the phrase 'let them eat cake'?

LEVANT: Well, it was ascribed to Marie Antoinette by MGM.

On December 10, 1939, Levant played Gershwin's "Rhapsody in Blue" under Canadian conductor Wilfred Pelletier for the CBS radio program *The Ford Sunday Evening Hour*. By late 1940, Levant had finished two orchestral works: "Caprice for Orchestra," a nine-minute piece conceived for Robert Russell Bennett's radio program, and "Overture 1912," also known at various times as "A New Overture and Polka for Oscar Homolka." The latter was premiered by Frank Black and the NBC Radio Orchestra in late 1940. "Caprice" would subsequently be promoted by conductor Sir Thomas Beecham and performed in Minneapolis, Pittsburgh, Rochester, and St Louis. Later, it would often be conducted by Levant himself. It was through Levant's insistence that Sir Thomas Beecham make an appearance on *Information, Please*, and Frank Black even sent in a musical question in hopes of stumping Oscar Levant.

During the December 1940 broadcast of Robert Russell Bennett's radio program over WOR in New York Levant gave the premiere of a short solo work, "Poem for Piano," renamed by Levant as "Insult for the Piano or The Lone Ranger in Vienna." After the performance, Bennett interviewed Levant: "I wonder if you remember the impression the work made on its first performance?" Levant replied, "Violently. It not only brought me obscurity but many enemies."

"Underneath this flabby exterior is an enormous lack of character."
—Oscar Levant

Levant, a musical-know-it-all, wrote a sell-out book, *A Smattering of Ignorance*. At a publicity appearance for the book, he played a snatch of music. "You know it?" Levant asked the audience. "Yes," they chorused. "Good," said Levant. "I don't." Playing the audience was what he did best, though his sharp wit and off-hand criticisms during *Information, Please* occasionally got him into trouble, and was guilty of professional discourtesy to Eddy Duchin in a 1939 broadcast, which received brief mention in the papers.

In 1936, Levant supplied the music for the 20th Century-Fox mystery, *Charlie Chan at the Opera*. On April 4, 1944, Levant played the "Gershwin Concerto" on radio, with Toscanini and the NBC Symphony Orchestra. In the summer of 1945 he appeared as himself in the Warner Brothers film *Rhapsody in Blue*, a loose-fitting biography of George Gershwin. Levant could also be seen playing the same concerto in the 1947 20th Century-Fox film, *You Were Meant For Me*. In the 1949 MGM film *The Barkleys of Broadway*, Levant was seen playing excerpts from Tchaikovsky's "Piano Concerto No. 1," and Khachaturian's "Sabre Dance," a recital and recording favorite of his. Both works offer unusually good aspects of his technique. In *An American in Paris* (1951), Levant plays every instrument in the orchestra during a fantasy concerto.

FADIMAN: (After Levant answered movie questions) Mr. Levant, you do go to the movies, don't you?

LEVANT: They come to me, too.

"Behind the phony tinsel of Hollywood lies the real tinsel."
—Oscar Levant

"Happiness isn't something you experience. It's something you remember."
—Oscar Levant

"I am no more humble than my talents require."
—Oscar Levant

"I envy people who drink. At least they have something to blame everything on."
—Oscar Levant

"I'm going to memorize your name and throw my head away."
—Oscar Levant

"The only difference between the Democrats and the Republicans is that the Democrats allow the poor to be corrupt, too."
—Oscar Levant

HOW TO FOOL THE EXPERTS: BLOOPERS AND TRUE STUMPERS

Don't look now, but how many times is the numeral "1" used on a dollar bill to indicate its denomination? What letter of the alphabet is missing on the telephone dials? Which traffic light is on top, the red or the green? If these simple questions stop you cold, don't apologize for a low I.Q. These same questions have stumped some of the greatest "experts" of the twentieth century. Economist Leon Henderson didn't know that the number "1" appears nine times on the dollar bill. Author Christopher Morley failed to recall that "Q" is the only letter absent on the telephone dial. And automobile-maker Henry Kaiser's face went red when he incorrectly stated that green occupies the upper position on the traffic light.

Although Clifton Fadiman's brain trust—Franklin P. Adams, Oscar Levant and John Kieran – enjoyed the reputation of knowing almost everything, they were stopped almost 2,000 times before the program went off the air. Everybody enjoyed seeing the masterminds take a tumble, and that's why Americans sent in thousands of trick questions in the unceasing war of wits.

On one particular broadcast, John Kieran was able to recite Shakespeare line by line at the request of Fadiman. Yet, when one Midwestern housewife asked interlocutor Fadiman to quiz Kieran on the birth date of Mrs. Kieran, the living library was stumped! Franklin P. Adams was bowled over when one of his fans submitted a poem, specifying that F.P.A. could identify it. He admitted that he didn't know. The poem as it turned out, was his own and originally appeared in his column, "The Conning Tower," several years before.

"It was upsetting when Clare Booth Luce appeared as a guest with us in Baltimore at the time, when, as a Congresswoman, she had incited the wrath of President Roosevelt," recalled Oscar Levant. "Bright as she is, the questions simply weren't geared for her. She was very well informed about politics and should have made a better showing." When asked to mention a character from a stage play who portrayed a member of the German diplomatic corps in the U.S., letter-perfect Luce was stumped. The character, she learned to her chagrin, was in her own play, *Margin for Error*, then doing big business on Broadway.

Guest celebrities included Gene Tunney, Stuart Chase, Sinclair Lewis, Will Durant and hundreds of other "Who's Who" folk. While many of these luminaries performed admirably, scores of them flopped miserably. James Roosevelt, son of President F.D.R., for example, appeared on the show and a bright quizzer submitted a quoted comment on current affairs, requesting Jimmy specifically identify its author. Jimmy was nonplused. To his embarrassment he learned that the quote came from his mother's syndicated column, "My Dad" and had appeared in the newspapers only the day before!

When Sing Sing warden Lewis E. Lawes was asked to supply the name of a man who had served time as a common criminal in a New York State penitentiary, then became a warden of Sing Sing prison, he was stumped. The answer was Thomas Mott Osborne who, in October 1913, entered Auburn Prison disguised as a convict and served one week in order to study prison conditions before being appointed warden at Sing Sing.

Rex Stout, famed mystery writer and creator of the fictional detective Nero Wolfe, a culinary crook-catcher, appeared on one program amid a fanfare that touted his latest book, *Too Many Cooks*. On the same program Stout, the armchair chef, was asked to name the savory dish that would result from a given list of ingredients. Stout fumbled and gave up. The recipe, Fadiman told the author faster than he could flip a pancake, had been culled from Stout's own book!

Questions involving simple powers of observation most frequently knocked the mental marvels off their five-foot shelf. When one ingenious contestant asked the experts to name the congressmen of their respective districts, the oracles were silent. Then on different occasions, the wise guys of the air failed to remember their home telephone numbers, their social security numbers, their automobile license numbers and other personal memoranda!

Think you could do better? Then see if you can answer this question, which baffled James Farley and Alben Barkley, as well as the regulars. "If the inscription on a penny reads one cent, what words indicating their value are stamped on the nickel, dime and quarter?" A nickel reads five cents; a dime reads one dime; a quarter reads a quarter dollar. If you survived that one, test your powers on this lulu, which stumped the wizards of wit and guests Sir Thomas Beecham and Cornelia Otis Skinner. First, put your hands behind your back. Now, starting with the shortest, name your fingers in order of length. Very few people ever guess the exact correct order, which is thumb, little finger, index finger, ring finger and middle finger.

Harold Stassen and William Beebe were stumped when asked, "What routine function does the average person perform daily that involves seven arc-like motions of the index finger?" The answer was dialing the telephone.

Early in the summer of 1942, when the experts had gone through an entire program without a single miss, it took an eleven-year-old quiz kid to stump them. Little Reyna Cooper of New Haven, Connecticut asked, "If the Commissioner of Baseball died and the two major leagues had a tie in the vote for his successor, who would cast the deciding vote?" It was a tough one and famed Kieran, the show's expert on "Bees, birds and batting averages," should have known. It cost the brainy team an encyclopedia set and a war bond to learn the answer—the President of the United States!

Now this isn't to say that the experts were wrong all the time. Sometime during the first two years of the series, the panel was asked for the life expectancy of an elephant. Kieran answered this question as "120" and protested when Fadiman rang up the register. "Sorry John," Fadiman said. "You're wrong. It's 140 according to the *World Almanac*." As a matter of fact, as naturalists the world over were quick to point out, the

World Almanac was wrong on this occasion. Though the sender got cash and credit for a stump, the experts knew better than the books.

"I myself attended an *Information, Please* broadcast [c. 1945] and watched the experts strut their stuff," recalled columnist Mort Weisinger. "I noticed one fact. While Fadiman was busy introducing the question, the experts would all study the audience, or keep an eye on the clock. The next day I mailed in my own question. It was accepted and when Fadiman read it over the air it went like this: 'The next question, gentlemen and Miss Barrymore, demands your closest attention. It cannot be repeated. It comes from Mr. Mort Weisinger, of Great Neck, New York, and is divided into two parts. The first part: what is the name of the author of this question? The second part: where does he live?' Not a soul could answer."

A similar stunt was pulled in a Canada Dry broadcast when a listener submitted a question, asking the experts to repeat the opening lines of each *Information, Please* broadcast that was recognized as the signature opening. No one could answer, "Wake up America! Time to stump the experts!"

When Randolph Churchill was a guest, he was supposed to be an authority on United States geography. When he was asked to name a river that divided two New England states, he replied with great authority, "The Delaware." Scientist Paul de Kruif, author of *Microbe Hunters*, did not know that "rubeola" was the name for measles. Stuart Chase did not know that "multiple shops" was British for chain stores. Playwright George Kaufman did not realize that the distinctive thing about his and Marc Connelly's play, *Deep Tangled-Wildwood*, was that it flopped.

On the broadcast of January 2, 1940, when asked who the author of *Rebecca of Sunnybrook Farm* was, none of the panelists knew the answer. Gloria Stuart, guest for the evening, admitted her embarrassment on the air for not knowing, when Fadiman pointed out that she actually played the role of Gwen Warren in the 1938 film of the same name!

THE ERRORS OF THEIR WAYS

Some questions wrongly answered on the program prompted letters from faithful listeners asking that the incorrect answer be amended. On a number of occasions, the letters were so overwhelming that the following week, Clifton Fadiman was given the chore of explaining the mistake, and setting right that which was wrong.

John Kieran made an error in an answer about baseball on one broadcast, giving the wrong name of the town in which the game was supposedly played. Apparently, according to Fadiman, 724 letters were brought to Golenpaul's attention before the end of the week.

In October of 1938, a sports question was asked and someone made a mistake regarding 10 men on a lacrosse team. This mistake was corrected by Fadiman before the program went off the air, because NBC was being swamped with phone calls.

On March 14, 1939, the question was asked: "Can you name the presidents of the colleges at which the following are the football coaches?" The wrong name was given for the President of the University of California, so Fadiman was forced to make the correction at the beginning of the next broadcast, admitting that they were wrong. This was apparently brought to his attention, as according to Fadiman, "the entire population of California apparently contacted us almost immediately after the broadcast."

On the broadcast of December 26, 1939, a question came about asking to name titles of books or plays in which there were only male characters—no females whatsoever. Adams remarked Eugene O'Neill's *Emperor Jones* and Fadiman accepted the answer. Shortly after the broadcast, a woman phoned Fadiman at the studio to inform him of the error, claiming she was an actress, and played a role in the very same play.

On May 22, 1942, the board of experts rejoiced at having a perfect score, and answering all of the questions correctly. Soon after, their rejoice turned to sorrow when they learned that one of the evening's questions, submitted by Mr. J. Burn from New York should have earned him a $50 Savings Bond and a set of *Encyclopedia Britannica* for his question about U.S. Presidents. Apparently they had made a slip in one of the answers.

On the September 10, 1940 broadcast, author Jan Struther answered the famous quotation, "What is better than rubies?" with "a virtuous woman." A great number of letters came in to her defense, because Fadiman had not accepted the answer. The answer he was asking for was "wisdom" from Proverbs 8:11. Fadiman stood vigorously on his answer, explaining the situation on air a month later (October 8), hoping his explanation would calm down the letter writers who were still upset over the verdict.

The broadcast of September 10, 1940 also marked Jan Struther's first of many appearances on the program. She was guest on at least eighteen broadcasts between 1940 and 1945. Struther was the author of *Mrs. Miniver* and delighted the experts with her charm, and ability to take a wisecrack—as well as give it back. Struther, however, was dropped abruptly years later after innocently answering an Agatha Christie question by using the English title *Ten Little Niggers*, released in the U.S. as *Ten Little Indians*.

On the broadcast of February 7, 1939, Fadiman announced another correction. In a previous episode from the weeks past, Cornelia Otis Skinner said "peeping" was a crime and Fadiman as the judge and jury did not accept it. Subsequent weeks, however, brought in a deluge of letters from attorneys disputing the ruling, claiming peeping was a crime, so Fadiman conceded.

Even though the United States was not at war with Japan at the time, very few letters arrived at NBC over a comment said on the broadcast of June 20, 1939. Foreign Correspondent John Gunther, when commenting about John Hay initiating the Open Door Policy, remarked over the air that "the Japanese closed it, a friend of mine said, so you can't even see a chink in it."

THE *INFORMATION, PLEASE* CARD GAME

As a promotional giveaway, Canada Dry arranged for a card game allowing fans of the program to play *Information, Please* at home with friends (of course, with the suggestion to have Canada Dry on hand for the gatherings and get-togethers). The card game contained enough questions to make up four full programs of *Information, Please*, numbered in the order in which they should be used. It was suggested that someone with a quick wit should be selected to play the part of Clifton Fadiman, who asked the questions on the program. The answers were printed on the cards, but in any case, the moderator was suggested to use their discretion in the judgements.

The moderator asked the questions clockwise and if an "expert" failed, they were fined ten points. The same question was then asked of the next expert. If none could answer it, the moderator was to start on a new question. When all questions on any single program had been asked, the person with the fewest points against them won the game. Like the radio show, the card players were instructed to collaborate if the question contained more than two parts. If the question was composed of one or two parts, both parts were to be answered by one person.

Extra copies of the card game were available for those who already purchased theirs, by simply sending the large label from two bottles of any Canada Dry Beverage and 10 cents to cover handling and postage to Canada Dry Ginger Ale, Inc., One Pershing Square, New York City.

Questions that were featured in the card game included:
- Name three sets of fathers and sons who have held high positions in the United States Government.

Answers: Roosevelts (Teddy Senior and Teddy Junior), Clark (Champ and Bennett Champ), Wallace (Henry Senior and Henry Junior), Adams (John, John Quincy and Charles Francis Adams).

- Name four ex-sovereigns, each of whom is now a "Man without a country."

Answers: Haile Selassie, Wilhelm of Hohenzollern, Alphonso of Spain and the Duke of Windsor.

- Name four comedians of the talkies who never talk, but who roll the audience in the aisles.

Answers: Charlie Chaplin, Harpo Marx, Charlie McCarthy, and Dopey.

- Define all of the following words: oca, ochre, okra, okum and okapi.
  Answers in order: A South American potato, a type of yellow clay, a green vegetable, a form of pitch used by sailors, and a rare African animal.

By February of 1939, a second edition of the card game was made available, with four times as many questions as the last one. The cost was still ten cents postage, and 2 bottle caps or labels supplying proof of purchase.

Other *Information, Please* premiums were starting to flood the market. In May of 1939, Simon & Schuster released a hardback collection of thirty-five "sessions" of ten questions each with challenging multi-part questions similar to those heard on the show. The *Information, Please Quiz Book* was available on newsstands and featured an introduction by host Clifton Fadiman, and producer Dan Golenpaul.

Later that year, Canada Dry produced a twelve-page booklet called *A Party Book for Adults* which included questions geared to special events (birthday parties, costume parties, etc,) as well as the inevitable sponsor plugs. This was another giveaway with the cost of bottle labels and sufficient postage. The questions featured in these books, giveaways and card games were the same questions submitted by listeners. Remember that the clause in each broadcast stipulated that all submissions "became the property of *Information, Please.*"

THE FIRST (TWO) OF MANY LAWSUITS

Months after *Information, Please* premiered on the radio, Dan Golenpaul found himself involved in the first of many lawsuits because of his intellectual program. A woman named Peggy Decker claimed she created a program along similar lines on WRNL, Richmond, four months before NBC started to broadcast its own version. Her program likewise offered to pay a prize for any question that she and her associated experts could not answer. In the fall of 1938, Peggy Decker brought the matter to NBC's attention. Later she retained Julian T. Abeles as counsel to press the matter. NBC at no time denied the claim, and after a couple of months of inquiry and discussion with all concerned (including Dan Golenpaul), the network submitted a settlement offer. In March of 1939, the priority claim made by Peggy Decker had been settled by NBC through a cash payment of $1,500. The agreement also arranged for Miss Decker to become a freelance continuity writer in New York for various radio programs, including *Information, Please*!

On March 12, 1940, an injunction restraining the publication of a magazine called *Information, Please* was granted by Supreme Court Justice Carroll G. Walter on application of Golenpaul Associates, stagers of the radio quiz program. Against complaints of the owners of

a magazine of the same name, published two years before the radio program was broadcast, Ann and Daniel Golenpaul instituted a suit, restraining the two principal defendants, Stanley S. Boressoff and Information Publications Corporation, from using the name for a magazine they proposed reissuing for publication (obviously to cash in on the program's name). The court held that the defendants had lost their right to the name after the magazine ceased publication about two years before the radio production started. Mr. Boressfford was the principal stockholder of the corporation and during that tenure, published two issues of the magazine under the title *Information, Please* in September and October of 1936. These were the only two issues printed and published.

At the trial before Justice Walter the defendants contended that they had a prior right to the title, but the court held that this right had been lost through disuse. He added that it was doubtful whether the publication of the two issues was sufficient to cause the title to be associated with the business of the defendants. "The evidence clearly established that such association had been terminated and disappeared long before the plaintiffs in good faith adopted that title for the radio program," Walter said.

AND THE WINNER IS...

In February of 1939, the radio editors of *United States and Canada* magazine voted *Information, Please* as the best radio quiz program. In April of 1939, the Women's National Radio Committee selected *Information, Please* as being the "Best Quiz Program on the Air." In April of 1941, the "Star of Stars Poll" in *Movie Radio Guide Magazine* revealed *Information, Please* as the winner of the National Awards for "Best Quiz Show" *and* "Best Educational Program." In February of 1941, the radio editors of *America* and the *New York World-Telegram* elected *Information, Please* as their "Favorite Quiz Program of the Year." In May of 1942, *Movie and Radio Guide* awarded *Information, Please* the "Best Quiz Program on the Air" for the fourth year in a row.

It was also selected by the editors of *The Saturday Review* to receive an award for "Distinguished Service to American Literature." Presentation of the award, a hand-carved and inscribed plaque, on the April 2, 1940 broadcast was made by Henry Seidel Canby, founder of *The Saturday Review* and was a member of the Editorial board. Dr. Canby's remarks accompanying the presentation summarized the reasons of the Editorial Board in making the award: "For sixteen years *The Saturday Review* has kept a weathered eye upon American literature. It does not usually make awards nor is this tribute to be regarded as a precedent. But the editors have felt that the contribution of *Information, Please* should not go unrecognized. The questions and answers which radiate from this room every week have sent thousands to useful reference volumes; they have brought to life good books long unopened; the wit and erudition in this hour have electrified the minds of thousands listening in. An intellectual curiosity aroused and active is the beginning of literature. I confer therefore upon Grand Inquisitor Fadiman and his conclave the ensignia of *The Saturday Review* award for the quickening of our intellectual life. Upon this plaque I hand you now, Mr. Fadiman, are inscribed the words, 'For Distinguished Service to American Literature'."

As Dr. Canby pointed out, this was the first time in the history of *The Saturday Review* that such an award had been made, and its editors were not sure whether it was likely to be made again. But *Information, Please* had performed a unique and important service to literature that deserved special recognition. It had enlivened an enthusiasm for knowledge and made information about good literature palatable to the millions, and in so doing, had helped destroy the myth – wherever it may still exist—that book publishing must depend upon a specialized market.

If it were not doing so already, the world of books should have been clapping its hands with delight at the spectacle of increasing numbers of people whose literary appetites were being sharpened and enlarged through the educational, yet vastly entertaining program. So wide was the appeal, so varied the audience, that the influence of the program was seen and felt almost everywhere. According to an issue of *The Saturday Review*, teachers in public schools and even colleges who had a difficult time persuading their students to read Shakespeare, Milton, Emerson or Whitman, were discovering that the literary giants had become overnight favorites.

And even those who made no effort to match knowledge with Clifton Fadiman's versatile savants, but sat back and waited for the quips, may be said to have derived some literary benefit; they were constantly exposed to lines from or titles of a wide range of books. Education, after all, is a matter of exposure; the rate of absorption and the saturation point depend upon the individual. But the most important thing was that education was made available for the willing, regardless of the intensity of willingness. That was the significant function of *Information, Please*. But some didn't think so.

MINORITY REPORT: THE QUIZZERS HAD THEIR SAY

Besides the usual submissions to "stump the experts," frequent listeners to *Information, Please* also wrote fan mail to the participants – Fadiman, Levant, Adams and Kieran – and the fan mail never stopped pouring in. It was very common for any radio program to receive letters from listeners but very rarely did fan mail get reprinted in the daily, weekly or monthly trade columns of journals and publications. Such was the incident of the *New York Times*, when on December 7, 1941, the *Times* reprinted a letter to the editor.

To the Radio Editor:
    This is a protest against the so-called *Information, Please* radio program. The public derives very little information from listening to the same. Here are two examples. Mr. Fadiman states that the studio pianist will play the first few bars of a musical composition. Oscar Levant is required to continue from there on. He does so. Where is there any information in this? It merely proved that Mr. Levant is a good pianist.
    Mr. Fadiman then recites the first line of a poem, then asks some of the brain department to recite the last line. John Kieran does so. This proves that Mr. Kieran has a good memory. No information for the public. We learn more from one program of the *Dr. I.Q. Quiz* or the *True or False* program than we do from a dozen *Information, Please* programs.
                      James S. Leith,
                      New York City, Dec. 2, 1941

Shortly after the letter appeared in the "Letter to the Editor" column (termed as "In the Radio Mailbag"), letters came in from New York residents, and on December 14, 1941, the following was reprinted:

To the Radio Editor:
> In answer to the protest of James S. Leith in today's *Times* concerning the *Information, Please* program, I should like to point out something he seems to have missed in connection therewith. The usual quiz program is one in which questions are asked of the audience. *Information, Please* reverses the usual order and asks a few experts questions which (the hope is) will stump these experts and put them on the spot. They sometimes do, much to the delight of everyone and the good-natured chagrin of the experts themselves.
> The idea is to find a question which will stump not the average I.Q. but the specialist. Mr. Leith has missed the point of the program (if he is really in earnest about the whole matter, which I doubt). It is not so much to give the public information as it is to see if one who is supposed to "know it all" can answer the question.
> However, many crumbs of knowledge fall from their table and, as one who is a devoted listener, I marvel at these men.
> Mrs. Olga F. De Gross,
> Lawrence, Long Island, December 7, 1941

So what is a Specialist? The week after resulted in a third letter reprinted in the December 21, 1941 issue of the *New York Times*:

To the Radio Editor:
> In last Sunday's *Times* Mrs. Olga F. De Gross says regarding *Information, Please*, "The idea is to find a question which will stump not the average I.Q. but the specialist."
> I take issue with this statement. I believe the idea is to find the questions which will not stump the "specialist." I am justified in this opinion by the fact that I have, on various occasions, submitted not less than twenty questions (chiefly on American History) which an educated person would have some chance of answering correctly, but on which not even one of the "experts" could hope to score 100 per cent.

Not one of these questions has been submitted to the "experts," who are too busy answering questions about fairy tales or quoting poetry, which I could have done equally well in my adolescent years, or in playing or identifying various musical compositions, which any first-class musician could do.

So the opinion stands that our "experts" have an alma mater who carefully shields them from the harder blows of the airwaves; and if they are nevertheless occasionally bowled over to the tune of $35 and a set of encyclopedias it is a regrettable accident.

W.D. Anthony,
Keyser, West Virginia, December 16, 1941

Perhaps one of the most surprising things about the program was that the only ones who did not recognize its popularity and merchandising value, and meticulously shunned its significant literary contribution, were prospective sponsors. The radio audience, apparently, was believed to consist largely of minor or sub-minor intellects who were spiritually, organically, and economically incapable of enjoying a reasonably intelligent program. *Information, Please* exploded that theory, with vibrations that were felt throughout the entire radio industry. Almost as a direct result of its success—financial as well as artistic—the conception of the average listener was being revised. Slowly the impression was gaining weight that the radio audience was not to be talked down to and that other programs of the *Information, Please* caliber and quality would be justified by the response.

This might have suggested to the book industry, which had always raised its collective eyebrows whenever the subject of radio was mentioned, that the time was at hand to drop its hardened attitude. It was true that in many of the tests made thus far results did not come up to expectations, but publishing, by its very nature, could not expect the same direct returns as the cereal manufacturer who received thousands of box tops after each broadcast. The only true index of a program's worth was the interest it created. And if there was still doubt that a program having literary merit can arouse interest, skeptics were referred to the 1,610,000 letters received by *Information, Please* in the twenty months since it began.

THE LUCKY STRIKE YEARS

As early as July 11, 1940, a press release was issued stating "Canada Dry will cease sponsoring *Information, Please* as of November 5. Another sponsor, name undisclosed, is now negotiating for the program." The undisclosed sponsor was the American Tobacco Company.

The contract between Daniel Golenpaul and Ann Golenpaul (doing business as Daniel Golenpaul Associates) and the American Tobacco Company was signed on August 5, 1940. For all services, talent, material and rights to be furnished by the producer, the sponsor agreed to pay Golenpaul the sum of $8,500.00 per broadcast performance. The contract also stipulated that recordings of each broadcast were to be made for the purpose of rebroadcast on the West Coast. The sponsor also retained the rights to make recordings or transcriptions of the broadcasts, and use any of them, as broadcast, for off-the-air sales promotion work, but not for public performances.

Paragraph twelve stipulated: "Sponsor shall have the right, which is hereby reserved to it, to prepare any and all commercials to be used on such programs and Producer undertakes to use the same in such manner as Sponsor may require."

Paragraph seventeen was offered a war clause: "If, during the term of this contract or any extension thereof, a state of war shall exist in the United States of America, Sponsor may at any time during such state of war cancel this contract by giving Producer notice in writing of its intention to do so and thereupon this contract and any extension thereof shall terminate and be cancelled at the conclusion of the last broadcast of the term then current thirteen (13) week cycle; but if such notice shall have been given less than thirty (30) days prior to the end of the term then current thirteen (13) week cycle, then this contract and any extension thereof shall terminate and be cancelled thirty (30) days after such notice shall have been given."

Paragraph 23 was not favorable for cigar-chomping Franklin P. Adams. "Producer agrees that it will not permit any cigarettes, cigars or tobacco products manufactured, sold or distributed by any person, firm or corporation other than Sponsor to be smoked in the broadcasting studio from which said programs may be broadcast or in any motion picture or other public performance of *Information, Please*, in so far as Producer shall be able to control the same. Producer agrees however to use his best efforts to do so."

With the contract signed, *Information, Please* was moving to a new day and time, Friday evening instead of Tuesday. With a ring of boldness yet confidence, the rotund, veteran barker of the wave lengths, Milton Cross, took to the air in late 1940 to announce that at last a board of tried-and-tested experts had been rounded up, ready to be stumped by questions from any one within the sound of his voice.

Off-mike, the board of experts knew each other by their first names but when they were on the air, they often referred to each other as Mr. Levant, Mr. Kieran and Mr. Adams. Levant would, on occasion, attempt to trick Fadiman into giving a clue or hint to clarify the answer. Often he failed, rarely he succeeded. Questions were often directed to specific guests that Fadiman announced the week before. As was most often the case, questions were set up regarding topics on which the weekly guest was supposedly an "expert." When a fashion expert was guest, a question was posed about 19th Century articles of clothing. When Shakespearean actor John Carradine was guest one week, many questions asking for quotes of the Bard were asked of the experts. When Larry McPhail, President of the Brooklyn Dodgers, made a guest appearance, many questions about baseball were pitched at him.

Listeners continued to accept the challenge. They shot an estimated 3,000,000 questions at the wise men by the end of 1939 alone. Modestly, the experts confessed at the end of eighteen months that they had missed less than 150 out of the thousands of answers, covering everything from mosquitoes to the sun, from mythology to Hollywood, from sapphires to soap.

Based upon surveys from the unseen audience the broadcasters were aware that "the walking encyclopedias" were not at the top of the popularity list. In the half-hour class Jack Benny was the leader, while Fibber McGee, *One Man's Family* and other shows of that caliber were far ahead in the popularity rating; in fact, *Information, Please* was reported to be ninth or tenth on the list.

Then why, it may be asked, did *Information, Please* score as a popular broadcast? Why had it survived and defied imitation? What qualified it for another year's run? The novel presentation of the questions sent the show off to a good start. They were never cut and dried. The wise men had been opportunists with wisecracks. And Clifton Fadiman had just the right voice and personality for his sort of professional role; he coupled wit with question marks. His tone of informality brought the questions into the home as if they were directed to the family grouped around the loud speaker. It was not as if he were asking the experts alone. Magnet-like, he pulled the listeners into the radio circle. In this strategy was found another element that accounted for the success of the broadcasts. It invited audience participation.

The folks at home listening in took part, for they too tried to find the answers; also they submitted questions and won a prize if their "stumpers" were used. Having heard hundreds of the broadcasts that survive in recorded form, it can be tempting, from the very first episode, to answer questions before the experts. Members of the audience found it a particular joy when they knew the answer and the experts stumbled. They were amazed when the experts knew some unheard-of thing and they didn't. In this show, the listener got a chance to pat himself on the back.

Generally, the guest celebrity was rather quiet. He seemed subdued or else playing it safe. It was charitable to remember, however, that his was a difficult role, for he was playing alongside seasoned experts to whom it was second nature to flash spontaneous answers; they had mastered the art of quick thinking. It was noted that the experts starred because they had a well-rounded knowledge, whereas it seemed that the guest was more of a specialist. Yet, his one-sidedness may be explained by the fact that he found it easiest to speak his specialized knowledge on the spur of the moment; he was too nervous, and too inexperienced at the microphone to dig down quickly into his store of information and draw up the right answer. In this sort of competition the clock was often quicker than the tongue. In this case, silence did not necessarily signify a dunce.

Occasionally, the experts, too, found that their brain waves were not spread over all fields; that they could not bring back the answers in the split-seconds allowed them. For some reason the board of experts was unable to answer questions about the Lone Ranger, his faithful Indian scout Tonto, or the names of their horses, regardless of how many times such questions kept coming back. If there were any wireless amateurs or radio engineers listening in they must have been surprised that no expert knew "DX" was the radio abbreviation of symbol for "distance."

The voices of the experts were not what the elocution teachers might rate as first class; in fact, the formula did not provide that the contestants be selected because of honeyed, serene or golden tongues. They spoke as themselves; they were natural, and some of them were poor broadcasters as compared to the trained announcers.

Listeners generally liked naturalness more than any other element in a program, and in this instance, naturalness was coupled with showmanship. There was nothing highfalutin' about it. The show was conducted as a game, and it was played in the parlor exactly as on the air. Informally, it became part of home life, sparkling with humor and friendliness. It is well to note, too, that commercial ballyhoo had been held in check on this program. Wisely the sponsor had not insisted on long talks about his product.

The opening broadcast under new sponsorship was on November 15, 1940, and featured radio comedian Fred Allen, supplied courtesy of Texaco Oil. With this launch, the prize money was given a boost. If the question was used, $10 was given plus the 1941 edition of the *Information, Please* quiz book. If the question stumped the experts, $25 more was added, plus a 24 volume set of the *Encyclopedia Brittanica*.

Also new to the program was Lucky Strike's famous tobacco auctioneer, L.A. "Speed" Riggs of Goldsboro, North Carolina. It was Speed Riggs who became a staple, best remembered for his shades of the auctioneer at work, ending with the catch phrase "Sold to American!" (Also spoofed in the 1940 movie *His Girl Friday*, based on the Hecht-MacArthur play *The Front Page*.) Remaining as the announcer was Milton Cross, and later, a commercial pitchman, Basil Ruysdael, was brought in.

Highlights of the *Information, Please* broadcasts during the Lucky Strike sponsorship included the broadcast of February 7, 1941 when author Jan Struther and writer Wilmot Louis met for the first time. Oddly enough, both were British and both worked at one time for the *London Times*, but never met until this broadcast.

On October 7, 1940, the vice president of Paramount Pictures, Inc., drafted a letter to Dan Golenpaul Associates offering to pay Golenpaul

$750.00 for the use of Levant in a motion picture!

Dan Golenpaul Associates, New York, N.Y.

Dear Sirs:
This will confirm our understanding and agreement covering the appearance by Mr. Oscar Levant in our motion picture tentatively entitled, *Kiss the Boys Goodbye.*

You have approved such appearance and as a consequence, Mr. Levant will not be able to make his regularly scheduled broadcasts of *Information, Please* program on January 17 and January 31, 1941. However, you are arranging to make up for one of these broadcasts so that Mr. Levant will actually miss only one broadcast, namely that on January 31, 1941. For this broadcast, you will have to use a substitute for Mr. Levant. To compensate you therefor, we agree to pay you the sum of $750.00, which sum you agree to accept. Should you have any difficulty in procuring a substitute for this sum, we shall use our best efforts to make one available to you; but in no event shall we be obligated to pay in excess of said sum of $750.00. Also, you shall not be obligated to use any substitute we suggest.

We further agree that Mr. Levant shall again be available for *Information, Please* broadcasts from New York City commencing February 21, 1941.

If the foregoing represents your understanding, will you please so indicate at the place provided below for that purpose.

Sincerely yours,

PARAMOUNT PICTURES, INC.

(signed) Vice President of Paramount

Accepted, Confirmed and Agreed to:

(signed) Dan Golenpaul

Much to the dislike of the radio audience, Levant's absence was noted by a large number of letters asking what happened to their favorite wit. So many letters, in fact, that Clifton Fadiman was instructed by Golenpaul to explain that the musician was in California filming, and would return shortly.

For the broadcast of February 28, 1941, actress Helen Claire made a quick appearance reciting lines from a role she played in New York, during a question in which the board members were asked to identify the source. Oscar Levant initially guessed incorrectly, but retracted his answer, realizing he was wrong. The answer which stumped Levant was *Kiss the Boys Goodbye*!

"My availability for a movie was limited to five weeks," recalled Oscar Levant, "the longest amount of time Dan Golenpaul would allow me to be absent from *Information, Please*. When I went to Hollywood for the third picture the starting date was postponed because of a studio problem, and since Golenpaul refused to let me stay for a longer period of time I couldn't do the part. I was asked by an executive at Paramount if I would accept half of the amount of money that I would have received had I done the picture. I agreed and signed the release only to discover later that his calculations had been in error and I had received less than the right sum. The picture turned out to be abominable; so what you don't do doesn't hurt you."

On February 28, 1941, *Newsweek* columnist John O'Hara was the guest expert. A month later, the April 14, 1941 issue of *Newsweek* featured O'Hara's latest column, describing his experience on the set, and a question asked of him by his real-life aunt:

"My Lyken's correspondent was particularly interested in her nephew's appearance a few weeks ago on *Information, Please*. She asked one particular question which revealed that she was asking it before I made my appearance. The question was: 'Now tell me the truth. Don't they rehearse it at all? Is it really spontaneous?' If she had heard the program when I was on it she would have known darn well that it was unrehearsed. Or, if not unrehearsed, that her nephew was the best stooge on the air. Aside from coming through with the recondite and breath-taking information that Covington, Kentucky is across the river from Cincinnati, my contribution to the program was decidedly negative. In fact, decidedly almost positively negative. I almost got the sponsors in a lawsuit by attributing to one playwright a work that belonged to another.

"My Lyken's correspondent is interested, she vows, in just what do you do when you go on *Information, Please*. Well, first of all, in my case at least, you play a few games of pool with F.P.A. You show an interest in the program by begging him for tickets, which he is unable to get (you're welcome, Frank). Then adroitly your steer the conversation around so that you can pop off with some forgotten fact like what was the interscholastic hop, step and jump record for Massachusetts high schools in 1904. The next week you allow him to "discover" you mumbling the first four bars of your own arrangement of, say, 'Comus Lycidas.' After that you're practically in.

"Next, a man named Dan Golenpaul, who is the boss of the program, calls you up, offers you $150, which you accept before he has a chance to change his mind, and he tells you you will go on next week. Until the night you go on the program you waste your time reading Spalding guides, World Almanacs, bound volumes of the *National Geographic Magazine*, and your own writings, if any, just in case some wise guy tries to trap you into a tacit admission that you have a ghost writer. You also waste your time and your friends' patience by trying to develop a mike personality.

"The night which you have not been afraid of at all, except secretly, comes. There is a fifteen-minute warm-up period, just before the program goes on the air, and you think this is the softest touch you ever made. You say to yourself: 'Why didn't I butter up Frank Adams years ago?' You are sure you're good for $150 a month from now on.

"Then you become aware that you are listening to the chant of the tobacco auctioneer, and for the next half hour you don't know your own middle name. But of course mine is Henry, so I'd just as soon forget it."

Many of the guests on *Information, Please* were paid low scale. Usually $150 per appearance but sometimes more. One exception was Eleanor Roosevelt, according to *Time* magazine, who reported she earned a hefty $500 for her sitting. Golenpaul wrote numerous letters and even used Franklin P. Adams' personal friendship in order to convince her to attend the panel, even against her advisors who felt that it would be undignified for the First Lady to appear on a quiz show, even though she endorsed products in women's magazines and had her own radio program.

What the weekly guests were really after was publicity. On April 25, 1941, Paul Muni, whose smash hit performance on Broadway's *Watch on the Rhine* was currently playing in New York, sat with the board of experts. On August 1, 1941, Professor Lyman Bryson of Columbia University appeared for the opportunity to retain his valedictorian presence, and arrange for a mention that he was the director of the radio program *The People's Platform*. On September 12, 1941, author Margaret Leech's best-selling book *Reveille in Washington* was presently the Book of the Month. (She missed a question about a character described in her own book!) The week after, poet and author of *The Devil and Daniel Webster*, Stephen Vincent Benet, appeared as a guest expert because the movie version of his classic story was soon to be seen in theaters under the title *All That Money Can Buy* (1941).

For trivia fans, the broadcast of September 26, 1941 featured a musical question and Oscar Levant supplied the music – even though he was not a guest expert on the panel that evening. Clifton Fadiman credited the music to Levant, but the musician, like the others before and after him, remained silent. On October 17, 1941, Fred Allen made a return visit to the program, and shortly before the end of the program, pulled a piece of paper from his pocket and turned the tables by asking the experts three questions of his own. The boys were unable to answer the third and last question—and Fred Allen embarrassed them by pointing out that it was the same question on which they stumped him with the last time he was on the program!

Just months before on July 2, 1941, Clifton Fadiman, John Kieran, Oscar Levant and Franklin P. Adams, along with Fred Allen, made a guest appearance on the premiere broadcast of *Millions for Defense*, a summer replacement for Fred Allen's *Texaco Star Theatre*. *Millions* was considered the first radio program to promote the sale of War Bonds during the war, and Golenpaul allowed his "brain trust" to guest on the program to help the war cause.

For New Yorkers, the broadcast of October 10, 1941 proved to be a broadcast worth tuning in for. Mayor La Guardia had only fair-to-middling luck as a member of the board of experts. He muffed several questions but easily identified as spaghetti sauce a mixture whose separate ingredients were listed by Clifton Fadiman.

John Kieran and Deems Taylor came to the mayor's rescue when he was unable to name two functions outside the administrative field that he could exercise that could not be exercised by President Roosevelt or Governor Lehman. The mayor wrinkled his brow, tugged at an ear and gazed into space, but the correct answer was not forthcoming. John Kieran noted that the mayor could sit as magistrate and Deems Taylor pointed out that he could perform marriage ceremonies. The mayor admitted he had exercised both functions a number of times.

In response to another question, the mayor wrongly named Philadelphia as the city where Market and Sutter Streets intersected. After Kieran identified New York as the place where Fourth and Tenth Streets crossed, the Mayor explained this variation from the usual layout of numbered streets in Manhattan. Fadiman joked, asking whether the mayor could do something about it. "It's historical," the mayor replied, "and the people of Greenwich Village kind of like it." "That takes care of the Greenwich Village vote," Fadiman suggested.

Another question fired at the experts concerned the number of mayors the city had. La Guardia said he was the ninety-ninth mayor, whereas the master of ceremonies contended he was the 103rd. Kieran declared that "the Little Flower is right." Mayor La Guardia dryly remarked that "I must have lost four of them." When Mayor La Guardia correctly answered a question relating to American politics, he made his reply just after a fellow-expert had given the wrong answer. Fadiman, as he usually did on the program, insisted that the mayor should have answered before his fellow-expert had given the incorrect reply. "Well, I'm very polite," the mayor explained. "It must have happened overnight," Adams remarked.

After the broadcast the mayor had to rush off to the studio where a program celebrating the twentieth anniversary of Station WJZ was in progress.

The broadcast of November 14, 1941 was a change from the normal routine. The two guests, journalist John Gunther and actor Leslie Howard both appeared via a "live" remote from London, England, leaving John Kieran and Franklin P. Adams the only guest experts in the studio that evening. Two weeks later, Drew Pearson and Robert Allen, writers who gained national prominence with their syndicated column, "Washington Merry-Go-Round," appeared on the program as guests, making a total of five guest experts for the evening! Oddly, neither man sat with the panelists that week. Each was seated at his own desk, with his own microphone, but away from the panelists.

The boys rang in the New Year of January 1942 with a change in the weekly winnings. To help support the war cause, any question used on the program earned the submitter $10 in Defense Stamps. If their question stumped the experts, they earned an additional $50 U.S. Defense bond, as well as the 24 volume set of *Encyclopedia Britannica*.

Hours before the broadcast of January 23, 1942, Clifton Fadiman was riding in a cab to the studio, with guest Alexander Woollcott. Woollcott informed the master of ceremonies that during a recent trip to England, he was invited to be a guest on the British version of *Information, Please*. Later that evening, Fadiman asked Woollcott what the difference was between the British equivalent and the U.S. version. "Oh, it's much pleasanter," remarked Woolcott. "We first get lunch, and you don't have to know anything to answer the question. They don't ask questions of fact. They asked questions of opinion. The first question they asked me was, 'What do you think about the future of the horse?' And the next question was, 'What did you think of the influence of parents on children?' Weeks later, Julian Huxley, one of the regular panelists, confirmed with Fadiman that the name of the program in England was entitled *The Brain Trust*, and definitely struck a sense of formality.

"During those semi-historical years of *Information, Please*," recalled Oscar Levant, "Alexander Woollcott was a frequent guest. He confided to me that he didn't intend to answer any of the questions—just to 'get even.' As he passed John Kieran's chair just before we went on the air he leaned over and said, 'I detest your World-Almanac mind'. Woollcott's eccentricities always delighted me."

Horror bogeyman Boris Karloff cancelled his invitation for the February 13th broadcast because of a superstition that he might fail at the questions because the date was Friday the 13th. He appeared as a guest the week after with another horror screen actor, John Carradine. Karloff's superstition was proved right as the board of experts answered every question correctly, earning a perfect score for the evening. The week after, a question was tossed at the experts, asking to name the guest of honor who substituted for Boris Karloff on Friday the 13th. No one knew the answer.

Singer Art Gentry, who would shortly become the announcer for *The Bob Hawk Show* and a regular cast member of the musical quiz program *Singo* (in which a jackpot was split with servicemen), supplied the accomplished whistling for a musical question on the broadcast of May 29, 1942.

For the broadcast of August 7, 1942, Ned Sparks, one of the most imitated actors in Hollywood history, replaced an ill Jimmy Gleason, who was originally scheduled as a guest expert for the evening. Sparks, apparently, was not familiar with the *Information, Please* program, and barely assisted in answering the questions. Still, the crew was able to pull off a perfect score, being able to answer all of the questions without any errors. The men celebrated that evening – but only for a limited time. Before the week was over, it would be brought to their attention that they actually flopped on a question about Mother Goose.

As of the broadcast of August 21, 1942, the folks of *Encyclopedia Britannica* got a little more generous. Besides the ten dollars in war stamps if their question was used, submitters also received a 12-volume set of the *Junior Encyclopedia Britannica*. This offer only lasted a few weeks, but long enough to have their Junior set advertised on the program.

On September 18, 1942, Orson Welles appeared courtesy of producer Dan Golenpaul: shortly before the program, Welles placed a side bet with the producer, that Golenpaul would have to buy himself a $500.00 war bond for every answer Welles gave incorrectly. Golenpaul felt sure that Welles would impress the boys, and Welles did – only making one acknowledged mistake during the program.

The third question of the evening was more on the humorous side:

FADIMAN: Who frightened the inhabitants of Grover's Mills, New Jersey?
ADAMS: Mr. W.
FADIMAN: Do you remember that, Mr. Welles?
WELLES: It comes back to me.
FADIMAN: Mr. Welles, have you had any success in scaring people ever since that famous Martian broadcast of yours?
WELLES: No, naturally everything has been anti-climatic.
ADAMS: Well, maybe now people scare *him*.

During the broadcast, Welles corrected Fadiman when the answer to a question was revealed—and then corrected Fadiman a second time by pointing out an error on his card, proving he knew more than Fadiman's answers. After the third correction, Fadiman joked, "Welles, this is your last appearance on this program..."

In 1959, the headlines of major newspapers were addicted to the quiz show scandal—game shows that American audiences were hooked into watching, only to learn slowly but surely that the contestants were being given answers in advance to create higher ratings. Gregory Ratoff, the Russian-born actor/director, recalled his very first appearance on *Information, Please*, the broadcast of October 9, 1942.

"It was in 1942. At that time *Information, Please* was the biggest radio show in the United States. It was the mother of all quiz programs. I was sitting at the 21 Restaurant with Darryl Zanuck, who was in uniform at the time, and the producer of the show, Dave Golenpaul, came up to the table and told Darryl he should be the guest on the *Information, Please* show. Darryl said he couldn't do it for two reasons. One, he was going away to war, and two, he didn't know the answers to anything. 'But,' he said, 'why don't you use Gregory as a guest star?' Golenpaul said, okay, he would.

"The show paid $300 for a guest appearance, so I didn't agree to do it for the money. But I thought a good intellectual show like this would be good for me and besides, I was sure it was fixed. I figured they wouldn't let somebody like me go on without knowing the answers, particularly when Golenpaul assured me that I would have no trouble on the program. I remember the show was to go on at 9 o'clock, and Golenpaul said he would have dinner with me at 7. I assumed he would give me all the answers at dinner. But when we met he talked about movies and never said anything about the show. Finally I said: 'So what are the answers to the questions you're going to ask me?'

"He said: 'I'm not going to tell you the answers to any of the questions.'

"So I got mad and I said: 'You mean you asked me to go on the show and you're not going to tell me what they're going to ask me? What kind of an idiot do you think I am? I'll make a complete idiot of myself. If you don't tell me the answers I'm not going on.'

"He said I shouldn't worry, I had to go on. It was announced all over the country. It was too late to find somebody else. I said: 'I don't care. Look, I'll make a deal with you. You're paying me $300 to go on the show. I'll pay you $2,500 not to go on. I'll give you my check right now.'

"He said: 'Are you serious? You'll give me a check for $2,500?'

"I said: 'Sure I will. I'll do anything except go on the program.'

" 'All right,' he said, 'write it out.' So I wrote out a check for $2,500. 'Are you sure it's good?' he asked me. I assured him it was. So he took the check and tore it up into a hundred pieces. 'Now,' he said, 'this will be a lesson to you. You're going on the show tonight, and no ifs, ands or buts about it. Don't forget we have a 15-minute warm-up period. You'll get the whole pitch during this time.'

"I'm thinking to myself, I've committed the greatest mistake of my life, but in thirty minutes it will be over. Okay, so the commercial is over and the questions start. I don't know anything. They ask questions about movies but I haven't seen the movies they ask about. Levant not only knows all of the answers but he's making wisecracks about me. I don't say so much as a peep. Fadiman says: 'Gregory, even if you don't know the answers, say something, just so we can hear your accent.'

"Now the clock has come by and there are only six minutes left. I'm a dead cookie. But then they play a piece of music and asked us to identify it. I remember having to learn this piece as a child in Russia. Levant, who knows so much about music, doesn't recognize it. He asks the music to be played again. Still he doesn't know. Kieran and Adams don't know either, so I raise my hand and say: 'I not only know it, but this is the greatest moment of my life, because Oscar Levant doesn't.'

"Well, the studio roared and I was such a success I went on forty times after that. No guest had ever been asked to come back forty times."

HOW THE QUESTIONS
WERE CHOSEN

Of the estimated fifteen million people who listened to the program every week, a staggering number must have wondered whether their names would be mentioned during the half-hour that followed, and if so whether they would receive the $10 in Defense Stamps or the $50 Defense Bond plus a set of the *Encyclopedia Britannica*. It all depended, of course, on whether their questions stumped the experts.

The prerequisite, however, was the submitted question itself. Why would Clifton Fadiman use it—if he did—and what were the requirements of a question aimed at baffling the board? Let the letter writer who submitted his or her questions be advised that they found themselves in the company of 15,000 others. That was the average number of letters which poured in each week into the offices of Dan Golenpaul. Since each letter carried an average of three or four questions, a barrage of 60,000 puzzles per week, or 10,000 questions per working day, was thrown on the desks of the eight staff readers. (Volume of mail statistics according to the *New York Times*, Curt L. Heymann, editor, March 15, 1942.) They saw to it that each letter—after its receipt had been acknowledged—was read and that nothing "interesting" was omitted. Each communication was carefully examined and its possibilities scrutinized. But, since as many as twenty questions could be used for every program, it went without saying that the chances of the majority were slim. Only five hundred letters survived the first elimination, and then, with the hardest task over, the remainders were again squeezed until fifty to one hundred contestants faced the final selection.

The final selection of quizzes was made by a board of five members and every question intended for use was checked and counter-checked by a research director. Golenpaul took nothing for granted and, unlike the experts, did not rely on his memory. He doesn't trust Shakespeare or Walt Whitman, Lin-Yutang or Madame Pompadour. He wanted to know the truth and nothing but the truth and find facts and figures, quotations and data in a most complete reference library.

What happened then to the thousands of letters whose questions had been eliminated? They were kept on file under the writers' names for any eventual claim. But there was another, though much smaller category, consisting of questions selected but put aside for later use. They were filed according to subjects and formed the programs' reserves. It often happened that a question was used a year or two after the writer had not only given up hope, but had almost forgotten that he once had a splendid question. A superb question on a Marx Brothers movie would be pulled months later for a broadcast, when it was learned that Groucho Marx was scheduled to be the next guest of honor.

After a final selection of questions was made, they were edited and laid out in conformity with the forthcoming program—painstaking routine work in which none of the experts had any part. In fact, only Fadiman had an idea of things to come. About three hours before the broadcast, an outline of the show was placed before him, giving him two and a half hours to figure out how to make it tough for the wise men.

THE WAR BOND TOURS

In November of 1942, it was publicly reported that *Information, Please* was going on tour for the War Savings Staff of the Treasury Department. Never seen outside New York except for the movie versions, the program visited cities along the eastern seaboard in an ambitious attempt by its creator and owner, Dan Golenpaul, to raise several million dollars for the war effort. The first stop was Symphony Hall, Boston, on December 4, 1942, where it was hoped that at least $1,500,000 would be realized. The three regulars, Levant, Adams and Kieran, and their presiding officer Fadiman, participated on the tour, which for starters was limited to one out-of-town appearance a month. According to a press release, a visit to Philadelphia was scheduled in January of 1943 and, if all went well, future visits in Baltimore, Washington, Hartford and perhaps Rochester or Buffalo.

Dan Golenpaul, who was meeting the expenses of the tour, said that tickets would be priced from a $25 Bond for balcony seats to perhaps as high as $50,000 for an aisle chair in Row A. In Boston, the ticket distribution would be handled by the local War Savings Staff. The day before the Friday broadcast, Adams, Kieran and Levant were on hand for a little personal bond selling at strategic points in Boston.

Aside from the regular broadcast, bond buyers would see the usual "warm-up" period of questions before the formal program and, in addition, Adams and Kieran, who were considered "wonderful material for vaudeville" by Golenpaul, would do a little extra business. Levant also addressed himself at the piano. Golenpaul was not inclined to reveal the names of guest experts far enough in advance for local areas to advertise, pending their acceptance of invitations to participate.

Golenpaul's initial intention of selling $1,500,000 worth in bonds was realized by their second visit. The January 9, 1943 issue of the *New York Times* reported: "Philadelphia, Jan. 8 – Thirty-four hundred persons who crowded the Academy of Music tonight to hear the *Information, Please* radio program, now on tour, bought a total of $6,314,123 in war savings bonds. The experts of the show were joined by Representative Will Rogers, Jr. of California, son of the humorist."

Evidently the war bond drive was extremely successful, and Golenpaul extended his tour along the East Coast for the rest of the 1943 calendar year.

For the broadcast of June 28, 1943, Chicago got its first look at *Information, Please* in action. The 3,500 or so people who filled all but a couple of the seats in the giant Civic Opera House enjoyed the radio experts' performance to the maximum, and went home feeling that the price of admission—a war bond from $50 to $5,000 in denomination—had been well-spent in more ways than one. The total war bond "take" for this trip was $6,818,107.

Richard K. Bellamy, radio editor of the *Milwaukee Journal*, was in the audience to get a first look and report on the visual aspect – the part a radio audience could not get at home. "As a radio show this one is very smartly staged," Bellamy wrote. "Even to the lone feminine aspect, a lovely, anonymous girl with a rose in her hair who sang several snatches to illustrate a song question on the broadcast.

"First Levant played some Gershwin on the piano with professional skill. Then Kieran arose, strapped on an accordion and slaughtered 'I'm Just Wild About Harry' (we think that's what it was) as cruelly as any tavern player has ever slaughtered it. He grinned from ear to ear all the while, and the crowd loved him. Adams put a pencil in his teeth and knocked off an unidentified melody on that crude instrument with his fingers. Kieran and [Walter] Yust closed the performance with a piano duet, 'Chopsticks.' It's amazing how little it takes to win over 3,500 people. At 9:15 Fadiman started asking some preliminary questions to get the board into the swing of things. He warned the audience: 'You, the cream of Chicago, will know the answers before these lugs up here on the stage. But please don't coach them.' Even during the broadcast Fadiman seemed perfectly relaxed, always waiting, like a cat, for an opening. He seizes openings lightning fast and without any visible effort."

In Chicago, Golenpaul played the role of director with perfection. He often sat with Fadiman, whispering occasional comments, and once or twice he crossed to the other table and nudged Yust a little closer to the microphone. He had decreed, "No photographers at the broadcast." Apparently his rule was law because no pictures were taken.

"We did a lot of travelling with *Information, Please*," recalled Oscar Levant, "and we were celebrities wherever we went. In Hartford, we dined at the governor's mansion. Fadiman sometimes wrote the speeches with which the dignitaries welcomed us. In Cleveland, Senator Lausche – the alleged Democrat who was to the right of Goldwater – was the mayor and greeted us. In Toronto, Lester Pearson made a speech, presented us with gifts, and thousands of crack troops paraded in front of us in tribute. It was mighty flattering but I was embarrassed. I didn't think we rated that."

On September 27, 1943, *Information, Please* originated from the stage of the Mosque Theatre in Newark, New Jersey, with two very special guests: Vice President of the United States Henry A. Wallace and Representative James W. Fulbright of Arkansas. Exactly $277,398,975 in war bonds were sold that evening as a result. $275 million dollars of the total came from a group of local business concerns. V.P. Wallace said that the "common man" was buying 50 percent more bonds in 1943 compared to 1942. "And he is going to do still better," he added. "He must do better so as to put our armies into Berlin and Tokyo as soon as possible. He must be better if we are to have a stable peace without inflation."

Asked by reporters after the broadcast what he had meant by his reference to a "partial alliance," Henry A. Wallace laughed and said, "You'll have to figure that one out for yourself." The Vice President, incidentally, was to have appeared as a guest on the quiz program, but he shuddered at the prospect and took no part in it other than to give a brief talk during the opening minutes. Representative Fulbright substituted for him in the question-and-answer period. Clifton Fadiman announced that the war bond total had been contributed by 3,277 people for the broadcast, all of whom bought bonds ranging from $50 to $5,000 to gain audience admission to the broadcast.

THE "LUCKY STRIKE GOES TO WAR" LAWSUIT

Radio programs made their way on air in two ways. They were underwritten by big name sponsors, who were expected to be involved with the show, or they were funded by individual producers, making them self-sufficient. Dan Golenpaul, the producer for *Information, Please*, earned kudos when he fired the American Tobacco Company, which had run a series of untruthful commercials and also demanded that panelists on the show smoke its cigarettes.

Dan Golenpaul's relationship with the American Tobacco Company was not without disputes. As producer of the program, Golenpaul had a financial interest in the quality of the *Information, Please* broadcasts. The sponsor, Lucky Strike, obviously had input regarding the advertising of its product, and the placement of the commercials within the show. Regrettably, Golenpaul wanted to keep the program as honest and true to the faithful listeners, without disturbing their enjoyment of the question and answer forum. Lucky Strike, however, had other ideas.

The very literary radio quiz fought a valiant rear guard action in Radio City against the crass commercials of its sponsor, Lucky Strike cigarettes. Shortly after signing the contract, George Washington Hill, President of the American Tobacco Company, sent Dan Golenpaul a list of those he wished barred from the program. Hollywood actors and radio comedians sponsored by Lucky Strike's competition, were at the top of his blacklist. At the time, Hill was being forced to testify in a stockholder scandal. Anyone butting heads with him as a result of the scandal also appeared on the list. Not one to allow anyone to interfere with *his* program (the contract between the two stipulated that Golenpaul was not only the creator and producer, but controlled 100% ownership of the program), Golenpaul sent his refusal.

In the fall of 1942, shortly before Golenpaul went duck hunting on Monkey Island in North Carolina, he was informed by an employee that his sponsor had only a three months' supply of green ink for the Lucky Strike packaging. Golenpaul returned from vacation with a newly-designed slogan, "Lucky Strike Green Has Gone to War!" The reason behind the slogan was obvious. Chromium, an element essential to solid green ink, was a war material in short supply, and since data indicated that women were smoking in increasing numbers, and attracted to archrival Chesterfield's white packaging, Hill took it upon himself to initiate the hard sell. Instead of the usual dark green and gold packs, the packaging was changed to white with red trim. On the bottom of the new packs was a curious abbreviation, "L.S./M.F.T." which meant "Lucky Strike Means Fine Tobacco."

Beginning with the broadcast of November 6, 1942, Basil Ruysdael, the pitchman for Lucky Strike on *Information, Please*, was instructed to pitch the product at any opportunity fate allowed. Whenever there was a brief pause in the conversation between Clifton Fadiman and the panelists, the phrase was presented over the microphone, with no regard for traditional commercial breaks. Golenpaul, on one account, accosted Hill and shouted, "You're lousing up my program and I won't stand for it!" Hill informed Golenpaul that contract or no contract, the American Tobacco Company was paying the bills, and therefore could do what it pleased. Golenpaul filed suit, and the story spilled onto the front pages of every major newspaper in the country.

Crusaders of the free press had a field day. One critic years later even commented that the dispute between Golenpaul and Lucky Strike was the basic theme of the motion picture, *The Hucksters* (1947) starring Clark Gable, Deborah Kerr and Sidney Greenstreet, a film about the advertising and radio industries, with Gable battling for integrity among yesmen. The press coverage of this dispute was very wide. There was reference to the litigation in *Advertising Age* (November 16, 1942 and November 23, 1942). An article which appeared in *Printers Ink* publicly claimed that the "Lucky Strike Green Has Gone to War" slogan was not a war priority at all. (In fact, in a 1943 poll conducted by *Woman's Day* magazine, "Lucky Strike Green Has Gone to War" was voted one of the most disliked radio commercials by the listeners who participated. It just so happened World War II was in progress – and the "sacrifice" of the green dye made the American Tobacco Company look good with the public.)

The case was ultimately dismissed, but the stormy program/sponsor relationship would come to a merciful end, with Golenpaul a national hero.

"From the first broadcast of *Information, Please*, May 17, 1938, I always insisted upon and obtained control of the entertainment portion of the program and the manner of its presentation," stated Golenpaul. "My contract with the American Tobacco Company cleverly provides for this control. However, there is more than a matter of contract rights involved. It involves the maintenance of the high standards of *Information, Please* which the public demands, has the right to expect and which we make every effort to provide. When these standards were interfered with several weeks ago by the sponsors with their 'Lucky Strike Green Has Gone to War' campaign, which incidentally was abandoned without explanation before the original plan for it was completed, I requested and obtained a release from my contract with the American Tobacco Company."

With only three air weeks remaining on its contract with the American Tobacco Company, following the spirited conflict over the recent cigarette slogan, Dan Golenpaul made an attempt to restrain Lucky Strike from further damaging *Information, Please*'s dignity with G.W. Hill's try at a new slogan.

Shortly before the *Information, Please* program began over the NBC network on the evening of January 22, 1943, the two announcers were served notice to appear in court on January 26 to determine whether repetition of a "teaser slogan" in their radio script was "annoying listeners." The notices were personally served by Golenpaul himself on Milton Cross and Basil Ruysdael. Dan Golenpaul disclosed that earlier that afternoon he had obtained a court order from Justice Carroll G. Walter of the New York Supreme Court.

The teaser slogan heralded a new American Tobacco Company Lucky Strike program and was: "The best tunes of all move to Carnegie Hall. Yes, the best tunes of all move to Carnegie Hall." These very two sentences were repeated a total of twelve times during the broadcast of January 22 and with their court orders in their pockets, Cross and Ruysdael stuck to the slogan as scripted, while Fadiman, Kieran, Adams and Levant winced noticeably on stage.

The cryptic slogan was never explained to the audience and it was

Lucky Strike's intention to officially explain the slogan on the two remaining *Information, Please* programs, meaning that the sponsor would replace *Information, Please* with a weekly *All-Time Hit Parade* program from Carnegie Hall beginning Friday night, February 12.

"It is my firm belief that the repetitive use of this slogan on *Information, Please* would annoy listeners and mar the entertainment value of the program," Golenpaul said in a statement. "I always insisted upon and obtained control of the entertainment portion of the program and manner of its presentation. My contract with the American Tobacco Company clearly provides for this control.

"I took no action until four and a half hours before the scheduled time of the broadcast of *Information, Please*, still hoping we would come to an understanding on a more reasonable use of the slogan. At 4 o'clock my attorneys, Damman, Roche and Goldeberg, 22 East 40 Street, New York City, asked for and obtained a court order from Judge Carroll G. Walter of the New York County Supreme Court. With respect to the present situation after every effort to come to a reasonable understanding had failed, the only course left was the legal action which I have taken."

The newspapers had a field day with the news. The *New York Times* headlined "*Information Please* Fights for Its Honor." The January 1943 issue of *Bridgeport Life* featured an article mentioning:

"One of the most interesting and certainly one of the best programs on the air is *Information, Please*. Last week on its hour the ears of the listeners were assailed something like twenty times by iterations of a meaningless jingle which from the tone of Mr. Fadiman's remarks was as irksome to him as it was to those who heard it. It seems the sponsors of this hour are having a new program opening in February and this inane method of attracting public attention to it was selected as good advertising. It is becoming more and more apparent those in charge of preparing commercial announcements are going on the premise the nation is composed of a bunch of morons. Nothing else could account for the drivel that is embodied in them and which are so senseless they cause one's sensibilities to crawl.

"However it is pleasing to know that one producer has the nerve to protest and Daniel Golenpaul Associates have sought an injunction to prevent its sponsor, the American Tobacco Company, from using on the show the jingle, 'the best tunes of all move to Carnegie Hall.' Now, is that not a nifty? One wondered what mastermind thought up this elegant bit of advertising tripe. In the argument against use of the jingle it was characterized as 'meaningless' and 'irritating' and it was stated it was used some twenty times in the thirty minute program.

"The advertising portion of radio in too many instances is hitting a new high for bad taste. Not a few complaints flooded in to *Information, Please* over the inane jingle which repetition made worse. The moronic chant of the tobacco auctioneer is quite bad enough in all conscience but this latest idea caps all previous efforts. It is an insult to the persons who appear on the program, all of whom are of exceptionally high standing and an insult to the public intelligence as well. There is a great deal of room for some really clever advertising but those who have it in charge now are not only lacking in good taste but in brains as well."

Golenpaul explained in court that he had asked the sponsors to limit the slogan to usage twice during the half-hour broadcast. Golenpaul even took a clipping of the *Bridgeport Life* article (among others) as witness to public opinion. The announcers Cross and Ruysdael testified that guests and audience members were disgusted over the slogan.

On January 27, 1943, Judge J. Shientag gave his verdict. "The contract entered into between the producers of *Information, Please* and its present sponsorship, defines the rights and obligations of the parties. The producers reserve to themselves the fight 'to determine all matters and things pertaining to the entertainment portion of the program, the artistic material to be broadcast and the manner in which the program shall be presented.' Defendant was granted the right 'to prepare any and all commercials to be used on such program and producer undertakes to use the same in such manner as sponsor and producer undertakes to use the same in such manner as sponsor may require.' The American Tobacco Company has used a 'jingle' in its broadcast evidently designed to advise radio listeners that it would no longer continue to sponsor *Information, Please* but would present a different program in Carnegie Hall.

"The attorney for the plaintiffs stated in open court that he did not charge the present sponsor with any conscious or malicious intent to injure the *Information, Please* program. It would undoubtedly have been in much better taste and more in conformity with the general character of the *Information, Please* program and the standing of those who participate in it if the sponsor had acceded to the request of the producers and cut down the number of times the 'jingle' complained of was used. Whatever bad taste may have been displayed in this connection does not, however, warrant a court of equity in granting a preliminary injunction before trial. The motion is accordingly denied."

The day after Judge Shientag delivered his ruling, Dan Golenpaul addressed the press with a formal statement: "The court felt that the irritation of the radio audience would be directed primarily against the American Tobacco Company. That may be true but why irritate an audience at all and interfere with their enjoyment of entertainment? Irrespective of the American Tobacco Company's standards of taste, or its respect for the judge's suggestion, I can assure the public that the new sponsor, H.J. Heinz Company, will not employ commercials that are apt to be irritating and annoying to the listeners."

The situation was not without merit. The letters written in support of Dan Golenpaul, venting their frustration in the Lucky Strike teaser slogan arrived in large volumes. Golenpaul had a courtesy letter composed in reply to everyone who wrote in regarding the listener's sympathy to Golenpaul's point of view. The composition dated February 10, 1943, was sent out to an estimated 1,000+ letter writers. Apparently the radio listeners were glad to know that Lucky Strike's tactics would be applied to a different program other than *Information, Please*.

Support for Golenpaul was evident during the broadcast of February 5, 1943 – the final broadcast sponsored by Lucky Strike. The announcer spoke up for the entire *Information, Please* panel and master of ceremonies during the broadcast, thanking Lucky Strike for their many hours of enjoyment. With sympathy for Golenpaul's stance on everyone's mind, when Fadiman asked, "Why couldn't Narcissa keep Ulysses?" Oscar Levant immediately remarked, "He got a new sponsor." The audience attending the broadcast laughed and clapped in recognition.

THE HEINZ SEASONS

Having lost his injunction for the American Tobacco Company, Golenpaul employed the same annoying tactic as the old sponsor for *Information, Please's* next sponsor. During the last week of January and first week of February, Clifton Fadiman and John Kieran helped support the new sponsor by appearing in a brief, sixty-second commercial teaser of their own, broadcast after various evening programs over NBC. The publicity stunt was designed to feature the crow of the rooster not once, but four times during the sixty seconds. The short, two-page skit was prepared for Fadiman and Kieran, is reprinted below:

CROW OF ROOSTER

FADIMAN: This is Clifton "*Information, Please*" Fadiman speaking.

KIERAN: And this is John Kieran, same address.

CROW OF ROOSTER

FADIMAN: And that's our old "*Information, Please* rooster who's come back to the old barnyard and whose voice you'll hear again on Monday evening, February 15th, at 10:30, when he and John Kieran and Franklin P. Adams and Oscar Levant and yours truly go to work for our new sponsor, the H.J. Heinz Company. John, you're a scholar – has our rooster got a Latin name?

KIERAN: Certainly. _____ (fill in Latin). And I'm delighted to hear that the rooster will raise his voice on our program again. You know, Kip, he's a noble bird.

FADIMAN: Got something to crow over, eh?

KIERAN: Sure thing. Henry David Thoreau said once that all climates agree with Chanticleer, and his shrill cry, if heard often enough, would serve to keep nations on the alert.

FADIMAN: That's a fine sentiment, John.

KIERAN: Yes, Kip, and that rooster is a fine bird too, a sign of civilization, a voice of the wilderness that has become tamed for the benefit of mankind. The rooster is enshrined in Aesop's Fables, in the Bible, in the legends of all nations. He's the proud symbol of the France that was and will be again. Why, this noble boss of the barnyard...

FADIMAN: Hey John, pipe down on the ornithology or folks will forget that the rooster is also the symbol of *Information, Please* and that we'll all be listening to him again when *Information, Please* starts its new series for the H.J. Heinz Company on Monday evening, February 15th, 10:30 p.m. Eastern War Time on the National Broadcasting Company Network. John, they tell me you've got a pretty good memory. Think you can repeat that?

KIERAN: *Information, Please* starts its new series, rooster and all, on Monday evening, February 15, 10:30 p.m. Right?

FADIMAN: Right.

CROW OF ROOSTER

KIERAN: So it's—Wake Up America!

FADIMAN: And time to stump the experts!

CROW OF ROOSTER

Beginning with the broadcast of February 15, 1943, it was like old times again for the *Information, Please* listeners, with no tobacco auctioneers, no cockeyed slogans, and for a complete change, no sales message of any kind despite a new sponsor who paid $10,000 a week for the privilege of staging the show. In short, there was nothing but change for the better as the best of the radio quiz shows went to work for the H.J. Heinz Company, also broadcast at a new time (Monday evenings at 10:30 p.m., EST).

NBC had apparently dug out the long-silenced cock-crow sound effect which traditionally opened the program in its pre-Lucky Strike days, and the Heinz Company, known as "the house of 57 varieties," understandably upped the ante for questions missed from $50 to $57 in War Stamps and Bonds, plus the usual set of *Encyclopedia Britannica*. For the premiere broadcast of the season, Fred Allen, radio's humorist, was the guest and during the last ten minutes of the program Allen changed places with Clifton Fadiman as quiz-master. (This style of Fadiman and Allen switching positions was done for many broadcasts when Fred Allen was signed up to appear.) Fadiman made no particular splash as an expert, but Allen was not a man to waste such an opportunity. He promptly posed a question calling upon the experts to identify the authors of three cosmic hypotheses, which he quoted. The authors were Spencer, Kant, and Hegel, but the experts muffed badly (even suggesting "your gag writers"), even with philosopher Fadiman among them. "Thank you, gentleman," said Allen, "I've always wanted a set of Britannica." The question was submitted by Fred Allen himself. Kieran even asked on the air if the whole charade was on the level, but later learned that the cash prize was to be donated to charity. Allen kept the set of Britannica.

The new sponsor was widely accepted by radio critics, when compared to the Lucky Strike commercials. According to the February 16, 1943 issue of *P.M.* magazine: "The Heinz Co. commercials were models

of institutional advertising. Not a pickle got mentioned. Heinz pledged itself to devote its commercial time to important information about food in wartime. For the first week, the company settled for urging its listeners to make this 'Be Kind to Your Grocer Week'."

The February 17th issue of *Variety* (a magazine hard to please when it came to reviews) was exceptionally impressed:

"*Information, Please* emerged unaltered, save for a few minor details. Instead of the sonorous voice of Milton Cross intoning the virtues of 'pin point carbonation' there was a brisker, more business-like delivery of Ben Grauer discussing the Heinz products. Since many of the latter were now virtually unobtainable, Grauer merely mentioned their past glories and devoted himself to the more pertinent topic of food rationing, the problems of the grocer, and added that future advertising interludes would be devoted to a discussion of specific food problems.

"Another innovation was the shrewd change in prize total. When the experts failed to come through, as they did three times Monday night, the Heinz Co. awarded the questioner $57 in War Bonds and Savings Stamps plus the *Encyclopedia Britannica*.

"Neither the new sponsor nor the late hour slowed the swift pace of the show."

Although Heinz sponsored the program from February to July (technically speaking, half a season), they did sponsor two full seasons. The opening broadcast of the first of two full seasons, the broadcast of September 13, 1943 was reviewed by *Variety*.

"*Information, Please* pundits, after a summer layoff, were right back on the ball Monday night when Clifton Fadiman and his troupe teed off their second season under the Heinz banner. The stanza has the same provocative qualities as in past years—adult humor, plus a deep-rooted knowledge that left the impression that the boys browsed away the summer catching up on the latest encyclopedia footnotes. With standby Oscar Levant currently on the Coast making the George Gershwin biog film, and bowing in on the program next week, the initial broadcast lineup included Franklin P. Adams, John Kieran and guesters Deems Taylor and Marcia Davenport, the author, with the latter copping individual honors. It was a sock half-hour presentation of spontaneity and good fun. Ben Grauer's commercials are terse and effective."

According to a press release of June 2, 1944: "LaMoyne A. Jones resigned yesterday as assistant to Wendell L. Willkie to take charge of press relations for the radio program, *Information, Please*. 'Since my withdrawal from the Presidential race, there has been less work for Lem to do,' Mr. Willkie said. 'When the opportunity of joining *Information, Please* arose, I was happy to release him, since it will give him a chance to work in a field in which he has always been interested'." In fact, it was Willkie who suggested to Golenpaul that his assistant go to work for him.

"Wendell Willkie appeared as a guest almost every other week," recalled Oscar Levant. "Dan Golenpaul, the producer and owner of the show, was a great admirer of his, and Willkie's appearances made the former feel like a kingmaker. After Wilkie's unsuccessful race in 1940, he appeared with the panel of *Information, Please* at a bond rally in Hartford, Connecticut, and he made a picture short with us. The first reel [of the movie short] had to be thrown away because Willkie addressed Clifton Fadiman as 'Mr. McFadden.'"

FADIMAN: Name an author in one of whose works a married man elopes with his first wife and another of whose works a wife gives up her husband for two other men.

LEVANT: Well, in such wholesale style it would be Noel Coward.

As of the broadcast of September 11, 1944, Dan Golenpaul added an extra stipulation with the prize money. If all three questions submitted stumped the experts, the submitter won an additional $500 War Bond. By early September 1944, Golenpaul's office confirmed that the free-speaking Oscar Levant had not been re-engaged as a "regular" for the 1944-45 season. The reason for Levant's dismissal was not publicly known, but gossip columnist and Hollywood reporter Maurice Zolotow reported the reason for Levant's leaving the program was "when a series of arguments with Golenpaul culminated in a fistfight."

The September 13, 1944 issue of *Variety* magazine made a brief mention of Oscar Levant's lack of appearance in their review for the season opener of September 11, 1944:

"The champ quizzer is back on the air with a bit of refurbishing here and there and even though the teeoff show didn't come off as scheduled—Wendell Willkie, slated to be one of the guest know-it-alls, had to beg off because of illness—it was a first rate session, with plenty of laughs and what seemed to be a more sprightly pace than usual. Willkie apologized for his absence through a wire read by Clifton Fadiman and said he hoped to make it up later on. Jan Struther, novelist, subbed, rounding out the show with Alexander ("Wilson") Knox, and Franklin P. Adams and John Kieran, the program's stalwarts. Oscar Levant, who in past sessions has been on the show regularly every fortnight, does not figure in *Info*'s plans this season.

"Second innovation is increase in prize money, giving listeners a $500 War Bond (plus the standard *Britannica* giveaway), should the experts muff all three parts of question submitted. This announcement makes for a good flash, but Heinz isn't gambling much—that kind of thing happens to these guys about once every sixth Michaelmas. Other prizes remain the same. All four experts, as well as Fadiman, were on the ball for the first show, creating laughs all along, stemming mostly from the smart insults Fadiman trades with his vis-à-vis brainsters. Knox gave an excellent account of himself, exhibiting a good knowledge of Shakespeare, poetry and music. His voice and accent are excellent for radio and he can do a repeat any time.

"Where the first show fell down was on commercials. It was an unhappy choice to pick tomato catsup as the sales leader item, emphasized by the plugs themselves, which conjured up visions of gooey tomatoes dripping a la Mack Sennett off some comic's puss. *Info Please*'s I.Q. calls for more commercial subtlety than manifested, but there's still no need to worry about this entry."

The November 13, 1944 broadcast featured two guest experts to the panel. Emily Kimbrough, and Diana Lynn, whose 18 years made her the youngest wit ever entered in the bench show of intellects. This joint appearance was obviously a publicity stunt. Emily Kimbrough co-wrote with her good friend Cornelia Otis Skinner, *Our Hearts Were Young and Gay*. In the picture of the same name, as the saying goes, Diana Lynn portrayed Kimbrough. The picture was playing all over the country and a large number of people, most of them pretty important, rubbed their hands delightedly over the evening's billing. Emily Kimbrough's latest book was released in bookstores the same day.

Like a true friend, Cornelia Otis Skinner sent over a question to trip her collaborator. Would Miss Kimbrough identify and date certain caprices in lady's fashion, among them "the cootie's nest"? This struck a mournful chord in John Kieran, who remembered at once that "cootie's nest" was the unofficial designation for G.I. uniforms in World War I. Not at all, Kimbrough informed him. It was a kind of underpinning for milady's hair, to make it bulge in the proper places. Clifton Fadiman seemed inclined to accept this answer as correct. "My cooties," said Kieran, "are very much hurt."

The talk of cooties was a little disconcerting to Diana Lynn. "I went to the bookstore and bought poetry anthologies," recalled Lynn, "and then I went to record shops and read their classical catalogs. Oh, I really studied." She acquitted herself nicely, too, even to knowing what a duster was and where it was worn.

In the same month of November 1944, the prize-money contest—a gimmick that was in abeyance for the last few years—popped up again when a Monday night show starring Frank Sinatra offered $5,000 in a letter-writing competition.

On the broadcast of February 5, 1945, Broadway director Moss Hart suffered a humiliating opening, proving that after eight years on the air, the program was still as spontaneous and entertaining as the first broadcast. The first question of the evening was, "How many toes would you see in a footprint of a chicken?" John Kieran debated with Fadiman for about thirty seconds over the answer to that question, whereupon Moss Hart remarked, "I think this has to be one of the silliest questions ever asked on *Information, Please*, really." When the next question asked how many toes would you see in a footprint of a cow, Kieran said two.

FADIMAN: I'll take that. Suppose the dust were very deep.

KIERAN: Three?

ADAMS: No, four.

FADIMAN: How did you know that, Mr. Adams?

ADAMS: Because that's how many feet a cow has.

FADIMAN: Now wait a minute. Now wait a minute. This is going to take the rest of the evening to straighten out. We are not talking about the number of feet on a cow, interesting as the subject may be. We are talking about the number of toes on each foot.

ADAMS: Two.

FADIMAN: Well, you're following Mr. Kieran's lead.

ADAMS: Because it's cloven.

FADIMAN: Depending on whether the dust is deep or shallow, you would see four or two.

HART: That's right, if you were interested.

FADIMAN: Yes, if you cared. If you were a cow following this cow, Mr. Hart, you might be conceivably interested.

HART: That's a fine speculation. (*Audience laughs*)

ADAMS: Suppose the cow wasn't a criminal?

FADIMAN: And you didn't care?

ADAMS: Then you wouldn't go after the footprints.

FADIMAN: Adams, you have something there.

Sponsorship by the H.J. Heinz Company lasted two full years from February of 1943 through February of 1945. On December 18, 1944, a press release issued from the Pennsylvania Newspaper Publishers Association reported that an advertising budget for 1945 which was "many times greater" than the previous year, had been adopted by the H.J. Heinz Company. The P.N.P.A. said in a statement that H.J. Heinz II, president of the company, reported that the company would discontinue sponsorship of the radio program, *Information, Please* and place most of its future advertising in newspapers. Mr. Heinz told the association that the decision was made as the result of comprehensive surveys before Pearl Harbor to determine the best advertising media for food products. "We feel that newspaper advertising will better enable the company to reach all kinds of people in selected markets," Mr. Heinz explained, "and to concentrate on the best markets depending upon changing economic conditions. We can also improve our advertising timing and allow for geographical and seasonal differences in food tastes throughout the nation."

According to Sally Ashley's 1986 biography *FPA: The Life and Times of Franklin Pierce Adams*, Heinz objected strongly to the appearance of several guests panelists, and decided to tender the option of not renewing their contract when the present term expired. The next sponsor, the Socony-Vacuum Oil Company, was "even more rigid and conservative."

THE MOBIL SEASON

Needing a sponsor to fill in the remainder of the season's broadcasts, the Socony-Vacuum Oil Company, Inc. agreed to sponsor the program. The terms and agreements of the contract changed. As of the February 12, 1945, *Information, Please* would be broadcast as a weekly one-half hour show over national hook-up. Previously, since the program's premiere in 1938, each and every broadcast was recorded and transcribed for later playback. Radio programs originating from the East Coast often included a repeat performance for the West Coast, two hours later, for the benefit of time zones. Thus, when the program was broadcast at 8:30 on the East Coast (at Eastern War Time), the West Coast could tune in to the same broadcast at 8:30 on the West Coast (at Pacific War Time). Because the program was not scripted, Golenpaul insisted that each and every broadcast be transcribed.

Beginning with the broadcasts in February of 1945, the program was to be heard on a later time slot on the East Coast, thus assuring the West Coast of hearing the same questions and answers in a convenient time slot. (This also explains why over 200 broadcasts of *Information, Please* exist in recorded form, dated before February of 1945, and an estimated 3 broadcasts of *Information, Please* exist in recorded form, dated after February of 1945.)

A clause in the contract stipulated that the partnership gave the Compton Advertising, Inc. (the agency representing the Socony-Vacuum Oil Company) the right, at the Agency's expense, to make off-the-line transcriptions of the show. However, such transcriptions could not be broadcast in any manner without the consent of the partnership.

With Oscar Levant no longer involved with the program, Golenpaul guaranteed in the contract dated February 10, 1945 (and previously in a "Memorandum of Agreement" dated November 21, 1944) to supply two guest experts for each broadcast. The price tag? $11,000 per broadcast. In addition, the sponsor was to pay the producer at the rate of $60,000 per year to cover promotion of *Information, Please* to be used at his discretion. According to the contract:

"For promotion of the show, to be used by the partnership in its sole discretion and without any obligation to account therefor, Sixty Thousand Dollars ($60,000) annually payable in installments as follows: $3,000 on March 1, 1945, $5,000 on the last day of March, 1945, and $5,000 on the last day of each month thereafter during the term or any renewals hereof."

Remembering the problems he suffered with the American Tobacco Company, Dan Golenpaul established a clause on pages thirteen and fourteen of the contract, protecting him from any further legal complications.

"For purposes of this Agreement, the entire half-hour show shall be deemed the 'entertainment portion of the show,' with the exception of material advertising the Sponsor, its subsidiaries or affiliates, and/or the products of the Sponsor, its subsidiaries or affiliates, (hereinafter referred to as commercials). The Partnership agrees that it will endeavor to place the first commercial during the first one-third part of the show and the second commercial during the last one-third part of the show.

"The Agency shall have complete control over the selection and identity of the Announcer and of the content and wording of the commercials, except that the Partnership shall have the right to disapprove any copy prepared by the Agency intended to be read by the Master of Ceremonies."

The duration (initially to commence on February 19, 1945) began with the broadcast of February 12, 1945, and was to continue for a period of seventy-two consecutive weeks ending June 24, 1946, provided, however, the show would not be broadcast during the summer months for a said term of not less then eight consecutive weeks and no more than ten consecutive weeks, the precise number to be determined by the Agency. The sponsor had the option for one additional year, an additional fifty-two weeks.

Most interesting was the clause on page sixteen which read:

"In no event during the term or any renewal hereof shall the aforesaid television rights be given to any sponsor of products competitive with the products of the Sponsor shown on said Schedule 'A' annexed, except paints, tires, batteries, spark plugs, chemicals, power fuels, solvents, synthetic rubber plasticizers from petroleum and sealing compounds."

Schedule A listed at the end of the contract, initialed by all parties signing, included a list of 34 products of the Socony-Vacuum Oil Company, Inc., its subsidiaries and affiliates: Automotive Gasoline (Mobil Oil), Aviation Gasoline, Bunker Oil, Heating Oil, Kerosene, Cutting Oils and Coolants, Insecticides, Fruit Sprays, Herd Oils, Anti-Freeze, Automotive Car Polish and Wax, Rust Preventives, Petroleum products used in processing other manufactured goods (Microcrystalline Waxes, Tanner's Oils, Wool and Rayon Oils), Water Conditioners, Polishing Cloths, Anti-Squeak Compounds, Religious and Table Candles, White Shoe Cleaner, Floor Wax, Furniture Polish, Automotive – Aviation – Marine Industrial Lubricants (oils and greases), Tires, Window Cleaner, Batteries, Spark Plugs, Paint, Chemicals, Asphalt, Wicks and Boat Bumpers, Road Oils, Power Fuels, Solvents, Synthetic Rubber Plasticizers from Petroleum, and Sealing Compounds.

And why was this schedule drawn up in advance? For Golenpaul's security, of course. This prevented the new sponsors from advertising any products without having notified Golenpaul in advance. This also prevented him from entering suits against the Socony-Vacuum Oil Company for false advertisements when describing their products, and the parts they manufactured and serviced. For the most part, the company merely pitched Mobil Oil as its prime product, which was targeted at the largest consumer base available.

The prize money was given another boost. If the submitter's question was used, they received $10 in War Stamps and a complimentary copy of the World Atlas. If they stumped the experts, they won a $100 War Bond, plus the usual encyclopedias. If all three of the questions stumped the experts (which was a very rare moment indeed), the submitter received a $500 War Bond and the Britannica set.

Very little is known about the incidents that occurred on the program, beginning with the Socony-Vacuum Oil Company sponsorship, since hardly any recordings of the broadcasts exist after February of 1945. (Three recordings exist from the Mobil season, at the date of this printing.)

With the war nearing an end, Golenpaul inaugurated a new guest policy beginning with the episode of October 22, 1945, when Lieutenant

Col. Gregory "Pappy" Boyington, ace Marine flier, appeared as "co-guest" with Quentin Reynolds. Adding a new category to its visitor lists, the quiz program would present, from time to time, guests of outstanding ability in war as information experts.

On October 28, 1945, the Sunday edition of the *Cleveland Plain Dealer* listed the results of a poll taken by readers of the publication. The poll represented the "people's choice" in Cleveland, ninety-five other cities and towns in Ohio with a few returns from Missouri, Oklahoma and Pennsylvania. *Information, Please* was rated as the fifth most popular radio program of the year, and voted as the best quiz program on the air. Popular opinion ranked the show highly. *Information, Please* was rated number five of the top ten most popular radio programs, while Bob Hope came in at ten!

THE 1945 *INFORMATION, PLEASE* EUROPEAN TOUR

During the summer of 1945, while *Information, Please* was off the air for a short hiatus, the *Information, Please* crew (which consisted of Fadiman, Adams, Kieran, Golenpaul and actress Beatrice Lillie) made a European tour for the program throughout all of July and early August. According to paperwork exchanged between Dan Golenpaul and Beatrice Lillie in September of 1964 (she was writing her autobiography and Golenpaul helped furnish material relating to the European tour), the itinerary included:

July 12, 1945 – Evening performance in a converted riding hall. Fourth guest was General Haislip.
July 13, 1945 – Two performances in Bahnhof (station) hall.
July 14, 1945 – Afternoon and evening performances on outdoor stage by the Neckar River.
July 15, 1945 – Performance in Gartenhalle (Hall in a Park) in Swäbisch-Gmund.
July 16, 1945 – Second performance in Swäbisch-Gmund. Forth guest was General Morris.
July 17, 1945 – Performance was on an open stage in field at Jugenheim.
July 18, 1945 – Performances from a bandstand in an area used for concerts in Spa days. Fourth guest was General Rheinhardt.
July 19, 1945 – Performance in Giessen, 20 miles away from Bad Nauheim, in a movie theater.
July 20, 1945 – Outdoor show in Marburg. Beatrice Lillie lost a fan in the after-performance crush.

July 21, 1945 – Remained in Marburg. Performance in "Tent City," an area housing 5,000 GIs awaiting reassignment.

July 22, 1945 – Performance in basement theater at Kassel.

July 23, 1945 – Another performance at Kassel, same as above.

July 24, 1945 – Same as above.

July 25, 1945 – Traveled by air to airstrip near Nuremberg. Then by car to Bamberg. No performance.

July 26, 1945 – Afternoon performance in a riding hall. Evening performance at Bayreuth at the Festspielhaus, how being used for G.I. movie house.

July 27, 1945 – Tortuous drive to Hamelberg, for an afternoon show in an open field. Later that evening an outdoor show for the 101st Infantry Regiment.

July 28, 1945 – By air to Regensburg. No show on this date.

July 29, 1945 – Show on banks of Danube.

July 30, 1945 – Outdoor show at Weiden.

July 31, 1945 – Performed a show in cow pasture in Kelheim, where the 9th Armored Division was stationed.

August 1, 1945 – By car to Munich. Show at Prinzregententheater. Broadcast by AFN (Armed Forces Network).

August 2, 1945 – Locale of Tutzing evening performance where there were more Germans and GIs.

August 3, 1945 – Dan Golenpaul returned to Paris. In Augsburg, for evening show at the Ludwigsbau, a theater in a park area.

August 4, 1945 – Crew made a visit to Richard Strauss in Garmisch. Evening show in Olympic Ice Stadium.

August 5, 1945. Golenpaul returns from Paris. Dinner and a late start in Linz by way of Salzburg. Guests included Sgt. Jimmy Shelton and Captain Frank Farrell.

August 6, 1945 – Performed a show in hangar at an airport.

August 7, 1945 – Midday show in outdoor area for only a handful of GIs. The men visited Adlershorst (Eagle's Nest) built by Hitler on top of the mountain. Built by Hitler for visitors, now used for Army brass.

August 8, 1945 – Outdoor show for a meager audience in the valley of Salzach in St. Johann. It is today that the men hear of news of Hiroshima.

August 9, 1945 – Return to Munich, await return by air to Paris. In the afternoon, rumors of Japanese surrender and end of the Pacific war. Weather is bad today.
August 10, 1945 – Another day of bad weather.
August 11, 1945 – Weather still bad, but flight comes in.
August 12, 1945 – Show at Salle Pleyel.
August 13 to 16, 1945 – At leisure in Paris. Golenpaul, Kieran, Adams leave for U.S.

During the tour, en route to the various locations where the performances were to take place for American troops stationed in Europe, Golenpaul and his crew (which also included actor Reginald Gardiner) traveled through many acres of rubble-covered ruins, and quartered in small private houses, a castle in Ludwigsburg, and even a Park Sanitorium! In some of the towns they toured, only buildings in town remained intact, while acres and acres of burned fields and residential houses had been blown to pieces.

"It's hard to believe these gentlemen are as intelligent as they sound."
—Clifton Fadiman

It was during this European tour in the summer of 1945 that, according to author/researcher Sally Ashley, Clifton Fadiman and John Kieran first noticed a change in Franklin P. Adams. Kieran had an eye infection and had to treat it several times each day. When Kieran asked Adams to help administer the medicine, Adams could not do so without his hands shaking violently. Late-night poker games also caused Adams to act strangely, almost as if intoxicated. The men later learned that their good friend Franklin P. Adams was afflicted with the early symptoms of Alzheimer's disease.

THE PARKER PEN SEASON

Three months after the cancellation of *Information, Please*, as a result of the Socony-Vacuum Oil Company's decision not to renew its contract, a press release dated September 1, 1946 dismissed the rumors that the program would never return to the airwaves again: "*Information, Please* is scheduled to be returning to the airwaves this fall after all. Dan Golenpaul, the show's producer, was said to have acquired a sponsor, but it was uncertain as to which network might be used." Within a couple weeks, Golenpaul found a new network in order to avoid the National Broadcasting Company, which had expressed a concern that the program was causing too much bad publicity surrounding Golenpaul's public disputes between the sponsors. The feuds were hitting newspapers, and NBC wanted to avoid this bad publicity, hoping it would not cause sponsors to abandon their quality programs.

Oscar Levant and Dan Golenpaul settled their differences for the moment, and Levant signed on as a member of the board of experts for one season on CBS. The broadcast of October 2, 1946 introduced to the listening public a new sponsor, the Parker Pen Company. This sponsor would only last one season, and would go down in history as the final sponsor for the *Information, Please* program. This was also the only season the program would be heard over the Columbia Broadcasting System. *Variety* reviewed the season opener in their October 9 issue:

"*Information, Please*, panting a little heavily with its years, was off on a new network, with a new sponsor, last Wednesday night. All the old familiar voices were present: Clifton Fadiman, the emcee; John Kieran and Franklin P. Adams, the regulars; Oscar Levant back after a two-year hiatus, as a guest, and Fred Allen, another old favorite, as additional guest. Show should have been a mellow breeze—not the wheeze that it was. The questions weren't too bright or interesting. They followed an old pattern, questions about names, gifts, racing terms, poetry, etc. Fadiman sounded a little labored as the emcee, and his voice, too, seemed muddled and indistinct at times. Impish Levant, for the first quarter-hour anyway, appeared subdued, while Allen was in only occasionally with a brief wisecrack. Kieran and Adams tried valiantly, but evidently hadn't gotten into the swing of things yet."

According to a critic at the *New York Times*, "The return of *Information, Please*, this time at 10:30 Wednesday evenings on CBS, can be described only as something of a shock to those who have followed the career of its determined producer, Dan Golenpaul. It may be recalled that some years ago Mr. Golenpaul engaged in a legal conflict with the American Tobacco Company, then his sponsor, because of the latter's strident advertising methods. Donning the mantle of ethereal purity, Mr. Golenpaul said such plug-uglies would not taint what was then and is now broadcasting's most adult quiz show. Alas, the hucksters grind slowly but infinitely fine. On the premiere of *Information, Please* this season where should the plug show up for the new sponsor but squarely in the body of a question asked of the Messrs. Kieran, Adams and Levant, et al. From hereon apparently it will not be enough for the experts to peruse the encyclopedia to cope with the tough ones; they'll also have to subscribe to Tide and Advertising and Selling. For Shame, Mr. Golenpaul!

"Other than that, *Information, Please* is much its old self, albeit not quite as lively as when it was younger. Mr. Kieran is the star, Mr. Adams admits he doesn't know the answer, and Mr. Fadiman tries not to be too condescending and pedantic. Mr. Levant this season is back in the good graces of Mr. Golenpaul and renewing his brash ways from time to time. *Information, Please* is still good fun."

On November 21, 1946, Stamford Connecticut newspapers reported that Randolph Churchill, son of Winston Churchill, former British Prime Minister, was charged the day before with driving at eighty miles an hour on the Merritt Parkway. He posted a $50 bond for appearance in New Canaan Town Court on December 9. The publicity was not helpful to the *Information, Please* program, because Churchill, who was staying at the Hotel Ambassador, was guest the night before on the show. He came to the United States recently from a tour of Europe, Palestine, North Africa and Egypt. He declined to discuss the charge against him, except to say that he hoped to controvert a charge of reckless driving, which is made part of speeding cases under Connecticut regulations, since he believed he was not driving recklessly.

Rivaling the "experts" on subjects varying from politics to poetry, Ellis Arnall, ex-Governor of Georgia, appeared on the *Information, Please* broadcast on January 29, 1947, and stole the show from such old-timers as Adams, Kieran and Levant. Moderator Fadiman repeatedly expressed his amazement, and the studio audience shouted encouragement as time after time the militant opponent of Herman Talmadge came up with quick answers that left his fellow-performers gasping. As a guest on the program that helped to project Wendell Willkie into national prominence in 1940, Mr. Arnall accomplished the rare feat of almost making *Information, Please* a one-man show.

"It would be pleasant to see a show of some other hands," Mr. Fadiman remarked sardonically toward the end of the program. On Georgia football history, even veteran sports writer John Kieran was left gasping as Ellis Arnall came up with the quick information that Charlie Trippi succeeded to the starring position held by Frankie Sinkwich, after the latter was injured in the 1943 Rose Bowl game. But it was on questions on poetry and literature that Arnall really showed up his rivals. A spontaneous recitation of Robert Burns' *Tam O'Shanter* rivaled Mr. Kieran's noted quick-wittedness, and his singing of "I Don't Want to Set the World on Fire" brought down the house.

Mr. Fadiman admitted that he would have been disappointed if Ellis Arnall had not been the first to associate a quotation with the Southern song, "Dixie." But a moment later the Georgia visitor astounded his listeners by identifying a particularly curious incident as coming from an O. Henry story.

"Mr. Adams knows those stories," he said slyly.

"But not tonight," came the reply.

But the true upstart was when a note of politics was injected into the program as two of the participants paid implied tributes to "the Governor Ellis Arnall." Referring to the mistake, Mr. Kieran called him "the former Governor, damn it!" In more dignified radio conversation, Mr. Adams quickly added, "the former Governor, alas." This did not go over well with William S. Paley, President of the Columbia Broadcasting System, who days before objected to the scheduling of the controversial ex-Governor of Georgia. Dan Golenpaul stood his ground and Paley threatened to cut him off the air. Golenpaul reportedly threatened a fight that would lead to bad publicity and strong public opinion in the newspapers if Paley dared to censor the show. According to radio historian John Dunning in his book *On The Air: The Encyclopedia of Old-Time Radio*: "Golenpaul was now widely known as a troublemaker, and when his Parker Pen contract expired, no further sponsor could be found."

The broadcast of April 23, 1947 featured Jackie Robinson hitting a high spot on the air when the Dodgers player appeared as a guest on *Information, Please*, along with the regular and invited literati. Robinson appeared for the benefit of the United Negro College Fund.

In late spring of 1947, Jack Gould of the *New York Times* reported: "*Information, Please* and its sponsor, the Parker Pen Company, are coming to the parting of ways soon, with the quiz program's producer, Dan Golenpaul, in the market for a new angle for next fall. Mr. G. acknowledged that he would like to obtain an earlier time for his weekly presentation, regarding its present spot on CBS – 10:30 p.m.—as too late in the evening. If it can find a spot for the Kieran-Adams-Levant display of knowledge, NBC reportedly would not be averse to playing host again to Mr. Golenpaul's package." This was just an understatement. CBS no longer wanted the program and NBC wouldn't accept any prodigal son. This left the door open for the Mutual Broadcasting System—and with two strikes against him, Golenpaul wouldn't leave well enough alone.

A MUTUAL UNDERSTANDING GONE BAD

In the summer of 1947, Jack Gould of the *New York Times* again reported: "*Information, Please* is being mentioned as a possible addition to the list of fall attractions on the Mutual network and WOR. Dan Golenpaul, producer of the quiz show, and network officials are discussing terms under which the program would be presented by a different sponsor in each city. If the negotiations are successfully concluded, the program might be offered at 9:30 Friday evenings, beginning on Sept. 26."

In August of 1947, Sidney Lohman of the *New York Times* broke the news that "persistent rumors that *Information, Please* would become a Mutual Broadcasting System feature, to be offered to affiliated stations on a cooperative basis, were confirmed last week by Phillips Carlin, Mutual Broadcasting System vice president in charge of programs, and Dan Golenpaul, producer of the program. Clifton Fadiman will ask the questions while Franklin P. Adams and John Kieran will be regular performers. They will be joined each week by two guests."

On September 19, 1947, the *New York Times* reported: "*Information, Please*, the quiz program wherein the radio audience attempts to stump the erudition of John Kieran, Franklin P. Adams and whatever guests happen to be at hand, will open for the season on WOR-Mutual Friday, Sept. 25 at 9:30 p.m. Clifton Fadiman will continue as quiz-master for the feature, while Fred Allen has been announced as guest for the premiere broadcast. A new sponsor for the program, which is being offered to advertisers on a cooperative basis, is the Chesapeake & Ohio Railroad, which will offer the program in New York, Chicago, Cleveland and Washington. According to Kenyon & Eckhardt, the advertising agency, the sponsorship agreement will run for forty-four weeks, beginning with the opening program."

What the *New York Times* did not report was that Mutual had already premiered the program a month before. From August 9 to August 30, 1950, the Mutual network presented four *Information, Please* broadcasts as a test run, to learn whether a radio audience was still interested in hearing a program that was already established and wasn't heard on the air for almost two years. Apparently there was interest because on September 26, 1947, *Information, Please* returned to the air. By this time, in its span of nine years on the air, the adult quizzer had been moved around the other three networks by five national advertisers. As Fadiman put it, on the debut of the Mutual series, "everything is now different." The series still depended on sponsors to pay the way. The Mutual Broadcasting System wouldn't know for a few days after the season opener how many of its affiliates had included local advertisers to put the coin on the barrelhead for the program. Nevertheless, the Chesapeake & Ohio Railroad's sponsoring of the show in the largest of areas such as New York, Chicago, Cleveland and Washington made a tidy little nucleus. In smaller areas like Omaha and Cincinnati, the program was sponsored by local advertisers.

The October 1, 1947 issue of *Variety* reviewed the official season opener:

"The unlimbering of *Information* on Mutual turned out one of those uncommon instances of best foot forward. Dan Golenpaul obviously made sure that it would be most approximately so by enlisting Fred Allen as guest. Everybody seemed quick on the up-pick. The quips, gags and general banter came off with consistent ease and spark, and the event was crowded with enough laughs to furbish adequately four or five regular installments of the show. Allen got an extra special opportunity for himself when one of the queries dealt with gag versions. The sequel was a succession of howls from the studio audience. F.P. Adams also fared big with his ultra-witticism, and Robert Montgomery showed up as no slouch himself at dishing 'em off the funny bone. Fadiman carried out the 'everything is different' theme to mirthful effect in the introduction of the expert panel. With a sly dig at the behaviourism of audience participation shows, Fadiman asked each his name and what he did. Allen's answer to the latter half of the questionnaire was: 'I'm a character analyst for a weighing machine company.'"

From what many considered a retirement, *Information, Please* emerged, thanks to the good graces of station WOR (part of the Mutual Network) in

New York. "It is good to have the show back because it still is the liveliest and most literate of the quiz attractions, even if the initial installment did sag rather badly in several spots," quoted one critic. Oscar Levant wanted no part of the program after the antics over the Columbia Broadcasting System, and retired from Golenpaul's employ for good. The panel consisted of the two tired-and-true veterans, Franklin P. Adams and John Kieran as regular experts, and Clifton Fadiman as the master of ceremonies.

With the help of Fred Allen (in what seemed like a yearly season-opener guest spot) the incidental ad-libbing still had the sparkle which always endeared the show to listeners who didn't conform to the radio industry's chart which placed the nation's mental level at eight years old. When Mr. Fadiman asked Mr. Lindsay in the August 9, 1950 broadcast if it was hard to be a good bad actor, Mr. Allen broke in: "It's hard to admit it."

Both Mr. Kieran and Mr. Adams got the proceedings beautifully balled up in trying to avoid answering the question of which of four cities were the most western—Des Moines, Birmingham, Forth Worth or Detroit? But *Information, Please* tripped over its own precocity when it introduced one of those pre-arranged, excessively involved questions which did not help the program even in years past. For several minutes, which could be a long time on radio, there was an inquiry calling for a knowledge of Mr. Kieran's book on birds, the idea being to use the name of a bird to answer a question on baseball. All it proved was that Mr. Kieran was the program's only ornithologist, and that was established during the program's first year on the air.

It was during this 1947-48 season that Dan Golenpaul reportedly wanted to learn if there was anyone not looking at television – the invitation did give listeners an opportunity for once to say what they wanted on the air. In the case of *Information, Please*, the answer could hardly help but be affirmative.

THE TAFT-HARTLEY ACT LAWSUIT

On November 10, 1947, Dan Golenpaul filed a complaint with the National Labor Relations Board accusing the American Federation of Musicians, headed by James C. Petrillo, of two violations of the Taft-Hartley law. Golenpaul alleged that his quiz show had been denied the services of a union musician beginning with the new season (now on Mutual) solely because the program was presented by a different sponsor in each city in which it was heard. In previous years, *Information, Please* had been sponsored by a single concern. It was his understanding, Golenpaul charged, that the only way his series could obtain the single pianist needed for the presentation of musical questions was to agree to hire 300 stand-by musicians—one for each local station carrying the program.

Under such a provision the cost of a pianist for the half-hour program would increase from $31.88 a week to approximately $9,564. In addition to his allegation of featherbedding, Golenpaul also offered the contention that *Information, Please* was the victim of an illegal secondary boycott, since legally Mr. Petrillo's union had contractual relations with the networks rather than with individual programs. Charles T. Douds, regional director of the National Labor Relations Board, said that under the Taft-Hartley law a charge of existence of a secondary boycott automatically received priority consideration by the board. He said that Dan Golenpaul's complaint was under investigation. If the board decided to act, it presumably would seek a restraining order in Federal Court.

While Milton Diamond, newly appointed counsel to Petrillo's union, declined to comment, union officials informally differed from Golenpaul's charge of featherbedding. They insisted that the use of musicians on cooperatively sponsored programs had been subject to an outright union ban for some years and that the union never had made any demand as a condition for authorizing such shows. Accordingly, they insisted, there was doubt whether there was a cause of action on the featherbedding issue.

Union spokesmen explained to the press that the federation objected to the cooperatively sponsored program on the grounds that such an arrangement discouraged a local concern from offering its own show with local musicians. In addition to affecting *Information, Please*, the union's ban during the start of the 1947 season had forced *The Joan Davis Show*, *Meet Me at Parky's* and *The Abbott and Costello Show* to use vocal choirs as a substitute for the usual orchestras on comedy offerings.

In his complaint, Golenpaul emphasized that he had been unsuccessful in obtaining a written copy of the union's ban and that he believed the edict was a part of the union's continuing controversy with the networks over the number of musicians employed in radio. Golenpaul stated that musical questions always had been among the most popular on *Information, Please* and that Joseph Kahn, pianist, previously had been regularly engaged to assist in their proper presentation.

Golenpaul insisted to reporters that "*Information, Please* never has and does not now have any labor dispute or controversy with the American Federation of Musicians. The basic dispute or controversy which the union has relates to the carrying of co-operatively sponsored shows by a network." Golenpaul did dispute, however, the union's contention that a "co-op program" jeopardized employment opportunities for local musicians more than did a conventional network show. "Certainly a network program which appropriates the available broadcast time of local stations reduces the employment of musicians just as much as a cooperative show which operates in exactly the same way except that instead of one sponsor, there are many."

In previous years, musical questions were presented to the pundits on the program by way of a few bars on the piano. These bars, it appears, were played by one Joseph Kahn, a member of Local 802 of the musician's union. Efforts to rehire Mr. Kahn before the program started this season, according to Golenpaul's complaint, had been unavailing because his union said no. The complaint filed at the regional office of the National Labor Relations Board in New York was really directed at Mr. Petrillo personally, charging him through the medium of his union with secondary boycott and the mandate to hire needless stand-by musicians. The charges alone made this an important case, the first of its kind to be brought against the A.F. of M. since the Taft-Hartley law took effect. It became even more important as a test of Petrillo's long-exercised tyranny over the radio industry.

The Taft-Hartley act, incidentally, declared it to be an unfair labor practice for a labor organization or its agents "to cause or attempt to cause an employer to pay or deliver or agree to pay or deliver any money or other thing of value, in the nature of an exaction, for services which are not performed or not to be performed." If this clause alone had been enforced against Petrillo, much of his despotism would have been abated.

Days later, Petrillo lifted the long-standing ban against instrumental music for network radio programs that were sponsored cooperatively by local interests in the various cities included in the chains. The union leader asserted that the ban's removal was in the nature of a trial. He said that the action would be studied in terms of the contention of the networks that lifting the ban would increase employment opportunities for musicians. Since the existent contracts between the networks and the union were scheduled to expire January 31, 1948, the trial was seen as being of that duration.

Petrillo stated that the union's action was in no way prompted by the complaint filed with the National Labor Relations Board by Dan Golenpaul. He said that the union had never demanded that the program hire 300 musicians—one for each program carrying the cooperatively sponsored program—as the price of receiving the services of a single pianist. "I have never talked to the man," Petrillo said.

The union president had explained earlier that the union refused to supply musicians under any circumstances to cooperatively sponsored programs on the ground that they jeopardized employment opportunities for local instrumentalists. At the same time he also asserted that no alternative proposal under which the ban would be lifted had been advanced by the union. Dan Golenpaul said that he did not know what disposition the NLRB would make of his complaint in view of the union's action. "I don't know what led Petrillo to reverse himself," he told the press. "Anyway, we claim a victory."

THE MUTUAL LAWSUIT

A suit to recover $500,000 damage from the Mutual Broadcasting System for alleged negligent handling on its network of the radio show, *Information, Please*, began on March 3, 1948 with the service of a complaint on the defendant by Dan Golenpaul Associates, owners and producers of the program. The complaint charged that a survey over a period of several months revealed that more than 100 Mutual stations around the country were committing acts in violation of the contract between the show owners and the Mutual Broadcasting System.

It also accused Mutual of making gross, reckless and intentional misrepresentations of the Golenpaul Associates in inducing them to enter into the present cooperative sponsorship of the show. *Information, Please* was being carried by Mutual on its coast-to-coast network. Unlike single-sponsored shows, it was presented in various localities around the country under local sponsorship, known as the cooperative sponsorship form of presentation. In New York and several other eastern cities, the Chesapeake & Ohio Railroad sponsored the program. The suit papers were served March 3rd at the offices of the attorney for the network.

Variety quoted the radio show owner as having said that he would continue with the Mutual network until the present sponsorship contracts expired in June. At that time, Golenpaul Associates emphasized Golenpaul would leave the broadcasting system.

Among the specific breaches of contract charged in the complaint were the following:
- A substantial number of stations were broadcasting the show for commercial sponsors for which no accounting was made.

- Sponsors were accepted by Mutual without the producers' approval—as specified in the original terms with the network.
- A substantial number of stations were not broadcasting the program at the scheduled time, but instead were giving delayed broadcasts without the producers' authorization.
- Some stations did not carry the program at all, and some only sporadically or at irregular times, making it impossible for listeners to hear the program consistently.
- Mutual permitted stations and networks outside its system to carry the show, on both commercial and sustaining basis, without the knowledge and consent of the producers.
- The continuity of the program was interrupted and abridged to accommodate spot announcements.
- Mutual permitted FM stations to carry the show in direct violation of the agreement.

Opportunities for obtaining a single sponsor for the complete regional networks affiliated with Mutual were lost when Mutual permitted individual stations of the regional networks to make sales, which was in violation of specific agreements not to do so.

When the *Information, Please* producers notified Edgar Kobak, president of Mutual, of these matters he expressed surprise and replied that he would verify them and see what corrective measures were instituted, according to the complaint. But, he added, the contract violations continued. Dan Golenpaul said that the suit would not affect the position of the sponsors, who would continue to the expiration of the contract between Golenpaul Associates and Mutual on June 24, 1948.

Two months later, on May 14, 1948, the Mutual Broadcasting System filed a general denial at the U.S. District Court for charges made against it by Dan Golenpaul Associates in the $500,000 damage suit. Asking dismissal of the action, Mutual entered a counter-claim for $100,000 on the grounds that Golenpaul and his firm, Dan Golenpaul Associates, had violated their contract with the network.

In reply, Mutual said the owners and producers of the show had breached the contract by refusing to approve sponsors procured by local stations and by declining to permit the broadcasting of *Information, Please* by individual stations at a time other than the time of broadcast at the originating studio. The network also charged that the Golenpaul firm had failed from time to time to provide programs of high quality and that it had produced programs unsuitable for broadcast. In addition, the network asserted that the plaintiffs had caused ill-will by being discourteous and insulting to representatives of stations and advertising agencies interested in the show.

Dan Golenpaul publicly stated later that evening, having learned about the counter-claim: "We are suing Mutual for gross incompetence and negligence in the handling of *Information, Please* for permitting stations to carry unauthorized sponsors and commercials and neglecting to account for same...*Information, Please* will let the public decide on the quality of the programs and will let the courts decide on the validity of our claims."

The Mutual contract was due to expire on Friday, June 25, 1948. It would mark a tragic date, establishing an end to the radio program so many Americans had enjoyed.

On July 4, 1948, nine days after the final sponsored broadcast, *Let's Talk Hollywood* premiered over NBC as a summer substitute for *The Jack Benny Program*, sponsored by Golenpaul's formal rival, the American Tobacco Company (Lucky Strike). *Let's Talk Hollywood* was an attempt to cash in on the success of *Information, Please*, in which listeners were optioned to submit questions about Hollywood movies and actors. A panel of comedic intellectuals attempted to answer the questions, awarding a prize to the person who submitted the question if it stumped the experts. For each question used on the program, a one-year subscription of *Photoplay* magazine was awarded. For stumping the panel, the submitter got a gold pass good for free admission to their favorite theater all year long. Eddie Bracken, film columnists Edith Gwynn and Erskine Johnson and various movie stars were members of the panel. The program lasted a mere three months.

THE FINAL SEASONS

Oddly enough, in May of 1949, between the Mutual cancellation and the final season (1950-51), Franklin P. Adams signed a letter/contract of acceptance with Dan Golenpaul modifying the existing agreement for his services as a member of the board of experts on the *Information, Please* program, even though the program was not being broadcast! According to the letter:

"We hereby agree that regardless of the number of weekly broadcasts that I may furnish you during 1949, our agreement shall continue for 1950 and thereafter. In other words, our agreement shall not terminate at the end of this year even though I do not furnish you with the minimum number of broadcasts specified."

This suggested Golenpaul was attempting to make good on his contract, since the previous agreements stipulated that he had to supply the board of experts a minimum number of broadcasts in order for all terms and conditions remain legally active. The next paragraph in the letter is interesting:

"In consideration of the foregoing, I am hereby paying you the sum of $200, receipt whereof you acknowledge, and, in addition, agree to pay you the sum of $50 per week commencing June 2, 1949 and on each Thursday thereafter up to and including December 29, 1949, irrespective of whether or not you perform on *Information, Please*. Of course, if we do go on the air during this period, either commercial or sustaining, I will pay you for each broadcast in accordance with our original contract, as modified, instead of in accordance with this letter."

In all other respects of the original contract, which remained in full force, Golenpaul was paying Franklin P. Adams even though the program was not being broadcast. Although this was the only 1949 contract found during this book's research, it would probably be a fair assumption that John Kieran and Clifton Fadiman were also being paid under said arrangements, but whether the amount of pay was the same as Adams' or not, remains to be seen.

In September of 1950, *Information, Please* returned to the radio for one final season (once again over the Mutual Network, having settled Golenpaul's suit against Mutual months before). Regardless of what is listed among many encyclopedias and reference guides, this final season did not consist of rebroadcasts of previous episodes. Like the previous seasons before, all of the broadcasts were new, with old friends Howard Lindsay and Russel Crouse appearing in many, and new guests including actors Gene Lockhart, John Lund and Richard Carlson. This final season differed only one way from all previous seasons—the broadcasts were not aired "live" over the network. Instead, they were recorded and played back days later over Mutual's affiliates. The final broadcast of *Information, Please* was heard on April 22, 1951, replaced with a serial action-drama, *The Count of Monte Cristo*, based on the novel by Alexander Dumas.

In the fourteen years and 510 broadcasts *Information, Please* attempted to stump the experts, and more than 1,800 dial-twisters had successfully hopped aboard radio and television's quiz program, throwing the experts for frequent losses and winning over $75,000 worth of savings bonds and exactly 1,366 free sets of the *Encyclopedia Britannica*.

THE THIRTEEN *INFORMATION, PLEASE* SHORT FILMS

Produced by Frederic Ullman, Jr.
Supervised/Directed by Frank Donovan.
Program Director, Dan Golenpaul.
Distributed by RKO Radio Pictures, Inc.

"If you've ever listened to *Information, Please* on the air, you know it's unprepared and unrehearsed. And that's the way we'll run it here and now. Here's the layout. I fire questions they've never seen or heard before at a quartet of experts. Any expert who thinks he knows the answer raises his hand. When a question is muffed, we ring a cash register, which means that Pathe is contributing $25 to the Will Rogers Memorial fund. Now—let me introduce our four authorities..." So opened each episode of the *Information, Please* movie shorts.

Clifton Fadiman, master of ceremonies and interrogator for both radio and the film versions of *Information, Please,* didn't have to worry about occupying his leisure time. Having a multitude of interests, the man of letters found spare time the least of his worries. Outside the studios he occupied himself in several ways. As literary critic for the *New Yorker*, he wrote the lead re-

views for the sprightly publication, and covered from one to four of the most important books of each week's crop. In addition, he reviewed from ten to twenty-five non-fiction books for each issue. Another chore was acting as editorial advisor for the publishing firm of Simon & Schuster.

Of "reel" interest to ardent radio listeners and film fans alike was news that *Information, Please* had reached the screen. The film versions took the form of a series of eighteen one-reel subjects scheduled for release during the years of 1939 to 1942.

Acting as the board of experts who answered a myriad of questions, contributed by a public determined to stump them, was the same trio of colorful personalities who appeared on the air show—Adams, Kieran and Levant—with Fadiman officiating. A different guest expert appeared in each release to swell the ranks of the above mentioned "wise men."

One of the most astounding stories in the annals of radio was the rapid rise to national prominence of *Information, Please*, sponsored over the air at the time by Canada Dry Ginger Ale, Inc, in less than a year after the premiere of the radio program. The supposition that it could have been made into a successful visual entertainment became an accomplished fact with the film adaptations by RKO-Pathe. (RKO teamed with the France-based production company Pathe in 1929 to produce theatrical newsreels under the name RKO-Pathe Newsreels, which lasted until 1950. These featured a logo variation in which the Pathe Rooster stood and crowed in place of the transmitter on the rotating globe.)

The method of producing the films captured the same spontaneous and exciting quality, which marked each radio session, and had incidentally, blazed a trail in motion picture technique. The participants came to the studio completely unrehearsed, with no hint of the questions in store for them. No script was used during the questioning and the only preparation, aside from technical details, attendant on shooting the films was the compiling of the questions which were typed and handed to Fadiman before work began.

Of course, there were visual questions, which were calculated to baffle the board still further. Those consisted of exhibitions of wrestling holds, photographs of well-known public figures disguised with skillful drawing, and other such puzzles in which screen audiences could match wits with the experts. This feature afforded a workout to the eye as well as the mind, and was said to heighten the interest which the radio program had. Even the familiar ring of the cash register when an expert missed a question was included in the short films. But where the radio program always turned bonus money over to the author of the muffed question, the film shorts donated it to a charity.

According to the press book issued through RKO, it was estimated at the time of the premiere of the first short that the radio program had an average of five million listeners. The quiz hour stood fourth in a recent poll on the popularity of all types of program, and was an undisputed winner of first among quiz programs.

The press book also offered theater managers numerous suggestions for cross-marketing the program to the movie-going public. Simon and Schuster's fast-selling *Information, Please* quiz game book, the material for which was taken from the actual radio programs, was suggested as a tie-in with bookstores and libraries. It could be offered as a prize in any contest staged in conjunction with the film. There was a distinctly educational side to *Information, Please* and it was suggested that theater managers capitalize on it by employing some sort of tie-up with schools. There was the possibility of setting aside a certain time for school classes to attend showings in a group. Prizes could be offered to students for the best essay on "What I Have Learned from *Information, Please*."

T. Orien Wright, New York display designer, devised a clever window display in McCutcheon's smart Fifth Avenue department store. The idea was simple and effective. A sign hanging between two well-dressed mannequins read: "Information Please! Question: What inspires many of the top ranking fashions of the year? Answer: Styles of your grandmother's day. From this period comes the glamour of jet black beads on smart matinee dresses."

Posters, lobby cards and one-sheets were designed featuring the characters of Fadiman, Levant and Adams for display in movie houses. For the price of $1.75 each, theater managers could purchase a larger banner measuring approximately 39 x 54 inches that advertised the series. Suitable for display, it was made of scarlet silk with brilliant gold, black and white imprinting.

Canada Dry Ginger Ale, Inc. distributed special displays advertising the film version to all their dealers throughout the United States and Canada. There were colorful pieces, which were attached to the tops of Ginger Ale and soda bottles. This proved a tremendous plug for the new series, as the displays would be seen on thousands of drug, grocery and refreshment counters.

Each *Information, Please* film short brought a new guest star before the cameras. Rex Stout and Gene Tunney were guest experts for the first and second pictures, and contributed their respective bits of knowledge about sleuthing and sports. Guests for the remaining reels were selected from the roster of those who had appeared on the radio program in the past.

Rex Stout, author of the widely-read Nero Wolfe mysteries, was the guest star for the first release of RKO-Pathe's *Information, Please* series of short subjects. While he handled questions outside his field with unusual competence, the creator of the master-sleuth failed to track down the answer to a question about famous mystery stories. He was particularly embarrassed when one of the plots under discussion turned out to be his own.

The Will Rogers Memorial Hospital benefited to the tune of $25 dollars each time a member of the board of experts muffed a question. The American Museum of Natural History helped RKO-Pathe stump the experts in the second release of the film series. Visual questions were added to the usual classic puzzles when the radio program was adapted to film, and the producers gathered an assortment of objects for the experts' powers of identification. The museum provided, among other things, a duck-billed platypus, an armadillo and a pelican. These were all stuffed specimens, which was just as well as the museum also sent along one skunk.

Producing the shorts was different from making any other movie. Of the five stars, four went before the camera without dialogue, direction or rehearsal. Like any movie production, the working day started at 9 a.m., when the minor members of the cast, who performed the visual parts of the questions put to the experts, arrived on the set. They rehearsed their business until Inquisitor Fadiman was ready. From 11:30 to 1:00, he was photographed asking the questions and giving every possible variation of "Very Good, Mr. Levant" (etc.) for the soundtrack. From 2:30 to 5:30 two cameras—one long shot and one close-up—worked on the experts. The close-up cameraman had a nerve-racking job because he never knew who might speak next. The experts had been carefully locked out of the room where Fadiman got his shots by exercising what was almost mental telepathy.

As a result, the movie shorts were as spontaneous, witty and informal as the radio program. After 5:30 the cast had its turn with the visual questions, some of which were performed before the camera. Visual questions and clues were given during the routines and with these, the experts were as much at home as with merely verbal problems. Stuffed birds, animals, football referees' hand signals and complex charades brought the standard average of flip and accurate answers. Charles Dickens' Mr. Micawber was one from a parade of fictional characters, speedily identified by guest expert Clarence Budington Kelland. On only one series, a group of stuffed fish, did the experts draw a blank. The worst performance in a film was by guest Gene Tunney who failed to identify four out of four wrestling holds!

A room dressed with desk and bookshelves marked the scenery and atmosphere for each filmed program. Between takes the experts relaxed, smoked and chatted with their friends. While the camera was grinding they were not allowed to smoke, but F.P.A., reluctant to give up his cigar, often held it under the table where he thought it was concealed from the camera. Levant hated movie makeup. During the scenes of display in which costumed men represented book titles, actors were invited for the brief appearances, including Milton Neil, Robert Lynd, Rollin Bauer, Joan McCarthy, Windy Russell and Howard Nelson. When Christopher Morley answered a question correctly, Adams put his hand down. When Fadiman asked him what title he had guessed, Adams also gave the right one and Fadiman remarked, "Mr. Adams always comes in a graceful second." Christopher Morley had good reason to appear on the film short. His best-seller, *Kitty Foyle*, had just recently been purchased by RKO for Ginger Rogers, the same studio that was releasing the *Information, Please* shorts. John Gunther received a perfect score for identifying various countries in South America. When Christopher Morley was guest, all four panelists sang a quartette version of "Old Black Joe."

Howard Nelson had wheeled a stove barely three feet into the room when Levant raised his hand and gave the answer. "Pretty fast," commented Fadiman. "Nobody will say this program has everything but the kitchen stove." When actor Robert Lynd played assailant with Milton

Neil as the victim in a physical illustration of a song title, Levant gave the correct answer. Fadiman remarked, "That's hitting it on the nose." "On the nose?" jeered Levant. At one point during one of the reels, Levant clamored to answer and Kieran said, "I've got a good title for it." Levant said, "I'll be a gentleman, which is difficult for me" and let Kieran answer.

"Gentlemen, what actor does this pantomime remind you of?" queried Interlocutor Fadiman. The long, lean arm of Franklin P. Adams waved in the air. "William Claude Fields," drawled Adams and stuck his own cigar back in his wide, whimsical mouth. "Very good, Mr. Adams. And now for our next question…" The smooth persuasive voice of Clifton Fadiman started to outline another query when, from the side of the stage, a little bearded man, looking like a refugee from an Orson Welles story conference, let out a cry that sounded like the grinding gears of an old car. Apparently the cast translated his speech as "Cut," for they relaxed and the cameras and sound recorders were reloaded.

Since the movie shorts were a visual medium, it seemed only appropriate that 90% of the questions involved some form of artwork, physical apparition, or pantomime. Questions were asked such as "Who trained himself in this fashion?" followed by an actor putting pebbles in his mouth and an actor putting wood between his fingers. (Answers were Demosthenes and Schumann.) When Fadiman asked what historic incident each pantomime suggested, men rushed after a gold-colored object and a woman wearing a fur coat marked 600 said, "Charge it." (Answers wee *The Gold Rush* and *The Charge of the Light Brigade*.)

The scene where all of the filming took place was a soundstage in New York City. For ten minutes, the time it took to unwind a reel, or 1,000 feet of film, through cameras and sound recorders, Fadiman shot questions at the Phi Beta Kappas of radio's most popular classroom. Six reels of questions and answers on every variety of subject from the stance of former champion prize fighters to the identification – by grimly munched sandwiches – of the various kinds of cheese, were filmed during one afternoon, just to compile what the editors would make into a ten-minute short! Call it speedy if you will, the shorts were just that. Fred Ullman, Jr. was the RKO-Pathe Vice President and producer of the shorts, and he explained to the men on stage that the sixty minutes of screen time would be cut down to one separate reel to join the parade of *Information, Please* shorts captivating the country's movie audiences as completely as the air show had won radio renown. According to Ullman, the *Informa-*

tion, Please shorts ranked second only to Disney's at the box office.

This might be why such a large number of shorts were produced—eighteen to be exact. When the first *Information, Please* short was released in 1939, the program was booked in 5,000 movie theaters across the country. Extremely impressive considering that movies released today rarely hit the 4,000 mark.

The *Information, Please* shorts were routinely released between double features in movie houses. Ruth Gordon appeared in the sixth short, released in March of 1940. At the Gramercy Park Cinema at Lexington Avenue in New York City, her short was shown between showings of *The Mortal Storm* (with James Stewart and Frank Morgan) and *Safari* (with Madeleine Carroll and Douglas Fairbanks, Jr.). In that same year, Wendell Willkie's short was shown at the same theater with *Devil's Island* (with Boris Karloff) and *My Love Came Back* (with Olivia de Havilland and Jeffrey Lynn). Willkie's movie short, unlike any of the other *Information, Please* shorts, spawned a short-lived controversy.

Wendell Willkie's personal charm was subjected to a test when he met Republican members of Congress in Washington in July of 1940. He was introduced to Senate Minority Leader McNary, his running mate, on his arrival to the capital. It was announced that Willkie was nominated for the Republican presidential ticket of 1940. Just days before, Willkie had gone to the Radio City Music Hall in New York for the premiere of the *Information, Please* movie short, in which he was the guest. Newspaper photographers soon drew the audience's attention to him and he was given an ovation. The publicity was not appreciated by members of both parties – obviously, it didn't look good for a possible future President to appear on a motion picture quiz short.

On October 4, 1940, Samuel F. Pryor, Jr., director of the Eastern division of the Republican National Committee, charged that the motion picture short entitled *Information, Please* was being suppressed under orders from the Democratic National Committee. The picture showed Wendell Willkie, appearing on the radio program and making a big hit by his answers to a variety of questions.

Mr. Pryor's charge was seconded by Clarence Kelland, assistant in charge of publicity at the headquarters, who stated that Edward J. Flynn, Democratic National Chairman, and the White House had united to stop further presentation. It was stated that the picture was very popular and that advanced bookings were heavy.

George J. Schaefer, president of RKO, made a public statement: "We have no right and we do not wish to use screens to show any picture at this time that would advocate or further the cause of either Willkie or Roosevelt." Schaefer said that he had no fear of retaliation and that no pressure had been brought to bear to suppress the picture. The failure to release the short constituted a threat to free speech and free press, Mr. Kelland said.

Once things got under way, the director, script girl, camera men, and all their various assistants were slightly breathless from their efforts to hide props. "It's really terrible. The minute you see one of those experts you start running around sticking things behind walls and under chairs." The experts were all upstairs, being made up. Reportedly, none of them were even slightly nervous. Radio had accustomed them to this. Motion pictures could not faze them. Besides, they had made one of these two-reelers before. Previews were not released until September of 1939 when the first short was released, and the financial figures made Pathe determine whether to make another and more elaborate film.

Once the actors had been separated from their friends in the audience and persuaded to take their seats before the cameras, the picture went ahead rapidly. Eileen Creelman of the New York *Sun* visited the set during filming, and recalled how "the actors were completely unabashed by it all. Even the cameras did not alarm them. Mr. Adams, when he did not know the answer and didn't care who knew that he didn't know, would fold his arms on the desk, put his head upon them, and apparently doze for a second. Mr. Kieran, silver-haired and quiet, seemed absorbed in each problem. Mr. Tunney was given to beaming and, until the sound man checked him, to drumming on the desk. Mr. Levant, young and round of face, was earnest as though this were really school days again. And he was more than a little embarrassed when Gene Tunney knew something about Mozart that he, the musical expert, had forgotten."

Two weeks after the signing of the RKO-Pathe contract, on April 8, 1939, Clifton Fadiman signed a three-page contract with Dan Golenpaul to perform the same services as described on the radio program, including the limit of hours required for filming per picture. Fadiman's contract was once again lucrative. Section eight stated:

"In the event that the first picture is released, I agree to employ you and you agree to render services in connection with six additional pictures upon the same terms and conditions that apply to the first picture, except your compensation shall be Eight Hundred and Fifty ($850) Dollars for each picture, plus an additional amount equal to 7 ½% of the gross receipts therefrom in excess of $15,000, such additional amount, however, not to be more than $150 per picture."

Two days later, on April 10, 1939, Oscar Levant signed a similar contract for Dan Golenpaul, including the same vital statistics as Fadiman's with the exception of the financial reimbursement. Section seven of the contract stated:

"If the first picture is released, I agree to pay you and you agree to accept for your services in the production thereof the sum of Three Hundred ($300) Dollars within five days after the picture is approved for release and not later than twenty-five (25) days after the filming."

That same week, both Franklin P. Adams and John Kieran signed the same contract, thus ensuring that the entire board of experts would.

The filming of the first seven movie shorts went along smoothly with expert precision-like care in the productions. On the evening of April 4, 1940, Fadiman, Adams, Kieran, Levant and guest Elmer Davis finished filming the seventh and final movie short fulfilling their contractual obligations for an initial seven shorts. Twelve days later, Dan Golenpaul and Pathe News, Inc. signed a revised contract dated April 16, 1940 with very little difference from the previous contract, except for the following four changes:

1. The numbers of hours for filming each short was lengthened from three to five, including the stipulation of the two additional hours if needed.
2. Subsequent filming of each short would take place approximately 45 days after the filming immediately preceding the completion of the previous short.
3. Pathe agreed to give Golenpaul a copy of the release schedule set up by RKO Radio Pictures, Inc.
4. In the event of the release of the first picture hereunder Pathe would pay Golenpaul $5,000 instead of the initial $3,000, though the rest of the financial agreements for the most part, pretty much remained the same.

On May 13, 1940, Levant, Adams and Kieran each signed a letter of acceptance, mutually agreeing to renew their written agreements to appear in the seven initial movie shorts. The amount of money paid to the board of experts remained the same throughout the entire series of filming. Clifton Fadiman signed his letter of acceptance on May 18, 1940, marking him as the only member from the original radio program to receive a pay raise. Instead of $850 plus a percentage of the gross receipts, Fadiman's new compensation was $1,150 for each single reel produced.

The following is a list of all eighteen *Information, Please* shorts and the guests who appeared on them. The dates listed below are that of the dates of filming, not the dates of release.

Movie Short #1	Guest: Rex Stout	May 26, 1939
Movie Short #2	Guest: Gene Tunney	August 3, 1939
Movie Short #3	Guest: Clarence Budington Kelland	October 13, 1939
Movie Short #4	Guest: Deems Taylor	November 22, 1939
Movie Short #5	Guest: Christopher Morley	January 10, 1940
Movie Short #6	Guest: Ruth Gordon	March 9, 1940
Movie Short #7	Guest: Elmer Davis	April 4, 1940
Movie Short #8	Guest: Wendell Willkie	June 13, 1940
Movie Short #9	Guest: Anna Neagle	August 8, 1940
Movie Short #10	Guest: Alice Marble	September 30, 1940
Movie Short #11	Guest: Louis Bromfield	November 19, 1940
Movie Short #12	Guest: Jan Struther	January 15, 1941
Movie Short #13	Guest: Boris Karloff	March 13, 1941
Movie Short #14	Guest: John Gunther	July 16, 1941
Movie Short #15	Guest: Howard Lindsay	September of 1941
Movie Short #16	Guest: Cornelia Otis Skinner	November 24, 1941
Movie Short #17	Guest: John Carradine	March 11, 1942
Movie Short #18	Guest: Russel Crouse	none available

The total of movie shorts filmed was seventeen, with the 18th planned for production. Very little documentation has been preserved and two sources suggest there may have been less. According to Ann Golenpaul, wife of Dan Golenpaul, the last movie short (with Russel Crouse as a guest expert) was fully written and rehearsed, but never filmed.

Golenpaul's papers suggested that all of the films were destroyed in a fire at the Pathe Warehouse. Golenpaul himself only owned 12 stills from the films, many of which have been reprinted in film magazines over the years.

HISTORY OF THE
INFORMATION, PLEASE ALMANAC

"When we decided to publish an almanac in 1946," recalled Golenpaul, "there were many almanacs in the country published by local newspapers and sold within their distribution areas. The only almanacs with national distribution were the *Farmer's Almanac* and the *World Almanac*. Since Ben Franklin's time, almanacs were considered more or less a throw-away, they were priced at 25 cents to 75 cents. Most of them were basically local directories, and the rest of the material was inconsequential. We decided to enter into the almanac field because of the tremendous amount of questions that the *Information, Please* radio program received from the listeners who were merely seeking information.

"When we made the decision to publish an almanac we decided it had to be more than a book of statistics. We felt that there was a need for a highly rated single volume reference book that was well organized and well written, and that it had to be modern in its concepts and treatments. We felt that our book should be a contemporary reference book combining scholarship and popular interest, and that while it should have a general appeal, the special appeal should be to students. This was our objective, and this is what we did."

According to a press release dated April 23, 1946, "John Kieran, former columnist and member of the quiz program, *Information, Please*, will edit *The Information Please Almanac and Year Book*, which Dan Golenpaul, producer of the program, is preparing for publication. It will be published annually by Doubleday."

John "walking encyclopedia" Kieran was Golenpaul's first choice. The first *Information Please Almanac* was published in 1947, and Kieran served

ALMANAC

444 MADISON AVENUE • NEW YORK 22, N. Y.

as editor until 1954 when he asked to be relieved because of a commitment to do a book on the nature life of New York State. During this period, Golenpaul participated and collaborated with John Kieran on editorial policies, so it was logical for him to take over the editorship which had been his responsibility to date.

Less than a year after the press release, the *Almanac* hit the grade when Bruce Rae reviewed the publication in the January 26, 1947 issue of the *New York Times Book Review*:

"In the past an almanac was known as a 'book or table containing a calendar of days, a register of ecclesiastical festivals and Saints days, and a record of astronomical phenomena.' But John Kieran, citing this encyclopedic definition in his forward, sponsors more pace and range in this 952-page volume of fact and comment, the first volume in a new series. Here is an almanac that can be read from cover to cover for its entertainment value. For more practical purposes it is a staggering compendium of facts, charts and statistical tables enlivened by resumes of current events written in the idiom of the day by leading authorities. 'Facts are fun,' Dan Golenpaul points out in explaining the purpose of the almanac. 'They should be presented in such a way that they don't scare you, but give you enjoyment.'

"He and his associates prove the point with their brisk and well-directed choice and use of material. This should be a revealing reference book for the people of tomorrow, since it has caught the tone and color of the dawning atomic age. Only the specialist is likely to spot the occasional gaps slurred over because of the breadth of the canvas covered.

"It has additional merits of being legible, well indexed and so smoothly strung together that the flow of information is easily absorbed. In the past when this reviewer has had to trail a segment of information to its liar, he has had many unhappy experiences with reference books. Usually after finding the index, it has proved inadequate and by the time he located the line sought, his depression was profound and was not lessened by the microscopic type in which the gem was imbedded. The index in this volume is masterly and you don't have to squint to read the type.

"Among the more unusual features of this almanac are a table on the world's riches and resources; a forty-page travel guide for every country in the world; and a chronology of world history in headline form from 4004 B.C. through 1946. The review of the past year goes beyond the news highlights, and includes articles by authorities in sports, drama, radio, music, art, letters and other fields. They are not dull, dragging doses of statistics. They are sprightly done, notably so in the piece on the evolution of the atomic age, as carefully traced by its Boswell, William L. Laurence.

"Does anyone wish to know what living costs in the United States today? *Information Please Almanac* supplies the answer. Or the summer temperature of Mozambique. Or the lend-lease aid received by Russia between 1941 and 1945. Or which airlines go to Iran. Or the names and dates of the Archbishops of Canterbury from Thomas à Becket and the Pontiffs from St. Peter. Or the world life expectancy. Or the text of the Gettysburg Address. Or where Aggtelik Cavern is. Or how many people in the world today speak the gypsy language.

"The book has its own Who's Who; it's 'The Rise of the United States' traced by Arthur M. Schlesinger; its biographies of all the Presidents by Arthur M. Schlesinger, Jr.; a history of the United Nations by Harold E. Stassen, and a strategical summary of World War II by George Fielding Eliot. Other contributors on the American scene are Elmer Davis, who writes of the year 1946 in Washington; Grantland Rice, who edits the thorough-going sports section; and Thomas Craven, Deems Taylor, John Mason Brown, Christopher Morley and Howard Barnes, who comment on the various arts in which they specialize. Walter Yust, editor in chief of *The Encyclopedia Britannica*, planned the section dealing with the historical, political, geographic, economic and social conditions of the other nations of the world."

The *Information Please Almanac* started as a hardback with a $2.00 list price and was published by Doubleday. The sale of the hardback edition was approximately one-quarter of a million and stayed around that figure for several years with future editions. In 1951, it was decided to bring out the paper edition at a $1.00 retail price. "When we made the decision to publish the paper edition we also developed a plan to sell the book through newspapers," recalled Golenpaul. "The first newspaper to sponsor the *Information Please Almanac* was the *New York Herald Tribune*. Many other newspapers took up the sponsorship. These changes resulted in a considerable increase in our sales. Our sales in the 1960s were approximately 700,000 which I believe for the first time exceeded sales for the *World Almanac*."

This technique was slightly original in the fact that paper edition copies of the Almanac would feature on the cover, custom-printed, the name of the newspaper. Example, "*The New York Herald Tribune* Edition." Thus newspapers could buy copies at a wholesale price, and sell them for profit. On May 3, 1951, Richard A.R. Pinkham, Circulation Manager for the *New York Herald Tribune,* wrote to Dan Golenpaul expressing his opinion for the test market:

"First and foremost, let me repeat to you that the sale of the *Information Please Almanac* in the greater New York area and in its surrounding trading zones far exceeded our original expectations. The book moved with great alacrity and many of our distributing agents sold out and were forced to reorder. I can't tell you how thoroughly gratified we are with this, and how confidently we can predict that the sale will grow and grow and grow as they say in your radio world."

Golenpaul reprinted this letter in his printed proposal, submitted to every major newspaper in the United States, in hopes that the letter would help convince other newspapers to purchase copies of the Almanac for resale.

The reviews were in. The *Atlanta Constitution* reviewed: "There's information galore in this fat volume. In addition to the facts and figures, it contains much interesting reading matter." The *San Francisco Chronicle* wrote: "One of the advantages to the reader of the increasing skill of the almanackists has been the fact that *Information Please Almanac* had not been a static, same-as-last-year kind of volume."

The clever marketing strategy of having newspapers order copies of the almanac with their names on the cover proved more than profitable: The *Chicago Sun-Times and Daily News* ordered 30,000 copies of the 1964 edition of the Almanac. The *San Diego Union and Evening Tribune* ordered 5,000 copies of the 1964 edition, then 5,000 copies of the 1965 edition. The *Portland Sunday Telegram* ordered 7,500 copies of the 1955 edition, 6,000 copies of the 1956 edition , 5,500 copies of the 1964 edition, and 5,500 copies of the 1965 edition. The *Washington, D.C. Evening Star and Sunday Star* ordered 15,000 copies of the 1956 edition, 7,500 copies of the 1964 edition, and 10,000 copies of the 1966 edition. The *Los Angeles Evening Herald-Express* ordered 20,000 copies of the 1955 edition, 25,000 copies of the 1956 edition, 40,000 copies of the 1964 edition, 40,000 copies of the 1965 edition, and 44,000 copies of the 1966 edition. The *Syracuse Herald-American* ordered 7,500 copies of the 1955 edition. The *Columbus Dispatch* ordered 7,500 copies of the 1955 edition.

The *Call-Bulletin* ordered 22,500 copies of the 1955 edition. The *Buffalo Courier-Express* ordered 7,500 copies of the 1955 edition. The *Patriot-News* ordered 5,000 copies of the 1955 edition, and 7,500 copies of the 1956 edition. The *Charlotte Observer* ordered 6,000 copies of the 1956 edition. The *Oregon Journal* ordered 15,000 copies of the 1955 edition. The *St. Paul Dispatch-Pioneer Press* ordered 5,000 copies of the 1955 edition, and 10,000 copies of the 1956 edition. The *Miami Herald* ordered 15,000 copies of the 1955 edition, and 10,000 copies of the 1956 edition. The *Winston-Salem Journal* ordered 5,000 copies of the 1955 edition, and 5,000 copies of the 1956 edition of the Almanac. The *Honolulu Advertiser* ordered 3,500 copies of the 1956 edition. The *Buffalo Courier-Express* ordered 12,000 copies of the 1956 edition.

Each newspaper had to sign an eight-page contract in agreement to the sale terms and shipment methods.

Dear Sirs:
This letter, when signed by both of us, shall constitute an agreement between us as follows:
1. You agree to purchase and we agree to sell and deliver to you _____ copies of the 19___ *Information Please Almanac*, _____(newspaper name)_____ edition (hereinafter referred to as the Almanac).
2. We shall not supply the Almanac to any other newspaper in your primary distribution area, which is defined as follows:
3. The _____(newspaper name)_____ edition of the Almanac will be identical with our regular paper covered edition, except that it will bear your imprint on the front cover and on the title page, and also have two pages for a local news chronology, which you shall prepare. You may substitute any other type of material of local interest for these two pages, such material to be subject to our approval.

4. The price of the Almanac to you shall be the retail less 50% F.O.B. Clinton, Massachusetts. Your retail price for the Almanac shall be _____ per copy, except for copies which may be mailed direct to the consumer by our printer, in which event you may, if you wish, add the handling and postage charges. Your price to retailers shall not be less than _____ per copy. The Almanac may be used by you as a free premium provided that no such promotion agreement shall have the effect of cutting the regular retail price of the book.
5. Your copies will be stored with our printer at Clinton, Massachusetts, subject to your delivery instructions for bulk shipments. Our printer will also fill your mail orders for which you furnish the addressed labels. On each such mail order there will be added to the above price 12 cents per copy handling, plus actual postage for ordinary book delivery. At this time, said postage is 15 cents per copy but is subject to change to conform with any change in the postage rules. The Almanac will be ready for shipment not later than _____, 19___. If, for any reason beyond our control, shipments cannot be made until later than _____, we will so advise you by _____ and you may modify your subsequent orders accordingly.
6. You shall confine distribution of your edition to the usual channels for newspaper distribution in your primary distribution area, such as newsstands, home delivery and mail orders solicited through your paper, and you will not distribute your edition through regular book dealers without our prior written consent.
7. We shall not be liable to you for our inability to deliver the books to you as herein provided because of war, accidents, factory breakdown, labor trouble, or causes or contingencies beyond our reasonable control.
8. If you so desire, you may review this arrangement for the 19___ and subsequent issues of the Almanac on terms mutually satisfactory to both of us, it being understood however, that this provision does not obligate us to publish any future editions of the Almanac.

Sincerely yours,
Dan Golenpaul

While the book would contain solid statistics and facts, Golenpaul and Kieran decided to use magazine techniques for organizing the Almanac so that it would not be used only as a reference book, but a book that would be read frequently. Golenpaul employed leading scholars and writers of the day to participate in the editorial development of the book. For example, in the 1947 edition, Elmer Davis wrote on Washington Politics, Grantland Rice on sports, Christopher Morley on books, John Mason Brown on the theater, Thomas Craven on art, and many others. Obviously, the majority were experts in their own field, and previous guests of the radio program *Information, Please* who had already proved their value.

With the 1948 edition, Golenpaul introduced a policy of special sections and special articles. In the 1948 edition, the special section was a "Politican's Guide" and some of the contributors were George Gallup, John Gunther, Mark Sullivan, Tom Stokes, Arthur Schlesinger, Sr. and Jr., Alan Nevins and many others. In the 1949 edition, "How Man Lives Under Capitalist-Socialist-Communist Governments" was the section. Some of the contributors included George Bernard Shaw and the U.S.S.R. Information Bureau, which had the first article to be released in an American publication.

Golenpaul continued the policy of special sections in future editions including:

"The Ten-Point Program to Abolish Poverty" by W.J. Cohen

"The 80-Billion-Dollar Defense System" by R.F. Kaufman

"American Education" by H. Rivlin

"Relearning Mathematics" by M.F. Rosskopf

"The Next Twenty Years in Space" by N. Panagakos

"The Houses Uncle Sam Builds" by Walter Rybeck of the Urban Institute of Washington

"Environmental Crisis" by Senator Edmund S. Muskie

"A Revolution in Foreign Policy" by Henry Steele Commager

"A Better Tax System" by Joseph A. Pechman

Some of the innovations during the many years of publication were the Crossword Puzzle Guide; Parliamentary Procedure; Recipes of Famous Restaurants; Your Family Name, What Does it Mean?; Breakthroughs in Science; Your Health and Long Life; What Price Common Market; and so on and so on.

By far the most fascinating part of the book was the miscellany of information, chiefly statistical, found among the pages. Page 278 offered the chance for the reader to know his life expectancy. Everyone knows that the Empire State Building is the tallest of all skyscrapers, but who can name the biggest outside New York? Page 636 will tell you that it is Cleveland's Terminal Tower, which is topped, by no less than seven of New York's giants. The results of every Olympic Games' events since their revival in Athens in 1896 were reprinted. If the reader wanted to know the population of Iraq, the rulers of Russia since 1462, the number of years Ty Cobb batted .300, the birth date of Lana Turner. or the number of people speaking Swahili, Uzbek or Rajasthani, those facts were included within the pages.

"Sales-wise, we have probably grossed about twenty million for the twenty-seven editions that we have published," recalled Golenpaul in April of 1972. "These books have gone into homes, libraries, schools and were probably used by about one hundred million people. It is particularly popular with students of all grades. They like our basic statistics which are excellent and our special articles which lend themselves to their social study courses."

Addendum: Over the years, Dan Golenpaul made numerous friends in every field of American politics, especially with powerful and influential figures. Having arranged for various men and women, experts and leaders of their original crafts to compose sections for the annual Almanac won him attention around the globe. Reprinted below are letters mailed to Golenpaul that might be of interest:

February 23, 1965
Dear Dan:
    Many thanks for all your kindness. You can certainly be proud of your latest fine edition of *Information Please Almanac*. I am doubly grateful for your warm recollections.

                              Best regards. Sincerely,
                              Hubert H. Humphrey

126 Information, Please

December 19, 1969
Dear Mr. Golenpaul:
    Thanks for thinking of me in such a fine way at Christmastime. The copy of the *Information Please Almanac* will certainly be put to good use and will be an appropriate and welcome addition to the Lyndon B. Johnson Library.
    Along with my gratitude, you have my warm good wishes for a Happy Holiday Season.
Sincerely,
Lyndon B. Johnson

December 30, 1969
Dear Mr. Golenpaul:
    I want to express my sincere appreciation for the copy of the 1970 *Information Please Almanac, Atlas and Yearbook* which you so thoughtfully sent to me. I am indeed pleased to have it.
Sincerely yours,
J. Edgar Hoover

(undated)
Dear Dan –
    Thank you so much for the 1972 Edition – I needed it badly.
Best,
Ed

(Ed Sullivan, 502 Park Avenue, New York City)

January 15, 1971
Dear Mr. Golenpaul:
    I was highly pleased to receive the new *Information Please Almanac Atlas and Yearbook.*
    Thank you for your continuing interest.
Sincerely yours,
Harry S Truman

November 11, 1971

Dear Mr. Golenpaul:

I have now received the 1972 edition of *Information Please Almanac* and have noted with interest the section on Politics – 1972. I appreciated having the opportunity to contribute to this edition, and I thank you for sending a complimentary copy to my attention.

Best wishes,
Bob Dole

This was just a sampling of the correspondence Golenpaul received from mailing complimentary Almanacs over the years. Among the correspondence was a Christmas card from Richard M. Nixon!

THE TELEVISION SERIES

SPONSOR: You can put your confidence in General Electric!

ANNOUNCER: Wake Up, America! Time to stump the experts! And now, for our first television performance, here is the master of ceremonies of *Information, Please* and regular essayist for *Holiday* magazine...Clifton Fadiman!

FADIMAN: Welcome to the debut on television of the one and only original *Information, Please*. Well, man and boy for many years, I've been announcing that *Information, Please* is spontaneous and unrehearsed. That has been true—and always will be. Now we know there are many old friends of *Information, Please* in the audience and we hope there are many new ones. All of you are probably interested to know how we play the game. We'll explain the rules in a few minutes, but just now, we are anxious to start playing. Our three-man panel consists of our two beloved *Information, Please* veterans...

So opened the premiere broadcast of television's counterpart of the radio program, *Information, Please*. Very little is known about the television program, except that it was broadcast over the network "live," and just like the radio counterpart, was just as spontaneous. What can be known about the program—both contents and quality—other than the assumption that the television program was devised in a similar format to the RKO shorts from 1939 – 1942, are the reviews from critics who stood to attention. On June 6, 1952 Jack Gould of the *New York Times* reviewed the series:

"As the first of the intelligent quiz shows on radio, *Information, Please* always has enjoyed a special niche in the affections of that section of the listening audience which somehow had been dimly aware that Washington's first name was George. Since it left the air some years ago a great many of the program's friends have repeatedly asked when the show would turn up on television.

"Well, the video version of *Information, Please* finally materialized last Sunday evening at 9 o'clock over the Columbia Broadcasting System network, but loyal followers of the program might as well be warned at the outset that they are going to have to be very understanding and patient. The premiere was easily the disappointment of the year. The questions put by Clifton Fadiman, resuming his familiar role as moderator, were far from interesting. The panel, consisting of Franklin P. Adams, John Kieran and James Michener, showed little relish for its assignment. And the staging and camera work were as amateurish as anything seen this year on video. It was an off night for everybody concerned.

"According to report, part of the troubles of the premiere of *Information, Please* can be traced to the political conventions. Together with the other networks, CBS has shipped much of its equipment to Chicago for the next three weeks, and *Information, Please* was caught with an outmoded camera and old-fashioned microphone equipment. There were other physical faults, too. The setting, for one, was most awkward. Mr. Fadiman was pushed off to one side of the panel and looked a little like a lonely coxswain in a rowboat. The experts were huddled together as in a dice game and were very ill at ease in not being able to see Mr. Fadiman face to face.

"But what really seemed missing on the debut was the spark of adult fun and spontaneous repartee which in years past has been the substance of *Information, Please*. In the main this was no doubt due to the unexciting questions, but the thought does occur that video has been burdened with so many quiz programs that *Information, Please* may have lost much of its novelty status. As a concession to television, Dan Golenpaul, the producer of *Information, Please*, arranged for the inclusion of visual questions involving drawings on placards. To change the placards there were a couple of girls in tights and long stockings. Just putting the placards on the screen without any distaff decoration would have been a more expeditious course. *Information, Please* doesn't need the Dagmarian touch.

"Despite all the handicaps on the premiere, *Information, Please* no doubt can ultimately make the grade after Mr. Golenpaul becomes familiar with the elementary requirements of television. He is in the unenviable position of a pioneer who must learn the ropes all over again."

The July 2, 1952 issue of *Variety* featured the following review:

"Dan Golenpaul's *Information, Please*, the daddy of all quiz shows, which for more than a decade was a weekly 'must' for the more literate radio listener, made its TV bow last Sunday (29) on CBS-TV as the thirteen-week summer replacement for General Electric's *Fred Waring Show*. Clifton Fadiman, doubling on the initial stanza from his regular *This Is Show Business* conferenciering, is back at his old emcee stand (he's presiding over the first eight programs), as are two of the old-time "*Info*" vets—Franklin P. Adams and John Kieran. Rounding out the panel of experts as the first of a weekly series of guests was James Michener, author of *Tales of the South Pacific*.

"As a TV entrant, *Information, Please* takes practically no concessions to the newer sight-and-sound medium. Nor, for that matter, to the changing tastes since its radio heyday. True, it is literate gab as projected by a group of warm, animated intellectuals who enjoy delving into their craniums.

"Their encyclopedic minds and the speed and deftness with which they can articulate their wealth of knowledge is as startling to TV viewing mortals as it was 15 years ago via the AM kilocycles. That Fadiman combines both a personal magnetism and unusual ability is, of course, no surprise to the TV audience. Kieran, with his complete ease, lack of self-consciousness and his ebullience (not to mention his almost-fabled memory) remains one of *Info*'s vital components. F.P.A. is a distinct personality who never projects himself—yet definitely belongs in the charmed circle. Michener, too, fitted into the cerebral pattern as though he were a longtime panelist on the show.

"*Information, Please* on the other hand, makes no pretensions of being anything but a showcase for picking the brains of some extraordinarily gifted people. There are no gimmicks, no low-cut femme fatales, no prizes. It retains its intellectual integrity and as such should recapture its audience. But it will be a limited segment of the TV viewers who will content themselves with this non-gimmicked form of entertainment offering little in the way of visual values. *Info* is still an interesting and entertaining show and it would be unfortunate if this limited audience were not to be considered in the scheme of TV patterns. There's something of a Ripley in sports announcer Red Barber showing up doing the GE commercials. Baseball or iceboxes, the Barber can do no wrong."

The July 12, 1952 issue of *Cue* reviewed the program as getting off to a slow start:

"Perhaps it's just that we've all become a little older, including the Messrs. Fadiman, Kieran and Adams, but the long-awaited TV debut of *Information, Please* was something of a disappointment. The wit and sparkle that distinguished the radio version for so many years were strangely absent on the video premiere. The panelists were as knowledgeable as ever, but what the hell—if it's straight information you're after, you can get it by dialing 411.

"As we watched the TV launching, we were thinking back to some of the classic exchanges that marked the program's career on dat ol' debbil radio. We remembered, with fondness, the session in which Fadiman asked Adams what the ruler of Persia was called. 'The Shah,' replied F.P.A. 'Are you Shah?' inquired Fadiman. 'Sultanly,' said Adams.

"If the video presentation of *Information, Please* continues to lack this kind of repartee, the fault may well lie with the questions, which, on radio, were as ingenious as the answers. By trying too hard for "visual appeal," the program may sacrifice the quality that endeared it to fans who felt that one bon mot was worth a thousand pictures.

"A particularly silly interlude on the opening TV show, for example, involved the identification of three ridiculously easy songs by the three-man panel of Adams, Kieran and author James Michener. Fadiman asked the board of experts to act out the titles rather than name them (we're on TV, boys). So after the first few bars of "Button Up Your Overcoat," Michener went through the motions of buttoning his jacket. With the opening strains of "Put Your Arms Around Me, Honey," Kieran embraced Michener good-naturedly, and a moment later, he was kissing Michener's hand as the music of "1 Kiss Your Hand, Madame," wafted through the blushing studio.

"This sort of horseplay is a crutch for many television programs which have nothing else to recommend them. But when you have men of the sharpness of Adams, Kieran and Michener (the *South Pacific* author will be a frequent guest), you just don't need it. Some of the questions on the show are based on drawings and word-cards shown to the panel and viewers simultaneously. And video also gives us a chance to study the facial expressions of the giants as they're thinking. Kieran, Fadiman and Michener are, of course, familiar figures to TV audiences, but Adams, the most attractively unattractive man to hit the channels since George S. Kaufman, is a television novelty.

"He and the others did right well by several difficult queries, and the spontaneously quoted poetry flowed as freely as seltzer. For Fadiman, who's been immersed in the lightweight atmosphere of *This Is Show Business* for so long, moderating *Information, Please* must seem like coming home. He'll serve as emcee for at least eight sessions, and there's little doubt that before long his charges will forget about those nasty cameras and begin punning and wise-cracking as fruitfully as they did on radio.

"Fadiman, who has never been averse to complimenting the *Information, Please* experts during the course of the program ("My, but you gentlemen are clever tonight") is even more demonstrative on the video version. Once, after Kieran correctly answered that a hare can travel as fast as 40 miles an hour, Fadiman reached over and patted him on the back in appreciation. Kieran smiled shyly, but recovered in time to quote a few million lines from Keats. The man's resiliency is amazing."

John Crosby in the July 4, 1952 issue of the *New York Herald Tribune* reviewed:

"The granddaddy of all quiz shows, *Information, Please*, made its television debut at long last, giving the populace its first clear look at the patriarch of quiz panelists, Franklin P. Adams, a sight to make strong men blanch. Actually, Mr. Adams' puckish face has adorned a good many movie shorts, but that's not the same thing as having him in your living room. This was his television debut. (There was a rumor afloat that Adams has never seen a television program, but this may be dismissed as heresy.) The first tussle with the cameras seemed to unsettle the old curator of popular songs. At any rate, he was unusually subdued, and beyond vouchsafing some poetry, he didn't have much to say. There were two other regulars around – Clifton Fadiman, the emcee, and John Kieran, the wildlife expert. Mr. Fadiman, the host of *This Is Show Business*, is an old hand at television and he had a real busy night of it Sunday. The guest was James Michener, author of *Tales of the South Pacific*.

"It was pleasant to hear the old rallying cry again—'Wake up, America. It's time to stump the experts—'and pleasant to report that *Information, Please* is still literate, deft and amusing. This is the old-fashioned type of quiz—dealing in history, politics, sports, the eccentricities of animals, poetry. It's a very masculine show. Women have been abroad from time to time, but you don't see much of them. Wrong type of mine to retain, say, children's verse.

"On the opening night the only women present were a couple of long-legged dolls whose function beside exhibiting their legs, was to change some large cards which were used as sight questions. They seemed to make Mr. Fadiman very nervous, these gals, and he drummed impatiently and made wisecracks about their intellects.

"There were few concessions to visibility—the girls' legs and the cards. The cards showed, among other things, a king sliding down a banister. Mr. Adams had his hand up on this one before Fadiman asked the question. (The question, as years of experience taught him, must certainly involve A.A. Milne's poem about the king who wanted a little bit of butter for his bread.) Another more or less visual gag demanded that Mr. Kieran and Mr. Michener act out the title of songs like "Button Up Your Overcoat," "Put Your Arms Around Me, Honey" and "I Kiss Your Hand, Madame." The idea here, in line with the current trend in these quiz operations, is to generate a little embarrassment among the experts in order to foster a feeling of complacency among the non-experts at home. It didn't work well. Mr. Michener and Mr. Kieran were just too dignified for this sort of thing.

"There was less badinage among the crowd than we're normally accustomed to, and the whole show needs a shaking down. But, on the whole, it's nice to welcome back so worthy an effort. If your question is accepted, incidentally, the prize is a $10 certificate to be used to buy books or magazines. You get an additional $50 certificate if you stump the experts. Dan Golenpaul, the producer, feels people ought to read in spite of television, a healthy note of optimism.

"*Information, Please*, as I say, is the old-fashioned type of quiz which might be described as intellectual mugging, a man showing off the contents of his brain as diffidently and charmingly as he knows how. I don't know whether it will survive against the other more recent type of quiz, a stentorian example of which follows *Information, Please* directly on CBS-TV."

The earliest contract relating to the television program dates January 4, 1952 when Dan Golenpaul sent a three-page contract to John K.M. McCaffrey offering to employ the editor of the *American Mercury* as one of the master of ceremonies (it being understood that Golenpaul was going to employ others to act in the same capacity) with the starter fee of $750.00 per performance, and $1,000.00 if the program exceeded the initial thirteen broadcasts. Golenpaul's contract also stipulated that "if we have not commenced television performances of *Information, Please* by April 1, 1952, this agreement shall terminate and thereafter neither of us shall be under any obligation or liability to the other."

The program didn't start until June, causing the contract to be voided, even though McCaffrey did play "master of ceremonies" for three of the broadcasts after Clifton Fadiman was unable to emcee half-way through the program's run. On March 25, 1952, the General Electric Company signed a contract with Dan Golenpaul Associates agreeing to sponsor the program over thirteen consecutive telecasts beginning with Sunday, June 29, 1952 and ending with the telecast of Sunday, September 21, 1952.

It was agreed between the producer and sponsor that each original telecast of the program would ordinarily be on a "live" basis. Golenpaul did pay money from his own pocket to film each telecast, in the format of 35 millimeter reels. The sponsor's cost involved? $10,500.00 for each broadcast. In June of 1952, John Kieran and Franklin P. Adams signed on to appear as regular panelists of the television program. According to the contract:

"We agree to pay you and you agree to accept an amount equal to seven and a half percent (7 ½%) of our gross selling price for the show, such amount, however, not to be less than Seven Hundred Fifty Dollars ($750) for each performance. In addition, we agree to pay you two and a half percent (2 ½%) of that portion of our gross selling price between Ten Thousand Dollars ($10,000) and Twelve Thousand Five Hundred Dollars ($12,500), and five percent (5%) of that portion of our gross selling price in excess of Twelve Thousand Five Hundred Dollars ($12,500). Gross selling price is defined as the gross amount each week received by us for the package consisting of all elements necessary for its presentation, including but not limited to all elements as furnished in the past in connection with radio broadcasts. You or your representative shall at all times have access to our sales contracts for the purpose of verifying the gross selling price."

Franklin P. Adams, however, only made an appearance on the premiere broadcast, and was forced to bow out afterwards, leaving John Kieran to handle the reins. Adams was replaced by guest panelists, which varied from telecast to telecast. Adams was in the early stages of Alzheimer's disease, which would take his life eight years later on March 23, 1960. Strangely enough, according to one source, Adams made two appearances on the program, but without having access to prints of this series, it is impossible to verify which source of information is accurate.

Both John Kieran and Clifton Fadiman were experienced with the expanding medium of television. Kieran hosted his own program, *Kieran's Kaleidoscope*. First aired in 1949, this fifteen-minute television program lasted 104 episodes and became known historically as the first syndicated television series. Each episode dealt with a different topic, using news footage and still photographs, with Kieran narrating such subjects as the solar system and the life of the beetle.

In July of 1949, Clifton Fadiman was hired as emcee for *This Is Show Business*, a long-running variety program in which he would briefly chat with guests before their on-screen performance, after which guest panelists (including George S. Kaufman) would place their votes on the best entertainment.

Information, Please studio pianist Joe Kahn reprised his position for the television series. Kahn was the father of Roger Kahn, who wrote the great baseball book, *Boys of Summer*. (In the book, incidentally, Roger recalled his appearance on the radio program and how he felt he was ignored by the members of the board because of his encyclopedic mind in the realm of sports and sports statistics, compared to that of Kieran's.)

TELEVISION EPISODE GUIDE

Production Credits
Producer and Editor – Dan Golenpaul
Associate Producer – Edith Schick
Associate Editors – Ann Golenpaul, Sophie Lippman and Gordon J. Kahn
Director – Bruce Andersen
Visual and Art Editor – Laverne Mock
Set Designer – Jo Mielziner
Commercial Set Designer – Samuel Leve

Episode #1   **Broadcast of June 29, 1952**
Panelists: John Kieran, Franklin P. Adams and James Michener
Master of Ceremonies: Clifton Fadiman
Announcer: Bud Palmer
Models: Polly Aaron and Anne Roberts
Pianist: Joe Kahn

Episode #2   **Broadcast of July 6, 1952**
Panelists: John Kieran and Gregory Ratoff
Master of Ceremonies: Clifton Fadiman
Announcer: Bud Palmer
Models: Anne Roberts
Ballerina: Anna Istomina
Pianist: Joe Kahn

Episode #3   **Broadcast of July 13, 1952**
Panelists: John Kieran and George Jessel
Master of Ceremonies: Clifton Fadiman
Announcer: Bud Palmer
Models: Anne Roberts
Pianist: Joe Kahn

Episode #4   **Broadcast of July 20, 1952**
Panelists: John Kieran, Charles Bolte and Sir Gladwyn Jebb
Master of Ceremonies: Clifton Fadiman
Announcer: Bud Palmer
Models: Anne Roberts
Actress: Lynn Merrill
Actor: Charles Aidman
Stand-ins: Frank Adamo, Eleanore Cohen, Frances Goram and John Conway
Pianist: Joe Kahn

Episode #5   **Broadcast of July 27, 1952**
Panelists: John Kieran, Gregory Ratoff and Cornelia Otis Skinner
Master of Ceremonies: Clifton Fadiman
Announcer: Bud Palmer
Actress: Lory March
Actor: James Monks and John Conway
Singers: Dianne De Sanctos and Mario Palermo
Stand-ins: Frank Adamo, Chloe Owen, Martha Larrimore and Bert Hunt
Pianist: Joe Kahn

Episode #6   **Broadcast of August 3, 1952**
Panelists: John Kieran, Gregory Ratoff and Ellis Arnall (former Governor of Georgia)
Master of Ceremonies: John K. M. McCaffery
Announcer: Bud Palmer
Actors: John Conway and Gordon West
Stand-ins: Frank Adamo, Chloe Owen, Martha Larrimore and Bert Hunt
Pianist: Joe Kahn

Episode #7   **Broadcast of August 10, 1952**
Panelists: John Kieran, Howard Lindsay and Franklin P. Adams
Master of Ceremonies: Russel Crouse
Announcer: Bud Palmer (live)
Actors: John Conway and Logan Field
Stand-ins: Frank Adamo and Martha Larrimore
Pianist: Joe Kahn
(There remains a possibility that Adams was not on this broadcast.)

Episode #8   **Broadcast of August 17, 1952**
Panelists: John Kieran, Gregory Ratoff and Charles Bolte
Master of Ceremonies: Clifton Fadiman
Announcer: Bud Palmer
Actress: Lynn Merrill
Actors: John Conway and Logan Field
Singer: Diane De Sanctos
Stand-ins: Frank Adamo, Ruth Elliot, Gerry Bolton and Bert Hunt
Pianist: Joe Kahn
Horn: Joseph Singer

Episode #9   **Broadcast of August 24, 1952**
Panelists: John Kieran, Burgess Meredith and Russel Crouse
Master of Ceremonies: Clifton Fadiman
Announcer: Bud Palmer
Actress: Diane De Sanctos and Lynn Merrill
Actors: John Conway and Logan Field
Stand-ins: Frank Adamo, Chloe Owen, Martha Larrimore, Ruth Elliot and Bert Hunt
Pianist: Joe Kahn

Episode #10   **Broadcast of August 31, 1952**
Panelists: John Kieran, Gregory Ratoff and Cornelia Otis Skinner
Master of Ceremonies: John K.M. McCaffery
Announcer: Bud Palmer
Singer: Diane De Sanctos
Actors: John Conway and Logan Field
Stand-ins: Frank Adamo, Chloe Owen, Martha Larrimore, and Bert Hunt
Pianist: Joe Kahn
Drummer: David Grupp

Episode #11   **Broadcast of September 7, 1952 (filmed)**
Panelists: John Kieran, Howard Lindsay and Franklin P. Adams
Master of Ceremonies: Russel Crouse
Announcer: Bud Palmer (live)
Pianist: Joe Kahn
Trivia: Episode eleven was probably a repeat of episode seven, as records indicate this episode as having been filmed and played back again, with the commercials being live.

Episode #12   **Broadcast of September 14, 1952**
Panelists: John Kieran, Dorothy Stickney and Gene Lockhart
Master of Ceremonies: Clifton Fadiman
Announcer: Bud Palmer
Actress: Diane De Sanctos and Lynn Merrill
Actors: John Conway and Logan Field
Stand-ins: Frank Adamo, Jean Westbrook, Martha Larrimore, and Dan Eriksen
Pianist: Joe Kahn

Episode #13   **Broadcast of September 21, 1952**
Panelists: John Kieran, James Michener and Gregory Ratoff
Master of Ceremonies: John K.M. McCaffery
Announcer: Bud Palmer
Actress: Lynn Merrill
Actors: Mario Palermo, Frank Palumbo, Al Silvani and Fred Catania
Singers: Diane De Sanctos
Stand-ins: Frank Adamo, Jean Westbrook, Chloe Adamo, and Dan Eriksen
Pianist: Joe Kahn
Drummer: David Grupp

According to memos in Dan Golenpaul's papers, at least 12 of the 13 broadcasts were preserved on kinescopes at one point in time. Since the episode guide was compiled by Golenpaul himself from paperwork and not from viewing the actual kinescopes themselves, it is not absolutely certain that the above list is accurate.

After the failure of TV's *Information, Please*, in the summer of 1954, Clifton Fadiman was hired as the moderator of *What's in a Word?*, a short-lived quiz program in which panelists had to guess a rhyme based on a two-word association provided by the contestant.

In 1955, Clifton Fadiman would become temporary host to *The Name's the Same*, a Mark Goodson-Bill Toddman production. The premise of the program was to have guests, who had the same name as famous people and fictional characters, quizzed by three celebrity panelists. If the panelists failed to determine the guest's name in ten questions or less, the guest received a check for $25.00. (Shades of repetition?) In 1956, Fadiman became the host of the television version of *Quiz Kids*, the same position he supported for the radio version years before.

PARTING IS SWEET SORROW

As with all good friends, the men stayed in touch throughout the years after the demise of *Information, Please*. "John Kieran had an incredible memory, particularly about Shakespeare, poetry, nature and birds," recalled Oscar Levant in his autobiography, "but Charlie Brackett of the incomparable movie team of Brackett and Wilder once told me that when they asked Kieran to appear in a small preface of a picture, he couldn't remember his lines. In the early days of *Information, Please* Kieran, who was a sportswriter for the *New York Times*, used to make predictions about the outcome of football games every Saturday. After each prediction he would make a comment in Latin—an amusing touch. Kieran is a lovable man."

John Kieran retired to Rockport, Massachusetts during the late fifties, and would outlive the rest of the "board of experts," passing away in December of 1981. On December 28, 1966, Kieran wrote to Dan Golenpaul:

Dear Dan:
    Sorry I missed you the other night. I was at my bad habit of stargazing. I think Margaret is frantically appreciative of that beautiful Hours production and I'm delighted with the beautiful martini mixer—I touch it reverently every hour on the hour, hoping it is real and wishing for sundown to make it legal. The almanac is as good as ever and I think the feature stuff up front is better than ever, particularly the lead piece on that God-awful mess in Southeast Asia. Ugh! Anyway, Happy New Year and love to you both from Margaret.
                            Yours on the rocks of Rockport,
                            John

November 3, 1971
Dan:

    Thanks for the stunning new edition of the *Information, Please Almanac, Atlas and Yearbook*. I read your opening political fusillade with enthusiasm. You didn't spare anybody – and deservedly so. It's great; no fooling. I can't wait to get on the voting booth in 1972. Right on! GOLENPAUL FOR PRESIDENT! Why not? Besides, we would love to be invited to dinner at the White House. In the interim, love and kisses to Anne and you from Margaret.

                                  Your current campaign manager in
                                  Rockport, Mass. and future
                                  Henry Kissinger in the White House,
                                  John

    During the late fifties, Golenpaul was in constant communication with members of business and politics including James A. Farley of the Coca-Cola Bottling Company, J. W. Fulbright and Albert Gore on the Committee of Foreign Relations, Jacob K. Javits on the Committee on Labor and Public Welfare, U.S. Senators Hubert Humphrey from Minnesota, Edward M. Kennedy from Massachusetts, Adlai E. Stevenson from Illinois, among others.

    On January 19, 1956, Haven Falconer of Loew's Incorporated, a distribution company for MGM Pictures, wrote to Dan Golenpaul asking permission for the use of the name *Information, Please* in one scene of *Somebody Up There Likes Me*, a movie dealing with the life and career of Rocky Graziano; on the same day, Dan Golenpaul granted permission. In one scene which takes place in Lou Stillman's Gymnasium, Rocky asks a man where he can find a friend he is looking for. The man replies substantially: "What is this—*Information, Please*? Can't you see I'm busy? I got a fighter here—in training. Try Lou Stillman."

    In February of 1956, Dan Golenpaul was invited by Gilbert Miller and Helen Hayes to attend the Tony Awards in April, to join an Honorary Committee of leaders in the civic, social and business circles who would sponsor the traditional presentation of the awards.

    In late March of 1961, *The Barry Gray Show* on radio's WMCA in New York featured a few guests who brought up the subject of the radio and television program, *Information, Please*. On April 3, 1961, Dan

Golenpaul wrote a letter to Barry Gray himself:

Dear Mr. Gray:
   One of your listeners reported to me that several days ago on one of your broadcasts with Mr. Jan Murray and some others, *Information, Please* was mentioned. The comments were highly complimentary to the *Information, Please* radio program and, as its originator and producer, I certainly appreciate your generous praise of our show.
   However, during the course of the discussion somebody stated that *Information, Please*, although one of the best shows on the air at the time, only received a rating of 4. This is an unfortunate error and someone was misinformed. *Information, Please* at its peak had a rating of approximately 20, and an average of 14 over many years. The significance of these ratings was that they were built up on a minor network with very strong shows playing opposite us. The purpose of this letter is to correct any unintentional error made about our rating.
   I share your despair about good shows getting lost in the mass media. But don't be too discouraged. You can't keep a good man down and you can't keep a good show down. Give the public a good show in radio, television, or any media, and they'll find it because they are a lot smarter than the people who are master-minding the mess of garbage deliberately designed for mass appeal. Let's face it – the people who are masterminding entertainment are just not masterminds.
   Thanks for any attention you may give this note. I hope you'll have time to read it and quote it on one of your programs.

Sincerely yours,
Dan Golenpaul

Clifton Fadiman's first marriage to Pauline Elizabeth Rush ended in 1949. He later married Annalee Whitmore Jacoby, a foreign correspondent for *Life* and *Time* magazines and co-author with Theodore White on *Thunder Out of China* in 1950. In addition to his wife and children Kim and Anne (both from his second marriage), Fadiman had a son from his first marriage, Jonathan Rush. (In fact, Fadiman had missed one week as emcee for *Information, Please* in the summer 1938 so he could take his son Jonathan on vacation to New Mexico.)

Although Fadiman was able to host the short-lived *Keep 'Em Rolling* program (from November 2, 1941 to May 17, 1942), a patriotic war-related variety show designed as a homefront morale-booster during the years of *Information, Please*, Fadiman was contractually unable to host any other program until the quiz program ended in 1948. Once free, Fadiman was highly sought after as a lecturer. During this same period, he also appeared on other radio quiz shows, most notably *Quiz Kids*, a juvenile version of *Information, Please* which put questions to bright young people. Other programs in which he participated included *Mathematics, Invitation to Learning* (on which he was a frequent guest), *Alumni Fun, Conversation*, and he also hosted *Words at War* for a short seven episodes in the summer of 1944. During the late fifties, Fadiman was a host in various segments of NBC's radio revival program *Monitor*.

While under contract with Golenpaul, Fadiman did manage to make a number of guest appearances on radio programs including *The Pursuit of Happiness*, short-term host of *This Is Broadway, The Cities Service Concert, We Refuse to Die, The Human Adventure, Over Here, Tomorrow Will Be Ours, Don't Let's Be Beastly to the Germans, Forecast, The NBC University Theatre, Breakfast with Burrows*, and he even attempted to teach Archie about literature during a guest appearance of *Duffy's Tavern*.

In April of 1955, Clifton Fadiman's first book was published, entitled *Party of One*. Lewis Nichols of the *New York Times Book Review* interviewed Fadiman. "I've always been scared to write a whole book," Fadiman explained. "I read a whole lot of them when I was young and that naturally frightened the wits out of me. Then, later, I was a publisher and helped publish a great many more books than were needed. But it's too late to go back now. This one's printed and everyone's stuck with it."

During his lifetime, Fadiman toyed with his own hobby of collecting and drinking wine. "It's a dandy hobby if the vocabulary weren't so la-di-da," said Fadiman. "You begin to sound a bit queer when you use it. A certain wine 'lacks finesse.' That sounds awful. But, damn it, that's just what it does."

Oscar Levant led the most unusual of lives after leaving the *Information, Please* program. On June 2, 1958, to the astonishment of a sold-out Royce Hall audience at U.C.L.A., gathered for the Los Angeles Music Festival, conductor Franz Waxman led Oscar Levant onstage. Together, they performed Shostakovich's second piano concerto. Playing from memory, Levant lost his place in its first movement, stopped, and declared to the audience, "I don't even know where I am. I'm going to start all over again." He did, succeeded, and earned a roar of applause from the audience.

Three days later he went to Columbia Records and recorded the album *Some Pleasant Moments in the Twentieth Century*, featuring music of Debussy, Mompou, Prokofieff, Ravel, and Shostakovich. His last album, *Oscar Levant at the Piano*, was recorded in the same period but not released by Columbia until 1961. His final public appearance in concert came on August 2, 1958. Although he attempted to cancel part-way through the Gershwin Concerto, while actually onstage, Levant was kept in motion by conductor André Kostelanetz. Levant finished the work, brilliantly. Before offering the first of two encores, he advised the audience that he was "playing under the auspices of Mt. Sinai."

In November of 1958, Levant was a guest on television's *The Jack Benny Program*, playing himself in an episode entitled "Jack Goes to the Doctor." In 1958 he became a guest panelist for one episode of *The Celebrity Game*. The year after, he appeared as a "mystery guest" on *What's My Line?* but his return to the quiz show arena was short lived.

It was during this same time (1958–60) that *The Oscar Levant Show* was being broadcast "live" over KCOP in Los Angeles with his wife and co-star June Gale. The program allowed Levant to perform complex piano pieces by Gershwin and Chopin, while giving him the opportunity to discuss any subject of the week, applying his trade as a sharp wit. While suffering breakdowns through the use of medications, some of which were illegal, Levant often made quips and remarks that gave the television viewers something about which to talk. On one particular week, Levant commented about Marilyn Monroe (who wasn't Jewish) and playwright Arthur Miller (who was) who were originally married in a civil ceremony, but who had recently renewed their vows in a Jewish ceremony performed by a Rabbi. Over live television, Levant quipped, "Now that Marilyn Monroe is kosher, Arthur Miller can eat her." Levant's show was immediately cancelled.

Almost right after the "Monroe" incident, Levant reportedly suffered his nineteenth breakdown. He was to live another fifteen years, addicted and repeatedly hospitalized, fitfully active in radio and television, and writing two autobiographies, confessing his favorite and not-so-favorite moments in *The Memoirs Of An Amnesiac* and *The Unimportance of Being*

Oscar. Increasingly reclusive, he passed away in Beverly Hills on August 14, 1972.

Two years after the death of Oscar Levant, and months after Dan Golenpaul passed away, there was an apparent attempt to revive the *Information, Please* program. According to the November 13, 1974 issue of *Variety*:

"*Information, Please*, a huge click in 1930s radio but which died after switching to television in the early 1950s, is being revived as a TV offering aimed at the syndicated prime access period. Dick Pack, onetime programming and production head of Group W, has acquired the radio-TV rights to the show from Ann Golenpaul, widow of Dan Golenpaul, who conceived and produced the program.

"The biggest problem with the new show, Pack admits, will be finding talent. What contributed largely to making the old show a hit was the lineup of regulars Clifton Fadiman, Franklin P. Adams (F.P.A.), John F. Kieran and Oscar Levant, plus top guests. Regulars have not yet been determined, but Pack expects production to begin early in 1975. Pack will produce in association with Ted Lloyd. What Pack is counting on is the appeal of the game-type format without the program being a real game show with piles of prizes and gimmicks."

Little more than two years later, *Variety* reported in its January 26, 1977 issue that Clifton Fadiman had signed on in the role of moderator:

"Producer Richard Pack is looking around town for a new Franklin P. Adams and/or John Kieran and Oscar Levant. Pack, an indie TV-film producer now packaging a pilot of *Information, Please* here for pubcaster KQED and PBS via a $48,000 CPB grant, will definitely be using the literate old show's moderator, Clifton Fadiman. But the panelists are yet to be selected. Pack says he hopes to find two here for permanent use on the show should it go beyond the pilot stage. There'll be a weekly guest expert, too. 'We're not looking for celebrities, necessarily,' said Fadiman. 'They're a dime a dozen. We want people of accomplishment with minds that know how to play.'

"The new *Information, Please* (NBC Radio aired the original in 1938-48) will feature the same mix of intellectualism and wit, with questions again coming from the audience. 'We expect the audience to be smarter and the questions tougher,' said Fadiman, now a writer-critic-editor in Santa Barbara. 'We don't intend to hype the show with elaborate production, unnecessary visual gimmicks and big prizes,' said Pack, former programming vice president with Westinghouse. Should the pilot succeed and financing fall in line, the KQED-produced series for PBS would begin late this year."

The revival fell flat and was never picked up as a prime-time series. Although Clifton Fadiman never got the opportunity to host the revival, his own accomplishments over the years included penning more than 65 introductions to a wide range of editions including Bradbury's *The Martian Chronicles*, *Six by Seuss* and Simon & Schuster's *War and Peace* (the latter of which was released under the "Inner Sanctum Mystery" byline.)

Of primary importance to Fadiman was *The World Treasury of Children's Literature*, which he assembled in the mid-1980s. There were volumes for children ages 4 to 8 and 9 to 14. He created the anthologies because he felt that it was necessary to involve children early in reading if literacy was to survive television. He was especially proud of his *Encyclopedia Britannica* entry on the history of children's literature. To study the subject he learned to read child-level Italian, Spanish, Swedish and Dutch when he was in his 70s.

In 1985, he won the Dorothy C. McKenzie Award for his contribution to children's literature for his work as an editor for *The World Treasury of Children's Literature*, the *Young Children's Encyclopedia* and other works. For those close to him, Fadiman was best remembered for his mostly anonymous role as senior judge for the Book-of-the-Month Club, a relationship he fostered for more than half a century, starting in the early 1940s. Despite losing his sight as a result of acute retinal necrosis in his late 80's, he continued to vet manuscripts for the Book-of-the-Month Club by listening to unabridged tapes of the volumes in question especially recorded for him by his son, Kim.

While blind he brought out a new edition of *The Lifetime Reading Plan*, a guide done with John S. Major that was intended to introduce Americans to the classics of civilization, and he was the general editor of *World Poetry: An Anthology of Verse from Antiquity to Our Time*. Late in his life the book world honored him for his love of the printed word by awarding him the 1993 National Book Foundation Medal for Distinguished Contribution to American Letters.

Fadiman spent his remaining years with his wife, Annalee Whitmore Fadiman, on Captiva Island, off Florida's Gulf Coast. When asked what hobbies were keeping him occupied, he stated they consisted of his wife and "the avoidance of exercise." He had a simple lifelong work ethic. "I can't retire," he said. "I wouldn't know what to do." Fadiman passed away on June 20, 1999 at his son's home on Sanibel Island, Florida of pancreatic cancer. He was 95.

In 2000 the Mercantile Library of New York established the Clifton Fadiman Medal for "Excellence in Fiction" to recognize an individual work of fiction by a living American author that merited rediscovery by the general public. The work may be in or out of print at the time of the selection. This medal is awarded annually.

In the April 20, 2003 edition of the *New York Daily News*, columnist David Hinckley wrote a piece for the weekly "Big Town Replay" column, containing a short biography about Franklin P. Adams and his famous baseball rhyme published in the July 10, 1910 edition of the *New York Evening Mail*. The rhyme went:

These are the saddest of possible words
  Tinker to Evers to Chance
Trio of bear cats and fleeter than birds
  Tinker to Evers to Chance
Ruthlessly pricking our gonfalon bubble
  Making a Giant hit into a double
Words that are weighty with nothing but trouble
  Tinker to Evers to Chance

"A prolific poet, his verse eventually was collected into 10 volumes, and his death in 1960 was mourned as another closure to the age of genteel wit," wrote Hinckley. In the saddest of possible words, paraphrasing F.P.A. himself, he walked the doggerel in 1910 and is still remembered to this day.

BROADCAST LOG

BROADCAST TIMES*

May 17, 1938 to November 8, 1938
Sustained, Blue Network, Tuesday, 8:30 to 9:00 p.m., EST.
(Broadcast originated from station WJZ in New York.)

November 15, 1938 to November 5, 1940
Canada Dry, Blue Network, Tuesday, 8:30 to 9:00 p.m., EST.
(Broadcast originated from station WJZ in New York.)

November 15, 1940 to February 5, 1943
Lucky Strike, NBC, Friday 8:30 to 9:00 p.m., EST.
(Broadcast originated from station WEAF in New York.)

Feb. 15, 1943 to July 12, 1943, September 13, 1943 to July 10, 1944, September 11, 1944 to Feb. 5, 1945
Heinz, NBC, Monday 8:30 to 9:00 p.m., EST.
(Broadcast originated from station WEAF in New York.)

February 12, 1945 to June 24, 1946
Mobil, NBC, Monday 9:30 to 10:00 p.m., EST.
(Broadcast originated from station WEAF in New York.)

October 2, 1946 to June 25, 1947
Parker, CBS, Wednesday, 10:30 to 11:00 p.m., EST.
(Broadcast originated from station WABC until the broadcast of November 6, 1946; they then originated from WCBS because the station in New York changed its call letters on November 2.)

September 26, 1947 to June 18, 1948
Sustained, Mutual Network, Friday, 9:30 to 10:00 p.m., EST.
(Broadcast originated from station WOR in New York.)

150 Information, Please

August 9, 1950 to August 30, 1950
Sustained, Mutual Network, Wednesday, 9 to 9:30 p.m., EST.
(Broadcast originated from station WOR in New York.)

September 10, 1950 to April 22, 1951
Sustained, Mutual Network, Sunday, 10 to 10:30 p.m., EST.
(Broadcast originated from station WOR in New York.)

* Keep in mind that the broadcast time varied from coast to coast. Also, in the cases of Daylight Savings Time, some areas did not recognize the change on specific weeks so the broadcast time can be listed an hour earlier or later than the rest of the same time zones (example: the broadcast of May 2, 1941). As an example, here is the complete list of radio stations over which *Information, Please* was heard during September of 1939. Time given was standard for the community opposite which it appeared.

WABY in Albany, NY	8:30 p.m.
KAGA in Atlanta, GA	7:30 p.m.
WBAL in Baltimore, MD	8:30 p.m.
WLBZ in Bangor, ME	8:30 p.m.
WJBO in Baton Rouge, LA	7:30 p.m.
WELL in Battle Creek, MI	8:30 p.m.
WBCM in Bay City, MI	8:30 p.m.
WSGN in Birmingham, GA	7:30 p.m.
KIDO in Boise, ID	6:30 p.m.
WBZ in Boston, MA	8:30 p.m.
WICC in Bridgeport, CT	8:30 p.m.
WEBR in Buffalo, NY	8:30 p.m.
WMT in Cedar Rapids, IA	7:30 p.m.
WLS in Chicago, IL	7:30 p.m.
WCKY in Cincinnati, OH	8:30 p.m.
WHK in Cleveland, OH	8:30 p.m.
KGKO in Dallas/Ft. Worth, TX	7:30 p.m.
KVDO in Denver, CO	6:30 p.m.
KSO in Des Moines, IA	7:30 p.m.
WXYZ in Detroit, MI	8:30 p.m.
WFDF in Flint, MI	8:30 p.m.
WOWO in Fort Wayne, IN	7:30 p.m.
KXYZ in Houston, TX	7:30 p.m.
WIBM in Jackson, MS	8:30 p.m.
WJTN in Jamestown, NY	8:30 p.m.
WREN in Kansas City, MO	7:30 p.m.
WJIM in Lansing, MI	8:30 p.m.
WMPS in Memphis, TN	7:30 p.m.
WTCN in Minneapolis/St. Paul, MN	7:30 p.m.

CFCF in Montreal, Ontario	8:30 p.m.
WNBC in New Britain, CT	8:30 p.m.
WDSU in New Orleans, LA	7:30 p.m.
WJZ in New York, NY	8:30 p.m.
KLO in Ogden, UT	6:30 p.m.
KTOK in Oklahoma City, OK	7:30 p.m.
WFIL in Philadelphia, PA	8:30 p.m.
KTAR in Phoenix, AZ	6:30 p.m.
KDKA in Pittsburgh, PA	8:30 p.m.
WMFF in Plattsburg, NY	8:30 p.m.
WEAN in Providence, RI	8:30 p.m.
WHAM in Rochester, NY	8:30 p.m.
KWK in St. Louis, MO	7:30 p.m.
KUTA in Salt Lake City, UT	6:30 p.m.
WBZA in Springfield, IL	8:30 p.m.
WSYR in Syracuse, NY	8:30 p.m.
WSPD in Toldeo, OH	8:30 p.m.
CBL in Toronto, Ontario	8:30 p.m.
KVOA in Tucson, AZ	6:30 p.m.
WMAL in Washington D.C.	8:30 p.m.

EPISODE GUIDE TO ALL 506 BROADCASTS

Regular panelists are listed first, followed by the guests of the week. All information to date, to the best of my knowledge, is accurate including spelling of guest panelists.

Episode #1 **Broadcast of May 17, 1938.**
Panelists: Franklin P. Adams, science writer Bernard Jaffe, columnist Marcus Duffield and Prof. Harry Overstreet

Episode #2 **Broadcast of May 24, 1938.**
Panelists: Franklin P. Adams, columnist Marcus Duffield, Louis Hacker and Paul de Kruif, author of *Microbe Hunters*

Episode #3 **Broadcast of May 31, 1938.**
Panelists: Franklin P. Adams and columnist Marcus Duffield. Other guests unknown.

Episode #4 **Broadcast of June 7, 1938.**
Panelists: Franklin P. Adams, Science writer Science writer Bernard Jaffe, columnist Marcus Duffield and John Kieran. John Erskine is the master of ceremonies instead of Clifton Fadiman for this broadcast.

Episode #5 **Broadcast of June 14, 1938.**
Panelists: Franklin P. Adams, John Kieran, columnist Marcus Duffield and playwright Marc Connelly

Episode #6 **Broadcast of June 21, 1938.**
Panelists: Franklin P. Adams, John Kieran, Science writer Bernard Jaffe and studio publicist Howard Dietz

Episode #7 **Broadcast of June 28, 1938.**
Panelists: Franklin P. Adams, John Kieran, columnist Marcus Duffield and Carmel Snow, editor of *Harper's Bazaar*

Episode #8 **Broadcast of July 5, 1938.**
Panelists: Franklin P. Adams, John Kieran, columnist Marcus Duffield and pianist Oscar Levant

Episode #9 **Broadcast of July 12, 1938.**
Panelists: John Kieran, Science writer Bernard Jaffe, radio commentator Quincy Howe, and playwright George S. Kaufman. (This was the first of three broadcasts Franklin P. Adams would miss because of a visit to the hospital.)

Episode #10 **Broadcast of July 19, 1938.**
Panelists: John Kieran, columnist Marcus Duffield, author Thomas Craven and playwright Ben Hecht

Episode #11 **Broadcast of July 26, 1938.**
Panelists: John Kieran, Oscar Levant, Science writer Bernard Jaffee and author/correspondent John Gunther

Episode #12 **Broadcast of August 2, 1938.**
Panelists: Franklin P. Adams, John Kieran, radio commentator Quincy Howe and playwright Moss Hart.
Playwright George S. Kaufman subs for Clifton Fadiman.

Episode #13 **Broadcast of August 9, 1938.**
Panelists: Franklin P. Adams, John Kieran, Alden Cook and Alice Newell

Episode #14 **Broadcast of August 16, 1938.**
Panelists: Franklin P. Adams, John Kieran, Oscar Levant and humorist Howard Brubaker

Episode #15 **Broadcast of August 23, 1938.**
Panelists: Franklin P. Adams, John Kieran, columnist Marcus Duffield and Percy Waxman, Associate Editor for *Cosmopolitan* magazine

Episode #16 **Broadcast of August 30, 1938.**
Panelists: Franklin P. Adams, John Kieran, Oscar Levant and Ben Hecht

Episode #17 **Broadcast of September 6, 1938.**
Panelists: Franklin P. Adams, John Kieran, Science writer Bernard Jaffe and Ben Bernie, musician conducting at the Strand Theatre in NY

Episode #18 **Broadcast of September 13, 1938.**
Panelists: Franklin P. Adams, Oscar Levant, columnist Marcus Duffield and Percy Waxman, Associate Editor for *Cosmopolitan* magazine

Episode #19 **Broadcast of September 20, 1938.**
Panelists: Franklin P. Adams, John Kieran and author Clarence Buddington Kelland

Episode #20 **Broadcast of September 27, 1938.**
Panelists: Franklin P. Adams, John Kieran, Sigmund Spaeth (the *Tune Detective*) and actor Basil Rathbone

Episode #21 **Broadcast of October 4, 1938.**
Panelists: Franklin P. Adams, John Kieran, journalist and radio commentator Dorothy Thompson and motion picture editor of the *New York World Telegram* William Boehnel

Episode #22 **Broadcast of October 11, 1938.**
Panelists: Franklin P. Adams, John Kieran, Oscar Levant and actress Lillian Gish

Episode #23 **Broadcast of October 18, 1938.**
Panelists: Franklin P. Adams, John Kieran, columnist Marcus Duffield and heavyweight boxing champion Gene Tunney

Episode #24 **Broadcast of October 25, 1938.**
Panelists: Franklin P. Adams, John Kieran, Oscar Levant, Science writer Bernard Jaffee and comedian Harpo Marx

Episode #25 **Broadcast of November 1, 1938.**
Panelists: Franklin P. Adams, John Kieran, columnist Marcus Duffield, and bridge expert Oswald Jacoby

Episode #26 **Broadcast of November 8, 1938.**
Panelists: Franklin P. Adams, John Kieran, Oscar Levant and W.E. Woodward. Playwright George S. Kaufman substitutes for Clifton Fadiman.

Episode #27 **Broadcast of November 15, 1938.**
Panelists: Franklin P. Adams, John Kieran, Oscar Levant and author/correspondent John Gunther

Episode #28 **Broadcast of November 22, 1938.**
Panelists: Franklin P. Adams, John Kieran, playwright Russel Crouse and author Hendrik Willem Van Loon

Episode #29 **Broadcast of November 29, 1938.**
Panelists: Franklin P. Adams, John Kieran, Oscar Levant and author Kathleen Norris

Episode #30 **Broadcast of December 6, 1938.**
Panelists: Franklin P. Adams, John Kieran, columnist Marcus Duffield, and critic Alexander Woollcott

Episode #31 **Broadcast of December 13, 1938.**
Panelists: Franklin P. Adams, John Kieran, Oscar Levant and Theodore Roosevelt, Jr.

Episode #32 **Broadcast of December 20, 1938.**
Panelists: Franklin P. Adams, John Kieran, columnist Heywood Broun and playwright George S. Kaufman

Episode #33 **Broadcast of December 27, 1938.**
Panelists: Franklin P. Adams, John Kieran, Oscar Levant and educator/journalist William Lyon Phelps

Episode #34 **Broadcast of January 3, 1939.**
Panelists: Franklin P. Adams, John Kieran, monologist and author Cornelia Otis Skinner, and Irwin Edmund, Professor of Philosophy at Columbia University

Episode #35 **Broadcast of January 10, 1939.**
Panelists: Franklin P. Adams, John Kieran, Oscar Levant and critic Alexander Woollcott

Episode #36 **Broadcast of January 17, 1939.**
Panelists: Franklin P. Adams, John Kieran, poet Ogden Nash and author Hendrik Willem Van Loon

Episode #37 **Broadcast of January 24, 1939.**
Panelists: Franklin P. Adams, John Kieran, Oscar Levant and General Hugh Johnson

Episode #38 **Broadcast of January 31, 1939.**
Panelists: Franklin P. Adams, John Kieran, Pulitzer Prize-winning author Gilbert Seldes and author Elizabeth Foss

Episode #39 **Broadcast of February 7, 1939.**
Panelists: Franklin P. Adams, John Kieran, Oscar Levant and University student Myron (Mike) Wallace

Episode #40 **Broadcast of February 14, 1939.**
Panelists: Franklin P. Adams, John Kieran, humorist Frank Sullivan and playwright Russel Crouse

Episode #41 **Broadcast of February 21, 1939.**
Panelists: Franklin P. Adams, John Kieran, Oscar Levant and baseball player Moe Berg

Episode #42 **Broadcast of February 28, 1939.**
Panelists: Franklin P. Adams, John Kieran, columnist Heywood Broun, and Rex Stout, creator of the Nero Wolfe mystery stories

Episode #43 **Broadcast of March 7, 1939.**
Panelists: Franklin P. Adams, John Kieran, Oscar Levant and author Morrie Ryskind

Episode #44 **Broadcast of March 14, 1939.**
Panelists: Franklin P. Adams, John Kieran, radio news commentator Elmer Davis and author Dorothy Parker

Episode #45 **Broadcast of March 21, 1939.**
Panelists: Franklin P. Adams, John Kieran, Oscar Levant and author/correspondent John Gunther

Episode #46 **Broadcast of March 28, 1939.**
Panelists: Franklin P. Adams, John Kieran, playwright Moss Hart and author Rex Stout

Episode #47 **Broadcast of April 4, 1939.**
Panelists: Franklin P. Adams, John Kieran, Oscar Levant and poet and author Dorothy Parker

Episode #48 **Broadcast of April 11, 1939.**
Panelists: Franklin P. Adams, John Kieran, musicologist Deems Taylor and columnist Marcus Duffield

Episode #49 **Broadcast of April 18, 1939.**
Panelists: Franklin P. Adams, John Kieran, Oscar Levant and radio commentator H.V. Kaltenborn

Episode #50 **Broadcast of April 25, 1939.**
Panelists: Franklin P. Adams, John Kieran, Alice Roosevelt Longworth (daughter of F.D.R.) and Arthur Krock, *New York Times* chief of the Washington Bureau

Episode #51 **Broadcast of May 2, 1939.**
Panelists: Franklin P. Adams, John Kieran, Oscar Levant and entertainer/composer George M. Cohan

Episode #52 **Broadcast of May 9, 1939.**
Panelists: Franklin P. Adams, John Kieran, author Rex Stout, and Bella Spewak, co-author of *Kiss Me Kate*

Episode #53 **Broadcast of May 16, 1939.**
Panelists: Franklin P. Adams, John Kieran, Oscar Levant and John P. Marquand, author of the *Mr. Moto* mysteries

Episode #54 **Broadcast of May 23, 1939.**
Panelists: Franklin P. Adams, John Kieran, Bernard Jaffee and author Clarence Buddington Kelland

Episode #55 **Broadcast of May 30, 1939.**
Panelists: Franklin P. Adams, John Kieran, Oscar Levant and author Stanley Walker

Episode #56 **Broadcast of June 6, 1939.**
Panelists: Franklin P. Adams, John Kieran, Deems Taylor and H.I. Philips

Episode #57 **Broadcast of June 13, 1939.**
Panelists: Franklin P. Adams, John Kieran, Oscar Levant and tennis player Helen Wills Moody

Episode #58 **Broadcast of June 20, 1939.**
Panelists: Franklin P. Adams, John Kieran, author/correspondent John Gunther and comedienne Gracie Allen

Episode #59 **Broadcast of June 27, 1939.**
Panelists: Franklin P. Adams, John Kieran, Oscar Levant and Wilbur L. Cross, former Governor of Connecticut

Episode #60 **Broadcast of July 4, 1939.**
Panelists: Franklin P. Adams, John Kieran, columnist Marcus Duffield and actress Lillian Gish

Episode #61 **Broadcast of July 11, 1939.**
Panelists: Franklin P. Adams, John Kieran, Oscar Levant and radio commentator Elliot Roosevelt (son of F.D.R.)

Episode #62 **Broadcast of July 18, 1939.**
Panelists: Franklin P. Adams, John Kieran, biologist William Beebe and author Clarence Buddington Kelland

Episode #63 **Broadcast of July 25, 1939.**
Panelists: Franklin P. Adams, John Kieran, Oscar Levant and Maurie Maverick

Episode #64 **Broadcast of August 1, 1939.**
Panelists: Franklin P. Adams, John Kieran, playwright Russel Crouse and James Kieran (brother of John Kieran, and press secretary for Mayor LaGuardia)

Episode #65 **Broadcast of August 8, 1939.**
Panelists: Franklin P. Adams, John Kieran, Oscar Levant and actress Ethel Barrymore

Episode #66 **Broadcast of August 15, 1939.**
Panelists: Franklin P. Adams, John Kieran, columnist Marcus Duffield and author Christopher Morley

Episode #67 **Broadcast of August 22, 1939.**
Panelists: Franklin P. Adams, John Kieran, Oscar Levant and columnist H. Napier Moore

Episode #68 **Broadcast of August 29, 1939.**
Panelists: Franklin P. Adams, John Kieran, Rex Stout and author Wilfred Funk

Episode #69 **Broadcast of September 5, 1939.**
Panelists: Franklin P. Adams, John Kieran, Oscar Levant and radio commentator Raymond Graham Swing

Episode #70 **Broadcast of September 12, 1939.**
Panelists: Franklin P. Adams, John Kieran, Bernard Jaffee and tennis champion Alice Marble (also a singer, and a designer of tennis shorts)

Episode #71 **Broadcast of September 19, 1939.**
Panelists: Franklin P. Adams, John Kieran, Oscar Levant and card shark/pool player P. Cal Simms

Episode #72 **Broadcast of September 26, 1939.**
Panelists: Franklin P. Adams, John Kieran, Rex Stout and author Carl Van Doren

Episode #73 **Broadcast of October 3, 1939.**
Panelists: Franklin P. Adams, John Kieran, Oscar Levant and C. Mildred Thompson, Assistant Prof. at Vassar

Episode #74 **Broadcast of October 10, 1939.**
Panelists: Franklin P. Adams, John Kieran, author Christopher Morley and journalist John T. Flynn

Episode #75 **Broadcast of October 17, 1939.**
Panelists: Franklin P. Adams, John Kieran, Oscar Levant and baseball player Moe Berg

Episode #76 **Broadcast of October 24, 1939.**
Panelists: Franklin P. Adams, John Kieran, Deems Taylor and poet/anthologist Louis Untermeyer

Episode #77 **Broadcast of October 31, 1939.**
Panelists: Franklin P. Adams, John Kieran, Oscar Levant and author Carl Sandberg

Episode #78 **Broadcast of November 7, 1939.**
Panelists: Franklin P. Adams, John Kieran, Christopher Morley and author Marquis James

Episode #79 **Broadcast of November 14, 1939.**
Panelists: Franklin P. Adams, John Kieran, Oscar Levant and U.S. Post Master James Farley

Episode #80 **Broadcast of November 21, 1939.**
Panelists: Franklin P. Adams, John Kieran, Moe Berg and screenwriter J.P. McEvoy

Episode #81 **Broadcast of November 28, 1939.**
Panelists: Franklin P. Adams, John Kieran, Oscar Levant and humorist James Thurber

Episode #82 **Broadcast of December 5, 1939.**
Panelists: Franklin P. Adams, John Kieran, Deems Taylor and Henry Pringle

Episode #83 **Broadcast of December 12, 1939.**
Panelists: Franklin P. Adams, John Kieran, Oscar Levant and author Walter B. Pitkin

Episode #84 **Broadcast of December 19, 1939.**
Panelists: Franklin P. Adams, John Kieran, Christopher Morley and violinist Albert Spalding

Episode #85 **Broadcast of December 26, 1939.**
Panelists: Franklin P. Adams, John Kieran, Oscar Levant and actor Sir Cedric Hardwicke

Episode #86 **Broadcast of January 2, 1940.**
Panelists: Franklin P. Adams, John Kieran, author Carl Van Doren and actress Gloria Stuart

Episode #87 **Broadcast of January 9, 1940.**
Panelists: Franklin P. Adams, John Kieran, Oscar Levant and Edna Ferber, author of *Show Boat*

Episode #88 **Broadcast of January 16, 1940.**
Panelists: Franklin P. Adams, John Kieran, Deems Taylor and Dr. Oliver St. John Gogarty

Episode #89 **Broadcast of January 23, 1940.**
Panelists: Franklin P. Adams, John Kieran, Oscar Levant and actor Dudley Digges

Episode #90 **Broadcast of January 30, 1940.**
Panelists: Franklin P. Adams, John Kieran, playwright Russel Crouse and U.S. Representative T.V. Smith

Episode #91 **Broadcast of February 6, 1940.**
Panelists: Franklin P. Adams, John Kieran, Oscar Levant and Nunnally Johnson, journalist for *New York Herald-Tribune*

Episode #92 **Broadcast of February 13, 1940.**
Panelists: Franklin P. Adams, John Kieran, Christopher Morley and actress Ruth Gordon

Episode #93 **Broadcast of February 20, 1940.**
Panelists: Franklin P. Adams, John Kieran, Oscar Levant and author Oliver LaForge

Episode #94 **Broadcast of February 27, 1940.**
Panelists: Franklin P. Adams, John Kieran, Dr. Roy Chapman Andrews and Dr. Oliver St. John Gogarty

Episode #95 **Broadcast of March 5, 1940.**
Panelists: Franklin P. Adams, John Kieran, Oscar Levant and author Frederick Lewis Allen

Episode #96 **Broadcast on March 12, 1940.**
Panelists: Franklin P. Adams, John Kieran, and Sam and Bella Spewack, authors of the later *Kiss Me Kate*

Episode #97 **Broadcast of March 19, 1940.**
Panelists: Franklin P. Adams, John Kieran, Oscar Levant and author John Chamberlain

Episode #98 **Broadcast of March 26, 1940.**
Panelists: Franklin P. Adams, John Kieran, Russel Crouse and Howard Lindsay (playwrights Crouse and Lindsay collaborated for 28 years on Broadway, on shows including *The Sound of Music*, *Life with Father* and *Arsenic and Old Lace*)

Episode #99 **Broadcast of April 2, 1940.**
Panelists: Franklin P. Adams, John Kieran, Oscar Levant and writer/critic Lewis Gannett

Episode #100 **Broadcast of April 9, 1940.**
Panelists: Franklin P. Adams, John Kieran, Christopher Morley and industrialist Wendell Wilkie

Episode #101 **Broadcast of April 16, 1940.**
Panelists: Franklin P. Adams, John Kieran, Oscar Levant and actor Ray Milland

Episode #102 **Broadcast of April 23, 1940.**
Panelists: Franklin P. Adams, John Kieran, Deems Taylor and military columnist Major George Fielding Elliot

Episode #103 **Broadcast of April 30, 1940.**
Panelists: Franklin P. Adams, John Kieran, Oscar Levant and actor Harry Carey

Episode #104 **Broadcast of May 7, 1940.**
Panelists: Franklin P. Adams, John Kieran, Russel Crouse and Carl W. Ackerman, Dean of the Columbia School of Journalism

Episode #105 **Broadcast of May 14, 1940.**
Panelists: Franklin P. Adams, John Kieran, author/correspondent John Gunther and Republican Committee Chairman Kenneth Simpson

Episode #106 **Broadcast of May 21, 1940.**
Panelists: Franklin P. Adams, John Kieran, Felix and author Christopher Morley

Episode #107 **Broadcast of May 28, 1940.**
Panelists: Franklin P. Adams, John Kieran, Oscar Levant and actress Dame Anna Neagle

Episode #108 **Broadcast of June 4, 1940.**
Panelists: Franklin P. Adams, John Kieran, Deems Taylor and playwright Robert Sherwood

Episode #109 **Broadcast of June 11, 1940.**
Panelists: Franklin P. Adams, John Kieran, Oscar Levant and actress Ruth Gordon

Episode #110 **Broadcast of June 18, 1940.**
Panelists: Franklin P. Adams, John Kieran, Rex Stout and publisher Ralph Ingersoll

Episode #111 **Broadcast of June 25, 1940.**
Panelists: Franklin P. Adams, John Kieran, Oscar Levant and actor Raymond Massey

Episode #112 **Broadcast of July 2, 1940.**
Panelists: Franklin P. Adams, John Kieran, Christopher Morley and comedian/actor Jimmy Durante

Episode #113 **Broadcast of July 9, 1940.**
Panelists: Franklin P. Adams, John Kieran, Oscar Levant and explorer Mrs. Martin Johnson

Episode #114 **Broadcast of July 16, 1940.**
Panelists: Franklin P. Adams, John Kieran, Deems Taylor and actor Monte Woolley

Episode #115 **Broadcast of July 23, 1940.**
Panelists: Franklin P. Adams, John Kieran, Oscar Levant and Erskine Caldwell (American novelist who wrote the novel *Tobacco Road*. Caldwell's recent novel was *Trouble in July*)

Episode #116 **Broadcast of July 30, 1940.**
Panelists: Franklin P. Adams, John Kieran, author/correspondent John Gunther and columnist Alva Johnston

Episode #117 **Broadcast of August 6, 1940.**
Panelists: Franklin P. Adams, John Kieran, Oscar Levant and author F. Van Wyke Mason

Episode #118 **Broadcast of August 13, 1940.**
Panelists: Franklin P. Adams, John Kieran, Republican Committee Chairman Kenneth Simpson and Sec. of Interior Harold Ickes

Episode #119 **Broadcast of August 20, 1940.**
Panelists: Franklin P. Adams, John Kieran, Oscar Levant and movie producer Walter Wanger

Episode #120 **Broadcast of August 27, 1940.**
Panelists: Franklin P. Adams, John Kieran, Christopher Morley and James Bennett

Episode #121 **Broadcast of September 3, 1940.**
Panelists: Franklin P. Adams, John Kieran, Oscar Levant and Henry Beedle Hough

Episode #122 **Broadcast of September 10, 1940.**
Panelists: Franklin P. Adams, John Kieran, John Gunther and author Jan Struther

Episode #123 **Broadcast of September 17, 1940.**
Panelists: Franklin P. Adams, John Kieran, Oscar Levant and Otto D. Tolischus, columnist for the *New York Times*

Episode #124 **Broadcast of September 24, 1940.**
Panelists: Franklin P. Adams, John Kieran, Oscar Levant and playwright Marc Connelly

Episode #125 **Broadcast of October 1, 1940.**
Panelists: Franklin P. Adams, John Kieran, Oscar Levant and playwright Clare Boothe Luce

Episode #126 **Broadcast of October 8, 1940.**
Panelists: Franklin P. Adams, John Kieran, author Jan Struther and author Louis Bromfield

Episode #127 **Broadcast of October 15, 1940.**
Panelists: Franklin P. Adams, John Kieran, Oscar Levant and Louis Hacker

Episode #128 **Broadcast of October 22, 1940.**
Panelists: Franklin P. Adams, John Kieran, Deems Taylor and editor/journalist Herbert Bayard Swope

Episode #129 **Broadcast of October 29, 1940.**
Panelists: Franklin P. Adams, John Kieran, Oscar Levant and author John Mason Brown

Episode #130 **Broadcast of November 5, 1940.**
Panelists: Franklin P. Adams, John Kieran, Oscar Levant and Christopher Morley

Episode #131 **Broadcast of November 15, 1940.**
Panelists: Franklin P. Adams, John Kieran, Oscar Levant and comedian Fred Allen

Episode #132 **Broadcast of November 22, 1940.**
Panelists: Franklin P. Adams, John Kieran, musician Deems Taylor and Lewis E. Lawes, warden of Sing Sing

Episode #133 **Broadcast of November 29, 1940.**
Panelists: Franklin P. Adams, John Kieran, Oscar Levant and American economist Leon Henderson

Episode #134 **Broadcast of December 6, 1940.**
Panelists: Franklin P. Adams, John Kieran, author Jan Struther and playwright Elmer Rice

Episode #135 **Broadcast of December 13, 1940.**
Panelists: Franklin P. Adams, John Kieran, Oscar Levant and anthropologist Ernest Albert Hooten

Episode #136 **Broadcast of December 20, 1940.**
Panelists: Franklin P. Adams, John Kieran, author Louis Bromfield and actor Herbert Marshall

Episode #137 **Broadcast of December 27, 1940.**
Panelists: Franklin P. Adams, John Kieran, Oscar Levant and Walter D. Edmonds, author of *Drums Along the Mohawk*

Episode #138 **Broadcast of January 3, 1941.**
Panelists: Franklin P. Adams, John Kieran, Deems Taylor and author Vincent Sheehan

Episode #139 **Broadcast of January 10, 1941.**
Panelists: Franklin P. Adams, John Kieran, Republican Committee Chairman Kenneth Simpson and Judge James G. Wallace

Episode #140 **Broadcast of January 17, 1941.**
Panelists: Franklin P. Adams, John Kieran, Oscar Levant and Owen Davis, author of *Mr. and Mrs. North*

Episode #141 **Broadcast of January 24, 1941.**
Panelists: Franklin P. Adams, John Kieran, actor Boris Karloff and Lewis E. Lawes, warden of Sing Sing

Episode #142 **Broadcast of January 31, 1941.**
Panelists: Franklin P. Adams, John Kieran, critic Alexander Woollcott and playwright S.J. Pearlman

Episode #143 **Broadcast of February 7, 1941.**
Panelists: Franklin P. Adams, John Kieran, Jan Struther and Latin singer Wilmot Louis

Episode #144 **Broadcast of February 14, 1941.**
Panelists: Franklin P. Adams, John Kieran, musician Deems Taylor and Henry Noble MacCracken, President of Vassar

Episode #145 **Broadcast of February 21, 1941.**
Panelists: Franklin P. Adams, John Kieran, Oscar Levant and songwriter/performer Jo Davidson

Episode #146 **Broadcast of February 28, 1941.**
Panelists: Franklin P. Adams, John Kieran, Oscar Levant and John O'Hara. Deems Taylor subs as master of ceremonies, for an ill Clifton Fadiman.

Episode #147 **Broadcast of March 7, 1941.**
Panelists: Franklin P. Adams, John Kieran, Christopher Morley and Elmer F. Leyden

Episode #148 **Broadcast of March 14, 1941.**
Panelists: Franklin P. Adams, John Kieran, Oscar Levant and Claude Rickard

Episode #149 **Broadcast of March 21, 1941.**
Panelists: Franklin P. Adams, John Kieran, Deems Taylor and actor Roland Young

Episode #150 **Broadcast of March 28, 1941.**
Panelists: Franklin P. Adams, John Kieran, Oscar Levant and actress Elsa Lanchester

Episode #151 **Broadcast of April 4, 1941.**
Panelists: Franklin P. Adams, John Kieran, John Gunther and Dr. Lyman Bryson of Columbia University

Episode #152 **Broadcast of April 11, 1941.**
Panelists: Franklin P. Adams, John Kieran, Oscar Levant and actor Philip Merivale

Episode #153 **Broadcast of April 18, 1941.**
Panelists: Franklin P. Adams, John Kieran, Rex Stout and Chief Magistrate Henry Curran

Episode #154 **Broadcast of April 25, 1941.**
Panelists: Franklin P. Adams, John Kieran, Oscar Levant and actor Paul Lukas

Episode #155 **Broadcast of May 2, 1941.**
Panelists: Franklin P. Adams, John Kieran, Deems Taylor and playwright Donald Ogden Stewart

Episode #156 **Broadcast of May 9, 1941.**
Panelists: Franklin P. Adams, John Kieran, Oscar Levant and heavyweight boxing champion Gene Tunney

Episode #157 **Broadcast of May 16, 1941.**
Panelists: Franklin P. Adams, John Kieran, humorist Frank Sullivan and press agent Richard Manney

Episode #158 **Broadcast of May 23, 1941.**
Panelists: Franklin P. Adams, John Kieran, Oscar Levant and Clifton Fadiman. Deems Taylor is the master of ceremonies for this broadcast while Fadiman got a chance to sit on the panel.

Episode #159 **Broadcast of May 30, 1941.**
Panelists: Franklin P. Adams, John Kieran, Jan Struther and author Cornelia Otis Skinner

Episode #160 **Broadcast of June 6, 1941.**
Panelists: Franklin P. Adams, John Kieran, Oscar Levant and actress Sally Benson

Episode #161 **Broadcast of June 13, 1941.**
Panelists: Franklin P. Adams, John Kieran, Oscar Levant and tennis player Bill Tilden

Episode #162 **Broadcast of June 20, 1941.**
Panelists: Franklin P. Adams, John Kieran, James G. Wallace and Al Smith, Ex-Governor of New York

Episode #163 **Broadcast of June 27, 1941.**
Panelists: Franklin P. Adams, John Kieran, Oscar Levant and director Alfred Hitchcock

Episode #164 **Broadcast of July 4, 1941.**
Panelists: Franklin P. Adams, John Kieran, John Gunther and Walter Durante

Episode #165 **Broadcast of July 11, 1941.**
Panelists: Franklin P. Adams, John Kieran, Oscar Levant and actress Mary Boland

Episode #166 **Broadcast of July 18, 1941.**
Panelists: Franklin P. Adams, John Kieran, Deems Taylor and biologist William Beebe

Episode #167 **Broadcast of July 25, 1941.**
Panelists: Franklin P. Adams, John Kieran, Oscar Levant and journalist/author William Shirer

Episode #168 **Broadcast of August 1, 1941.**
Panelists: Franklin P. Adams, John Kieran, Dr. Lyman Bryson of Columbia University and Henry Noble MacCracken, President of Vassar

Episode #169 **Broadcast of August 8, 1941.**
Panelists: Franklin P. Adams, John Kieran, Oscar Levant and baseball player Larry MacPhail

Episode #170 **Broadcast of August 15, 1941.**
Panelists: Franklin P. Adams, John Kieran, Deems Taylor and playwright Russel Crouse

Episode #171 **Broadcast of August 22, 1941.**
Panelists: Franklin P. Adams, John Kieran, Oscar Levant and short story writer Faith Baldwin

Episode #172 **Broadcast of August 29, 1941.**
Panelists: Franklin P. Adams, John Kieran, Christopher Morley and George V. Denny, Jr.

Episode #173 **Broadcast of September 5, 1941.**
Panelists: Franklin P. Adams, John Kieran, Oscar Levant and Deems Taylor

Episode #174 **Broadcast of September 12, 1941.**
Panelists: Franklin P. Adams, John Kieran, author Louis Bromfield and Margaret Leach

Episode #175 **Broadcast of September 19, 1941.**
Panelists: Franklin P. Adams, John Kieran, Oscar Levant and author Stephen Vincent Benet

Episode #176 **Broadcast of September 26, 1941.**
Panelists: Franklin P. Adams, John Kieran, Jan Struther and musician Sir Thomas Beecham

Episode #177 **Broadcast of October 3, 1941.**
Panelists: Franklin P. Adams, John Kieran, Oscar Levant and baseball player Lefty Gomez

Episode #178 **Broadcast of October 10, 1941.**
Panelists: Franklin P. Adams, John Kieran, Deems Taylor and NY Mayor Fiorello LaGuardia

Episode #179 **Broadcast of October 17, 1941.**
Panelists: Franklin P. Adams, John Kieran, Oscar Levant and comedian Fred Allen

Episode #180 **Broadcast of October 24, 1941.**
Panelists: Franklin P. Adams, John Kieran, Deems Taylor and author C.S. Forrester

Episode #181 **Broadcast of October 31, 1941.**
Panelists: Franklin P. Adams, John Kieran, Deems Taylor and comedian Groucho Marx

Episode #182 **Broadcast of November 7, 1941.**
Panelists: Franklin P. Adams, John Kieran, Oscar Levant and Douglas Miller

Episode #183 **Broadcast of November 14, 1941.**
Panelists: Franklin P. Adams, John Kieran, John Gunther and actor Leslie Howard

Episode #184 **Broadcast of November 21, 1941.**
Panelists: Franklin P. Adams, John Kieran, Oscar Levant and author Cornelia Otis Skinner

Episode #185 **Broadcast of November 28, 1941.**
Panelists: Franklin P. Adams, John Kieran, Oscar Levant, and columnists Drew Pearson and Robert Allen

Episode #186 **Broadcast of December 5, 1941.**
Panelists: Franklin P. Adams, John Kieran, Deems Taylor and author Edna Ferber

Episode #187 **Broadcast of December 12, 1941.**
Panelists: Franklin P. Adams, John Kieran, Oscar Levant and Dr. George N. Shuster, President of Hunter College in N.Y.

Episode #188 **Broadcast of December 19, 1941.**
Panelists: Franklin P. Adams, John Kieran, Jan Struther and Joseph E. Davies, U.S. Ambassador to U.S.S.R.

Episode #189 **Broadcast of December 26, 1941.**
Panelists: Franklin P. Adams, John Kieran, Oscar Levant and John Gunther

Episode #190 **Broadcast of January 2, 1942.**
Panelists: Franklin P. Adams, John Kieran, Deems Taylor and author Cornelia Otis Skinner

Episode #191 **Broadcast of January 9, 1942.**
Panelists: Franklin P. Adams, John Kieran, Oscar Levant and Paul V. McNutt, Chairman of the War Power Commission

Episode #192 **Broadcast of January 16, 1942.**
Panelists: Franklin P. Adams, John Kieran, Russel Crouse and sports editor Paul Gallico

Episode #193 **Broadcast of January 23, 1942.**
Panelists: Franklin P. Adams, John Kieran, Deems Taylor and critic Alexander Woollcott

Episode #194 **Broadcast of January 30, 1942.**
Panelists: Franklin P. Adams, John Kieran, Oscar Levant and Janet Flanner, author of *An American in Paris*

Episode #195 **Broadcast of February 6, 1942.**
Panelists: Franklin P. Adams, John Kieran, Christopher Morley and actress Ruth Hussey

Episode #196 **Broadcast of February 13, 1942.**
Panelists: Franklin P. Adams, John Kieran, Oscar Levant and T.T. Barrett

Episode #197 **Broadcast of February 20, 1942.**
Panelists: Franklin P. Adams, John Kieran, actor Boris Karloff and actor John Carradine

Episode #198 **Broadcast of February 27, 1942.**
Panelists: Franklin P. Adams, John Kieran, Oscar Levant and Emil Ludwig, German author of European history

Episode #199 **Broadcast of March 6, 1942.**
Panelists: Franklin P. Adams, John Kieran, Jan Struther and biologist Sir Julian S. Huxley

Episode #200 **Broadcast of March 13, 1942.**
Panelists: Franklin P. Adams, John Kieran, Oscar Levant and actor Adolphe Menjou

Episode #201 **Broadcast of March 20, 1942.**
Panelists: Franklin P. Adams, John Kieran, actor John Carradine and Sir Thomas Beecham

Episode #202 **Broadcast of March 27, 1942.**
Panelists: Franklin P. Adams, John Kieran, Oscar Levant and author Wallace R. Deuel

Episode #203 **Broadcast of April 3, 1942.**
Panelists: Franklin P. Adams, John Kieran, Madame Ivy Litvinov, author and translator, and wife of the Soviet Ambassador to the U.S., and Mrs. Maxim Maximovich

Episode #204 **Broadcast of April 10, 1942.**
Panelists: Franklin P. Adams, John Kieran, Russel Crouse and author John Mason Brown

Episode #205 **Broadcast of April 17, 1942.**
Panelists: Franklin P. Adams, John Kieran, Oscar Levant and sportswriter Grantland Rice

Episode #206 **Broadcast of April 24, 1942.**
Panelists: Franklin P. Adams, John Kieran, Christopher Morley and Eric Knight, author of *Lassie Come Home*

Episode #207 **Broadcast of May 1, 1942.**
Panelists: Franklin P. Adams, John Kieran, Oscar Levant and James M. Landis, Dean of Harvard University Law School

Episode #208 **Broadcast of May 8, 1942.**
Panelists: Franklin P. Adams, John Kieran, Margaret Webster and press agent Richard Manney

Episode #209 **Broadcast of May 15, 1942.**
Panelists: Franklin P. Adams, John Kieran, Oscar Levant and journalist Raymond Clapper

Episode #210 **Broadcast of May 22, 1942.**
Panelists: Franklin P. Adams, John Kieran, Deems Taylor and actor Roland Young

Episode #211 **Broadcast of May 29, 1942.**
Panelists: Franklin P. Adams, John Kieran, Oscar Levant and author Wallace R. Deuel

Episode #212 **Broadcast of June 5, 1942.**
Panelists: Franklin P. Adams, John Kieran, Deems Taylor and actress Madeleine Carroll

Episode #213 **Broadcast of June 12, 1942.**
Panelists: Franklin P. Adams, John Kieran, American economist Leon Henderson and author Frederick Lewis Allen

Episode #214 **Broadcast of June 19, 1942.**
Panelists: Franklin P. Adams, John Kieran, Christopher Morley and Cornelia Otis Skinner

Episode #215 **Broadcast of June 26, 1942.**
Panelists: Franklin P. Adams, John Kieran, Jan Struther and journalist Frederick C. Erksner

Episode #216 **Broadcast of July 3, 1942.**
Panelists: Franklin P. Adams, John Kieran, Oscar Levant and producer/director Gregory Ratoff

Episode #217 **Broadcast of July 10, 1942.**
Panelists: Franklin P. Adams, John Kieran, Deems Taylor and writer/composer H.I. Phillips

Episode #218 **Broadcast of July 17, 1942.**
Panelists: Franklin P. Adams, John Kieran, Oscar Levant and Major Henry Cabot Lodge, Jr.

Episode #219 **Broadcast of July 24, 1942.**
Panelists: Franklin P. Adams, John Kieran, Arthur Garfield Hayes and sports editor Paul Gallico

Episode #220 **Broadcast of July 31, 1942.**
Panelists: Franklin P. Adams, John Kieran, Oscar Levant and Helen MacInnis, author of two recent best-sellers, *Above Suspicion* and *Assignment in Brittany*

Episode #221 **Broadcast of August 7, 1942.**
Panelists: Franklin P. Adams, John Kieran, Russel Crouse and actor Ned Sparks

Episode #222 **Broadcast of August 14, 1942.**
Panelists: Franklin P. Adams, John Kieran, Oscar Levant and officer Mildred McAfee (just eleven days before this broadcast, Mildred McAfee became the U.S. Navy's first female officer)

Episode #223 **Broadcast of August 21, 1942.**
Panelists: Franklin P. Adams, John Kieran, American economist Leon Henderson and journalist Raymond Clapper

Episode #224 **Broadcast of August 28, 1942.**
Panelists: Franklin P. Adams, John Kieran, Oscar Levant and radio commentator Quincy Howe

Episode #225 **Broadcast of September 4, 1942.**
Panelists: Franklin P. Adams, John Kieran, Jan Struther and author C.S. Forrester

Episode #226 **Broadcast of September 11, 1942.**
Panelists: Franklin P. Adams, John Kieran, Oscar Levant and columnist Alva Johnston

Episode #227 **Broadcast of September 18, 1942.**
Panelists: Franklin P. Adams, John Kieran, Christopher Morley and actor Orson Welles

Episode #228 **Broadcast of September 25, 1942.**
Panelists: Franklin P. Adams, John Kieran, Oscar Levant and Leon Henderson

Episode #229 **Broadcast of October 2, 1942.**
Panelists: Franklin P. Adams, John Kieran, Deems Taylor and journalist Robert St. John

Episode #230 **Broadcast of October 9, 1942.**
Panelists: Franklin P. Adams, John Kieran, Oscar Levant and Gregory Ratoff

Episode #231 **Broadcast of October 16, 1942.**
Panelists: Franklin P. Adams, John Kieran, Cornelia Otis Skinner and Alexander Woollcott

Episode #232 **Broadcast of October 23, 1942.**
Panelists: Franklin P. Adams, John Kieran, Oscar Levant and actress Dame Anna Neagle

Episode #233 **Broadcast of October 30, 1942.**
Panelists: Franklin P. Adams, John Kieran, Christopher Morley and author Carl Sandburg

Episode #234 **Broadcast of November 6, 1942.**
Panelists: Franklin P. Adams, John Kieran, Oscar Levant and Pulitzer prize-winning author Hanson W. Baldwin

Episode #235 **Broadcast of November 13, 1942.**
Panelists: Franklin P. Adams, John Kieran, poet/anthologist Louis Untermeyer and author/poet Dorothy Parker

Episode #236 **Broadcast of November 20, 1942.**
Panelists: Franklin P. Adams, John Kieran, Oscar Levant and Louis Bromfield, author of *Early Autumn*

Episode #237 **Broadcast of November 27, 1942.**
Panelists: Franklin P. Adams, John Kieran, American economist Leon Henderson and Wilma Lord Perkins, editor of *Cooking School*

Episode #238 **Broadcast of December 4, 1942.**
Panelists: Franklin P. Adams, John Kieran, Oscar Levant and Major Henry Cabot Lodge, Jr.

Episode #239 **Broadcast of December 11, 1942.**
Panelists: Franklin P. Adams, John Kieran, Christopher Morley and William L. Shirer

Episode #240 **Broadcast of December 18, 1942.**
Panelists: Franklin P. Adams, John Kieran, Oscar Levant and actress Ilka Chase

Episode #241 **Broadcast of December 25, 1942.**
Panelists: Franklin P. Adams, John Kieran, Leon Henderson and James Wallace Beardsley, civil engineer

Episode #242 **Broadcast of January 1, 1943.**
Panelists: Franklin P. Adams, John Kieran, Oscar Levant and Gregory Ratoff

Episode #243 **Broadcast of January 8, 1943.**
Panelists: Franklin P. Adams, John Kieran, Oscar Levant and U.S. Representative Will Rogers, Jr.

Episode #244 **Broadcast of January 15, 1943.**
Panelists: Franklin P. Adams, John Kieran, Deems Taylor and actor Charles Coburn

Episode #245 **Broadcast of January 22, 1943.**
Panelists: Franklin P. Adams, John Kieran, Oscar Levant and Alfred Hitchcock

Episode #246 **Broadcast of January 29, 1943.**
Panelists: Franklin P. Adams, John Kieran, Cornelia Otis Skinner and author Emily Kimbrough (both guests were co-authors of the book *Our Hearts Were Young and Gay*)

Episode #247 **Broadcast of February 5, 1943.**
Panelists: Franklin P. Adams, John Kieran, Oscar Levant and Jan Struther

Episode #248 **Broadcast of February 15, 1943.**
Panelists: Franklin P. Adams, John Kieran, Oscar Levant and Fred Allen

Episode #249 **Broadcast of February 22, 1943.**
Panelists: Franklin P. Adams, John Kieran, Christopher Morley and Gregory Ratoff

Episode #250 **Broadcast of March 1, 1943.**
Panelists: Franklin P. Adams, John Kieran, Oscar Levant and Will Rogers, Jr.

Episode #251 **Broadcast of March 8, 1943.**
Panelists: Franklin P. Adams, John Kieran, Oscar Levant and Gregory Ratoff

Episode #252 **Broadcast of March 15, 1943.**
Panelists: Franklin P. Adams, John Kieran, Oscar Levant and Jan Struther

Episode #253 **Broadcast of March 22, 1943.**
Panelists: Franklin P. Adams, John Kieran, Christopher Morley and author Sinclair Lewis

Episode #254 **Broadcast of March 29, 1943.**
Panelists: Franklin P. Adams, John Kieran, Oscar Levant and General U.N. Ambassador Carlos P. Romulo

Episode #255 **Broadcast of April 5, 1943.**
Panelists: Franklin P. Adams, John Kieran, Cornelia Otis Skinner and Jan Struther

Episode #256 **Broadcast of April 12, 1943.**
Panelists: Franklin P. Adams, John Kieran, Oscar Levant and industrialist Wendell Wilkie

Episode #257 **Broadcast of April 19, 1943.**
Panelists: Franklin P. Adams, John Kieran, baseball commissioner Ford Frick and sportswriter Grantland Rice

Episode #258 **Broadcast of April 26, 1943.**
Panelists: Franklin P. Adams, John Kieran, Oscar Levant and Leon Henderson

Episode #259 **Broadcast of May 3, 1943.**
Panelists: Franklin P. Adams, John Kieran, John Hershey and Sinclair Lewis

Episode #260 **Broadcast of May 10, 1943.**
Panelists: Franklin P. Adams, John Kieran, Oscar Levant and George Denny

Episode #261 **Broadcast of May 17, 1943.**
Panelists: Franklin P. Adams, John Kieran, Jan Struther and Boris Karloff

Episode #262 **Broadcast of May 24, 1943.**
Panelists: Franklin P. Adams, John Kieran, press agent Richard Manney and actress Ethel Barrymore

Episode #263 **Broadcast of May 31, 1943.**
Panelists: Franklin P. Adams, John Kieran, Oscar Levant and Sir Thomas Beecham

Episode #264 **Broadcast of June 7, 1943.**
Panelists: Franklin P. Adams, John Kieran, Deems Taylor and novelist Marcia Davenport

Episode #265 **Broadcast of June 14, 1943.**
Panelists: Franklin P. Adams, John Kieran, Oscar Levant and author Hillary St. George Saunders

Episode #266 **Broadcast of June 21, 1943.**
Panelists: Franklin P. Adams, John Kieran, Christopher Morley and C. Mildred Thompson, Assistant Prof. at Vassar

Episode #267 **Broadcast of June 28, 1943.**
Panelists: Franklin P. Adams, John Kieran, Oscar Levant and Walter Yost, editor of the *Encyclopedia Britannica*. The June 28 broadcast of *Information, Please* originated from the Chicago Civic Opera House.

Episode #268 **Broadcast of July 5, 1943.**
Panelists: Franklin P. Adams, John Kieran, Oscar Levant and Gregory Ratoff

Episode #269 **Broadcast of July 12, 1943.**
Panelists: Franklin P. Adams, John Kieran, Oscar Levant and Jan Struther. The July 12 broadcast of *Information, Please* originated from the San Francisco Opera House.

Episode #270 **Broadcast of September 13, 1943.**
Panelists: Franklin P. Adams, John Kieran, Deems Taylor and novelist Marcia Davenport

Episode #271 **Broadcast of September 20, 1943.**
Panelists: Franklin P. Adams, John Kieran, Oscar Levant and playwright Clare Boothe Luce. The broadcast of September 20 originated from the stage of the Lyric Theatre in Baltimore, Maryland. During this broadcast, John Kieran read a paragraph from an item in his column as an appeal to buy war bonds.

Episode #272 **Broadcast of September 27, 1943.**
Panelists: Franklin P. Adams, John Kieran, Oscar Levant and James William Fulbright. The broadcast of September 27 originated from the Mosque Theatre in Newark, New Jersey. Vice-President Henry A. Wallace spoke on the program about "Bonds and Future Peace."

Episode #273 **Broadcast of October 4, 1943.**
Panelists: Franklin P. Adams, John Kieran, and two sports commentators Red Barber and Bill Stern

Episode #274 **Broadcast of October 11, 1943.**
Panelists: Franklin P. Adams, John Kieran, biologist William Beebe and Donald Culross Peattie, biographer and naturalist

Episode #275 **Broadcast of October 18, 1943.**
Panelists: Franklin P. Adams, John Kieran, Oscar Levant and novelist Marcia Davenport

Episode #276 **Broadcast of October 25, 1943.**
Panelists: Franklin P. Adams, John Kieran, author John Mason Brown and author Richard Lockridge

Episode #277 **Broadcast of November 1, 1943.**
Panelists: Franklin P. Adams, John Kieran, Oscar Levant and Betty Smith, author of *A Tree Grows in Brooklyn*

Episode #278 **Broadcast of November 8, 1943.**
Panelists: Franklin P. Adams, John Kieran, Sen. Lester Hill and Sen. Joseph H. Ball

Episode #279 **Broadcast of November 15, 1943.**
Panelists: Franklin P. Adams, John Kieran, Oscar Levant and Gregory Ratoff

Episode #280 **Broadcast of November 22, 1943.**
Panelists: Franklin P. Adams, John Kieran, Russel Crouse and playwright Moss Hart

Episode #281 **Broadcast of November 29, 1943.**
Panelists: Franklin P. Adams, John Kieran, Oscar Levant and pianist Artur Rubenstein

Episode #282 **Broadcast of December 6, 1943.**
Panelists: Franklin P. Adams, John Kieran, author/lecturer Louis Brown and Sinclair Lewis

Episode #283 **Broadcast of December 13, 1943.**
Panelists: Franklin P. Adams, John Kieran, radio commentator Quincy Howe and delegate Dr. T.F. Chiang

Episode #284 **Broadcast of December 20, 1943.**
Panelists: Franklin P. Adams, John Kieran, Oscar Levant and author/farmer Jesse Stewart

Episode #285 **Broadcast of December 27, 1943.**
Panelists: Franklin P. Adams, John Kieran, Jan Struther and Leon Henderson

Episode #286 **Broadcast of January 3, 1944.**
Panelists: Franklin P. Adams, John Kieran, Oscar Levant and author Louis Bromfield

Episode #287 **Broadcast of January 10, 1944.**
Panelists: Franklin P. Adams, John Kieran, Christopher Morley and U.S. Representative John M. Coffey

Episode #288 **Broadcast of January 17, 1944.**
Panelists: Franklin P. Adams, John Kieran, Oscar Levant and John P. Marquand

Episode #289 **Broadcast of January 24, 1944.**
Panelists: Franklin P. Adams, John Kieran, musician Deems Taylor and author Elizabeth Janeway

Episode #290 **Broadcast of January 31, 1944.**
Panelists: Franklin P. Adams, John Kieran, Oscar Levant and Clifton Fadiman. Wendell Wilkie is master of ceremonies, substituting for Clifton Fadiman who sits on the board.

Episode #291 **Broadcast of February 7, 1944.**
Panelists: Franklin P. Adams, John Kieran, George S. Kaufman and Fred Allen

Episode #292 **Broadcast of February 14, 1944.**
Panelists: Franklin P. Adams, John Kieran, Oscar Levant and scientist William H. Davis

Episode #293 **Broadcast of February 21, 1944.**
Panelists: Franklin P. Adams, John Kieran, author John Roy Carlson and author Elizabeth Janeway

Episode #294 **Broadcast of February 28, 1944.**
Panelists: Franklin P. Adams, John Kieran, Oscar Levant and actor Franchot Tone

Episode #295 **Broadcast of March 6, 1944.**
Panelists: Franklin P. Adams, John Kieran, author Edna Ferber and playwright S.J. Pearlman

Episode #296 **Broadcast of March 13, 1944.**
Panelists: Franklin P. Adams, John Kieran, Oscar Levant and author Quentin Reynolds

Episode #297 **Broadcast of March 20, 1944.**
Panelists: Franklin P. Adams, John Kieran, Sen. Theodore Green of Rhode Island and Sen. Alben W. Barkley of Kentucky

Episode #298 **Broadcast of March 27, 1944.**
Panelists: Franklin P. Adams, John Kieran, Oscar Levant and pianist Artur Rubenstein

Episode #299 **Broadcast of April 3, 1944.**
Panelists: Franklin P. Adams, John Kieran, screenwriter Marion Hargrove and playwright Russel Crouse

Episode #300 **Broadcast of April 10, 1944.**
Panelists: Franklin P. Adams, John Kieran, actress Florence Eldridge and actor Fredric March (real-life husband and wife)

Episode #301 **Broadcast of April 17, 1944.**
Panelists: Franklin P. Adams, John Kieran, Oscar Levant and choreographer/dancer Agnes de Mille

Episode #302 **Broadcast of April 24, 1944.**
Panelists: Franklin P. Adams, John Kieran, actress Irene Dunne and Deems Taylor

Episode #303 **Broadcast of May 1, 1944.**
Panelists: Franklin P. Adams, John Kieran, Oscar Levant and Lester B. Pearson, Minister-Counselor, Canadian Legation of Washington

Episode #304 **Broadcast of May 8, 1944.**
Panelists: Franklin P. Adams, John Kieran, author Elizabeth Janeway and Jan Struther

Episode #305 **Broadcast of May 15, 1944.**
Panelists: Franklin P. Adams, John Kieran, Oscar Levant and John Gunther

Episode #306 **Broadcast of May 22, 1944.**
Panelists: Franklin P. Adams, John Kieran, George S. Kaufman and Moss Hart

Episode #307 **Broadcast of May 29, 1944.**
Panelists: Franklin P. Adams, John Kieran, Oscar Levant and musician Leonard Bernstein

Episode #308 **Broadcast of June 5, 1944.**
Panelists: Franklin P. Adams, John Kieran, Christopher Morley and military analyst Major George Fielding Eliot

Episode #309 **Broadcast of June 12, 1944.**
Panelists: Franklin P. Adams, Oscar Levant, Russel Crouse and Admiral Emory S. Land

Episode #310 **Broadcast of June 19, 1944.**
Panelists: Franklin P. Adams, John Kieran, Sen. Harold Burton and Sen. Alben Barkley of Kentucky

Episode #311 **Broadcast of June 26, 1944.**
Panelists: Franklin P. Adams, John Kieran, Jan Struther and author Donald Culross Peattie

Episode #312 **Broadcast of July 3, 1944.**
Panelists: Franklin P. Adams, John Kieran, Oscar Levant and Deems Taylor

Episode #313 **Broadcast of July 10, 1944.**
Panelists: Franklin P. Adams, John Kieran, Oscar Levant and Christopher Morley

Episode #314 **Broadcast of September 11, 1944.**
Panelists: Franklin P. Adams, John Kieran, Jan Struther and actor Alexander Knox

Episode #315 **Broadcast of September 18, 1944.**
Panelists: Franklin P. Adams, John Kieran, Gregory Ratoff and actor Reginald Gardiner

Episode #316 **Broadcast of September 25, 1944.**
Panelists: Franklin P. Adams, John Kieran, entrepreneur Henry J. Kaiser and author Quentin Reynolds

Episode #317 **Broadcast of October 2, 1944.**
Panelists: Franklin P. Adams, John Kieran, Esme of Paris and Christopher Morley

Episode #318 **Broadcast of October 9, 1944.**
Panelists: Franklin P. Adams, John Kieran, pianist Alec Templeton and Leonard Bernstein

Episode #319 **Broadcast of October 16, 1944.**
Panelists: Franklin P. Adams, John Kieran, Senator Claude Pepper and Senator Harold Burton

Episode #320 **Broadcast of October 23, 1944.**
Panelists: Franklin P. Adams, John Kieran, Artur Rubenstein and author/lecturer Louis Brown

Episode #321 **Broadcast of October 30, 1944.**
Panelists: Franklin P. Adams, John Kieran, Bernard Jaffe and naturalist Robert Cushman Murphy

Episode #322 **Broadcast of November 6, 1944.**
Panelists: Franklin P. Adams, John Kieran, Christopher Morley and author/historian Will Durant

Episode #323 **Broadcast of November 13, 1944.**
Panelists: Franklin P. Adams, John Kieran, author Emily Kimbrough and actress Diana Lynn

Episode #324 **Broadcast of November 20, 1944.**
Panelists: Franklin P. Adams, John Kieran, Boris Karloff and Reginald Gardiner

Episode #325 **Broadcast of November 27, 1944.**
Panelists: Franklin P. Adams, John Kieran, Leonard Bernstein and Gregory Ratoff

Episode #326 **Broadcast of December 4, 1944.**
Panelists: Franklin P. Adams, John Kieran, Deems Taylor and actor Clifton Webb

Episode #327 **Broadcast of December 11, 1944.**
Panelists: Franklin P. Adams, John Kieran, pianist Alec Templeton and Gregory Ratoff

Episode #328 **Broadcast of December 18, 1944.**
Panelists: Franklin P. Adams, John Kieran, author John Mason Brown and naturalist Robert Cushman Murphy

Episode #329 **Broadcast of December 25, 1944.**
Panelists: Franklin P. Adams, John Kieran, Fred Allen and Judge James G. Wallace of the New York Court of General Sessions. Broadcast from the Naval Hospital in St. Albans, New York for the benefit of the veterans.

Episode #330 **Broadcast of January 1, 1945.**
Panelists: Franklin P. Adams, John Kieran, Moss Hart and harmonica player Larry Adler

Episode #331 **Broadcast of January 8, 1945.**
Panelists: Franklin P. Adams, John Kieran, Deems Taylor and Rep. Augustus Bennett

Episode #332 **Broadcast of January 15, 1945.**
Panelists: Franklin P. Adams, John Kieran, Howard Lindsay and cartoonist Basil O'Connor

Episode #333 **Broadcast of January 22, 1945.**
Panelists: Franklin P. Adams, John Kieran, pianist Erich Leinsdorf and naturalist Robert Cushman Murphy

Episode #334 **Broadcast of January 29, 1945.**
Panelists: Franklin P. Adams, John Kieran, Jan Struther and Russel Crouse

Episode #335 **Broadcast of February 5, 1945.**
Panelists: Franklin P. Adams, John Kieran, playwright Moss Hart and actor Clifton Webb. Hugh Thompson of the Metropolitan Opera House in New York made a brief appearance in this broadcast when he helped supply the vocals for three musical questions.

Episode #336 **Broadcast of February 12, 1945.**
Panelists: Franklin P. Adams, John Kieran, Fred Allen and short story writer Faith Baldwin

Episode #337 **Broadcast of February 19, 1945.**
Panelists: Franklin P. Adams, John Kieran, John Gunther and Gregory Ratoff

Episode #338 **Broadcast of February 26, 1945.**
Panelists: Franklin P. Adams, John Kieran, Christopher Morley and Colonel Edward Eagan

Episode #339 **Broadcast of March 5, 1945.**
Panelists: Franklin P. Adams, John Kieran, pianist Erich Leinsdorf and author Waverly Root

Episode #340 **Broadcast of March 12, 1945.**
Panelists: Franklin P. Adams, John Kieran, sports commentator Red Barber and author Betty Smith

Episode #341 **Broadcast of March 19, 1945.**
Panelists: Franklin P. Adams, John Kieran and controversial literary figure Bernard DeVoto

Episode #342 **Broadcast of March 26, 1945.**
Panelists: Franklin P. Adams, John Kieran, author Quentin Reynolds and author Ira Wolfert

Episode #343 **Broadcast of April 2, 1945.**
Panelists: Franklin P. Adams, John Kieran, Ellis Arnall, former Governor of Georgia and Marjorie Kinnan Rawlings

Episode #344 **Broadcast of April 9, 1945.**
Panelists: Franklin P. Adams, John Kieran, Donald Culross Peattie and author Glenway Wescott

Episode #345 **Broadcast of April 16, 1945.**
Panelists: Franklin P. Adams, John Kieran, sports commentator Red Barber and baseball commissioner Ford Frick

Episode #346 **Broadcast of April 23, 1945.**
Panelists: Franklin P. Adams, John Kieran, Clifton Webb and baritone Lawrence Tibbett

Episode #347 **Broadcast of April 30, 1945.**
Panelists: Franklin P. Adams, John Kieran, Ray Milland and author Louis Bromfield

Episode #348 **Broadcast of May 7, 1945.**
Panelists: Franklin P. Adams, John Kieran, novelist Marcia Davenport and author Waverly Root

Episode #349 **Broadcast of May 14, 1945.**
Panelists: Franklin P. Adams, John Kieran, Cornelia Otis Skinner and author John Mason Brown

Episode #350 **Broadcast of May 21, 1945.**
Panelists: Franklin P. Adams, John Kieran, Artur Robinstein and Deems Taylor

Episode #351 **Broadcast of May 28, 1945.**
Panelists: Franklin P. Adams, John Kieran, actress Beatrice Lillie and Clifton Webb

Episode #352 **Broadcast of June 4, 1945.**
Panelists: Franklin P. Adams, John Kieran, Marshall Field, Jr. (son of the famous founder of the department store chain), and Colonel Edward Eagan

Episode #353 **Broadcast of June 11, 1945.**
Panelists: Franklin P. Adams, John Kieran, actress Diana Lynn and musician Morton Gould

Episode #354 **Broadcast of June 18, 1945.**
Panelists: Franklin P. Adams, John Kieran, Russel Crouse and George S. Kaufman

Episode #355 **Broadcast of June 25, 1945.**
Panelists: Franklin P. Adams, John Kieran, Deems Taylor and actor Reginald Gardiner. This was the final show of the season, as the team (including Gardner) went on the 1945 European *Information, Please* tour.

Episode #356 **Broadcast of September 10, 1945.**
Panelists: Franklin P. Adams, John Kieran, Moss Hart and Fred Allen

Episode #357 **Broadcast of September 17, 1945.**
Panelists: Franklin P. Adams, John Kieran, journalist Marquis W. Childs and Dean Mildred Thompson of Vassar

Episode #358 **Broadcast of September 24, 1945.**
Panelists: Franklin P. Adams, John Kieran, Christopher Morley and mountain climber/author James Ramsey Ullman

Episode #359 **Broadcast of October 1, 1945.**
Panelists: Franklin P. Adams, John Kieran, Red Barber and Bill Slater

Episode #360 **Broadcast of October 8, 1945.**
Panelists: Franklin P. Adams, John Kieran, Bernard Jaffee and William Laurence

Episode #361 **Broadcast of October 15, 1945.**
Panelists: Franklin P. Adams, John Kieran, pianist Alec Templeton and violinist William Primrose

Episode #362 **Broadcast of October 22, 1945.**
Panelists: Franklin P. Adams, John Kieran, Lieut.-Col. Gregory Boyington and author Quentin Reynolds

Episode #363 **Broadcast of October 29, 1945.**
Panelists: Franklin P. Adams, John Kieran, Cornelia Otis Skinner and Artur Rubenstein

Episode #364 **Broadcast of November 5, 1945.**
Panelists: Franklin P. Adams, John Kieran, Boris Karloff and Corp. Arthur Schesinger, Jr.

Episode #365 **Broadcast of November 12, 1945.**
Panelists: Franklin P. Adams, John Kieran, cartoonist Bill Mauldin and composer/lyricist Frank Loesser

Episode #366 **Broadcast of November 19, 1945.**
Panelists: Franklin P. Adams, John Kieran and actor Robert Montgomery

Episode #367 **Broadcast of November 26, 1945.**
Panelists: Franklin P. Adams, John Kieran, Maj. Gen. Emmet O'Donnell and Colonel Edward Eagan

Episode #368 **Broadcast of December 3, 1945.**
Panelists: Franklin P. Adams, John Kieran, Deems Taylor and actor Douglas Fairbanks, Jr.

Episode #369 **Broadcast of December 10, 1945.**
Panelists: Franklin P. Adams, John Kieran, Christopher Morley and Captain Harold E. Stassen

Episode #370 **Broadcast of December 17, 1945.**
Panelists: Franklin P. Adams, John Kieran, actor Douglas Fairbanks, Jr. and actor David Niven

Episode #371 **Broadcast of December 24, 1945.**
Panelists: Franklin P. Adams, John Kieran, Boris Karloff and John Mason Brown

Episode #372 **Broadcast of December 31, 1945.**
Panelists: Franklin P. Adams, John Kieran, Gregory Ratoff and Fred Allen

Episode #373 **Broadcast of January 7, 1946.**
Panelists: Franklin P. Adams, John Kieran, author Charles Jackson and screenwriter Marion Hargrove

Episode #374 **Broadcast of January 14, 1946.**
Panelists: Franklin P. Adams, John Kieran, John Gunther and Col. Benjamin Davis, Jr.

Episode #375 **Broadcast of January 21, 1946.**
Panelists: Franklin P. Adams, John Kieran, journalist/author Thomas B. Costain and Charles G. Bolte, author of *Post-Atomic National Defense*

Episode #376 **Broadcast of January 28, 1946.**
Panelists: Franklin P. Adams, John Kieran, Lt. Col. James Warner Bellah and mountain climber/author James Ramsey Ullman

Episode #377 **Broadcast of February 4, 1946.**
Panelists: Franklin P. Adams, John Kieran, Moss Hart and Beatrice Lillie

Episode #378 **Broadcast of February 11, 1946.**
Panelists: Franklin P. Adams, John Kieran, Lt. Col. John H. DeWitt, Jr. and pioneer aeronaut Jean Piccard

Episode #379 **Broadcast of February 18, 1946.**
Panelists: Franklin P. Adams, John Kieran, Russel Crouse and Lieutenant Thomas Stokes

Episode #380 **Broadcast of February 25, 1946.**
Panelists: Franklin P. Adams, John Kieran, Artur Rubenstein and Cornelia Otis Skinner

Episode #381 **Broadcast of March 4, 1946.**
Panelists: Franklin P. Adams, John Kieran, Sen. Brian McMahon and John Gunther

Episode #382 **Broadcast of March 11, 1946.**
Panelists: Franklin P. Adams, John Kieran, Betty MacDonald, author of *The Egg and I* and pianist Eugene List

Episode #383 **Broadcast of March 18, 1946.**
Panelists: Franklin P. Adams, John Kieran, Ray Milland and Charles Jackson, author of *The Lost Weekend*

Episode #384 **Broadcast of March 25, 1946.**
Panelists: Franklin P. Adams, John Kieran, Gladys Schmitt, editor of *Scholastic Magazine* and author Thomas Costain

Episode #385 **Broadcast of April 1, 1946.**
Panelists: Franklin P. Adams, John Kieran, actor Walter Pidgeon and lyricist Walter Dietz. Clifton Fadiman was unable to attend this broadcast, so Fred Allen substituted for Fadiman.

Episode #386 **Broadcast of April 8, 1946.**
Panelists: Franklin P. Adams, John Kieran, Colonel Edward Eagan and athlete Mickey Walker

Episode #387 **Broadcast of April 15, 1946.**
Panelists: Franklin P. Adams, John Kieran, Cornelia Otis Skinner and author Charles G. Bolte

Episode #388 **Broadcast of April 22, 1946.**
Panelists: Franklin P. Adams, John Kieran, screenwriter Marion Hargrove and musician Max Schulman. On this same evening, Oscar Levant was playing piano on *The Percy Faith Orchestra* show.

Episode #389 **Broadcast of April 29, 1946.**
Panelists: Franklin P. Adams, John Kieran, John Gunther and Gen. George Churchill Kenny

Episode #390 **Broadcast of May 6, 1946.**
Panelists: Franklin P. Adams, John Kieran, Lillian Gish and actor Freddie Bartholomew

Episode #391 **Broadcast of May 13, 1946.**
Panelists: Franklin P. Adams, John Kieran, Max Shulman and Arthur M. Schlesinger, Jr.

Episode #392 **Broadcast of May 20, 1946.**
Panelists: Franklin P. Adams, John Kieran, Deems Taylor and actor Dennis King

Episode #393 **Broadcast of May 27, 1946.**
Panelists: Franklin P. Adams, John Kieran, actress Faye Emerson and Elliott Roosevelt, son of F.D.R.

Episode #394 **Broadcast of June 3, 1946.**
Panelists: Franklin P. Adams, John Kieran, author John Mason Brown and author Phyllis Bottome

Episode #395 **Broadcast of June 10, 1946.**
Panelists: Franklin P. Adams, John Kieran, Deems Taylor and Jimmy Durante

Episode #396 **Broadcast of June 17, 1946.**
Panelists: Franklin P. Adams, John Kieran, Russel Crouse and actor Robert Montgomery

Episode #397 **Broadcast of June 24, 1946.**
Panelists: Franklin P. Adams, John Kieran, Cornelia Otis Skinner and Fred Allen

Episode #398 **Broadcast of October 2, 1946.**
Panelists: Franklin P. Adams, John Kieran, Oscar Levant and Fred Allen

Episode #399 **Broadcast of October 9, 1946.**
Panelists: Franklin P. Adams, John Kieran, actor Robert Montgomery and actor/author Elliott Nugent

Episode #400 **Broadcast of October 16, 1946.**
Panelists: Franklin P. Adams, John Kieran, Oscar Levant and author Charles Jackson

Episode #401 **Broadcast of October 23, 1946.**
Panelists: Franklin P. Adams, John Kieran, Oscar Levant and comedian Bob Hope

Episode #402 **Broadcast of October 30, 1946.**
Panelists: Franklin P. Adams, John Kieran, Jan Struther and radio news commentator Elmer Davis

Episode #403 **Broadcast of November 6, 1946.**
Panelists: Franklin P. Adams, John Kieran, author/journalist Annalee Jacoby and journalist Theodore White

Episode #404 **Broadcast of November 13, 1946.**
Panelists: Franklin P. Adams, John Kieran, Russel Crouse and Captain Harold E. Stassen

Episode #405 **Broadcast of November 20, 1946.**
Panelists: Franklin P. Adams, John Kieran, Oscar Levant and Randolph Churchill

Episode #406 **Broadcast of November 27, 1946.**
Panelists: Franklin P. Adams, John Kieran, Reginald Gardiner and Fred Allen

Episode #407 **Broadcast of December 4, 1946.**
Panelists: Franklin P. Adams, John Kieran, Oscar Levant and actress Madeleine Carroll

Episode #408 **Broadcast of December 11, 1946.**
Panelists: Franklin P. Adams, John Kieran, Deems Taylor and Roland Young

Episode #409 **Broadcast of December 18, 1946.**
Panelists: Franklin P. Adams, John Kieran, Oscar Levant and George S. Kaufman

Episode #410 **Broadcast of December 25, 1946.**
Panelists: Franklin P. Adams, John Kieran, author Charles G. Bolte and Adeil Shepard

Episode #411 **Broadcast of January 1, 1947.**
Panelists: Franklin P. Adams, John Kieran, Jan Struther and pianist Alec Templeton

Episode #412 **Broadcast of January 8, 1947.**
Panelists: Franklin P. Adams, John Kieran, John Gunther and harmonica player Larry Adler

Episode #413 **Broadcast of January 15, 1947.**
Panelists: Franklin P. Adams, John Kieran, Oscar Levant and sports editor Paul Gallico

Episode #414 **Broadcast of January 22, 1947.**
Panelists: Franklin P. Adams, John Kieran, director Frank Capra and actor James Stewart. *It's a Wonderful Life* had been re-released in theaters just weeks before. This episode was set-up for publicity.

Episode #415 **Broadcast of January 29, 1947.**
Panelists: Franklin P. Adams, John Kieran, Oscar Levant and Ellis Arnall, former Governor of Georgia

Episode #416 **Broadcast of February 5, 1947.**
Panelists: Franklin P. Adams, John Kieran, Oscar Levant, and Gregory Ratoff

Episode #417 **Broadcast of February 12, 1947.**
Panelists: Franklin P. Adams, John Kieran, Arthur Schlesinger, Jr. and Raymond Massey

Episode #418 **Broadcast of February 19, 1947.**
Panelists: Franklin P. Adams, John Kieran, Oscar Levant, Howard Lindsay and Russel Crouse. This broadcast featured five guest panelists!

Episode #419 **Broadcast of February 26, 1947.**
Panelists: Franklin P. Adams, John Kieran, Oscar Levant and Sen. Charles W. Tobey

There was no Information, Please broadcast on March 5, 1947. because the Columbia Broadcasting System presented an hour-long special presentation that took up its regularly-scheduled time slot. The documentary presentation on juvenile delinquency was entitled The Eagle's Nest and featured Joseph Cotton as the narrator.

Episode #420 **Broadcast of March 12, 1947.**
Panelists: Franklin P. Adams, John Kieran, Oscar Levant and author Charles G. Bolte

Episode #421 **Broadcast of March 19, 1947.**
Panelists: Franklin P. Adams, John Kieran, violinist Yehudi Menuhin and pianist Hephzibah Menuhin

Episode #422 **Broadcast of March 26, 1947.**
Panelists: Franklin P. Adams, John Kieran, Oscar Levant and Max Shulman

Episode #423 **Broadcast of April 2, 1947.**
Panelists: Franklin P. Adams, John Kieran, Deems Taylor and Gregory Ratoff

Episode #424 **Broadcast of April 9, 1947.**
Panelists: Franklin P. Adams, John Kieran, author Charles Jackson and novelist Laura Z. Hobson

Episode #425 **Broadcast of April 16, 1947.**
Panelists: Franklin P. Adams, John Kieran, Oscar Levant and Fred Allen

Episode #426 **Broadcast of April 23, 1947.**
Panelists: Franklin P. Adams, John Kieran, baseball star Jackie Robinson and Dr. Rufus Clement, President of Atlanta University

Episode #427 **Broadcast of April 30, 1947.**
Panelists: Franklin P. Adams, John Kieran, Oscar Levant and actor George Sanders

Episode #428 **Broadcast of May 7, 1947.**
Panelists: Franklin P. Adams, John Kieran, Cornelia Otis Skinner and Gregory Ratoff

Episode #429 **Broadcast of May 14, 1947.**
Panelists: Franklin P. Adams, John Kieran, Oscar Levant and Dame Rebecca West

Episode #430 **Broadcast of May 21, 1947.**
Panelists: Franklin P. Adams, John Kieran, Oscar Levant and Ellis Arnall, former Governor of Georgia

Episode #431 **Broadcast of May 28, 1947.**
Panelists: Franklin P. Adams, John Kieran, Oscar Levant and John Gunther

Episode #432 **Broadcast of June 4, 1947.**
Panelists: Franklin P. Adams, John Kieran, author Charles G. Bolte and Raymond Massey

Episode #433 **Broadcast of June 11, 1947.**
Panelists: Franklin P. Adams, John Kieran, Howard Lindsay and Cornelia Otis Skinner

Episode #434 **Broadcast of June 18, 1947.**
Panelists: Franklin P. Adams, John Kieran, violinist Albert Spalding and Dr. R.C. Murphy

Episode #435 **Broadcast of June 25, 1947.**
Panelists: Franklin P. Adams, John Kieran, Russel Crouse and Cornelia Otis Skinner

Episode #436 **Broadcast of September 26, 1947.**
Panelists: Franklin P. Adams, John Kieran, Robert Montgomery and Fred Allen

Episode #437 **Broadcast of October 3, 1947.**
Panelists: Franklin P. Adams, John Kieran, baseball commissioner Ford Frick and sportscaster Mel Allen

Episode #438 **Broadcast of October 10, 1947.**
Panelists: Franklin P. Adams, John Kieran, Edward J. Flynn, author of *You're the Boss,* and author Robert C. Ruark

Episode #439 **Broadcast of October 17, 1947.**
Panelists: Franklin P. Adams, John Kieran, actress Pamela Kellino and actor James Mason

Episode #440 **Broadcast of October 24, 1947.**
Panelists: Franklin P. Adams, John Kieran, Deems Taylor and Jimmy Durante

Episode #441 **Broadcast of October 31, 1947.**
Panelists: Franklin P. Adams and John Kieran. Guests are unknown.

Episode #442 **Broadcast of November 7, 1947.**
Panelists: Franklin P. Adams, John Kieran, Robert Montgomery and Captain Harold E. Stassen

Episode #443 **Broadcast of November 14, 1947.**
Panelists: Franklin P. Adams, John Kieran, Russel Crouse and actor Louis Calhern

Episode #444 **Broadcast of November 21, 1947.**
Panelists: Franklin P. Adams, John Kieran, Sen. Charles W. Tobey of New Hampshire and Ellis Arnall, former Governor of Georgia

Episode #445 **Broadcast of November 28, 1947.**
Panelists: Franklin P. Adams, John Kieran, Robert A. Allen and Roger Butterfield, author of *Pride of the Marines*

Episode #446 **Broadcast of December 5, 1947.**
Panelists: Franklin P. Adams, John Kieran, Colonel Edward Eagan and Gen. John Reed Kilpatrick

Episode #447 **Broadcast of December 12, 1947.**
Panelists: Franklin P. Adams, John Kieran, actor Lew Ayres and actress Diana Lynn

Episode #448 **Broadcast of December 19, 1947.**
Panelists: Franklin P. Adams, John Kieran, John Gunther and cartoonist Bill Mauldin

Episode #449 **Broadcast of December 26, 1947.**
Panelists: Franklin P. Adams, John Kieran, Russel Crouse and Lawrence Tibbett

Episode #450 **Broadcast of January 2, 1948.**
Panelists: Franklin P. Adams, John Kieran, George Sanders and singer Maggie Teyte

Episode #451 **Broadcast of January 9, 1948.**
Panelists: Franklin P. Adams, John Kieran, Howard Lindsay and actor Burgess Meredith

Episode #452 **Broadcast of January 16, 1948.**
Panelists: Franklin P. Adams, John Kieran, Boris Karloff and George S. Kaufman

Episode #453 **Broadcast of January 23, 1948.**
Panelists: Franklin P. Adams, John Kieran, actress Pamela Kellino and actor James Mason (real-life husband and wife)

Episode #454 **Broadcast of January 30, 1948.**
Panelists: Franklin P. Adams, John Kieran, soprano Helen Traubel and tenor Lauritz Melchior

Episode #455 **Broadcast of February 6, 1948.**
Panelists: Franklin P. Adams, John Kieran, Moss Hart and author Quentin Reynolds

Episode #456 **Broadcast of February 13, 1948.**
Panelists: Franklin P. Adams, John Kieran, cartoonist Al Capp, creator of *Li'l Abner,* and cartoonist Milt Caniff, creator of *Terry and the Pirates.*

Episode #457 **Broadcast of February 20, 1948.**
Panelists: Franklin P. Adams, John Kieran, Charles Taft and Sen. J Howard McGrath

Episode #458 **Broadcast of February 27, 1948.**
Panelists: Franklin P. Adams, John Kieran and returning from last week, Charles Taft

Episode #459 **Broadcast of March 5, 1948.**
Panelists: Franklin P. Adams, John Kieran, Burgess Meredith and Fred Allen

Episode #460 **Broadcast of March 12, 1948.**
Panelists: Franklin P. Adams, John Kieran, John Gunther and Artur Rubenstein

Episode #461 **Broadcast of March 19, 1948.**
Panelists: Franklin P. Adams, John Kieran, Ray Milland and Captain Harold E. Stassen

Episode #462 **Broadcast of March 26, 1948.**
Panelists: Franklin P. Adams, John Kieran, Alfred Hitchcock and Dr. Flanders Dunbar

Episode #463 **Broadcast of April 2, 1948.**
Panelists: Franklin P. Adams, John Kieran, author Robert C. Ruark and Admiral W.H. Blandy

Episode #464 **Broadcast of April 9, 1948.**
Panelists: Franklin P. Adams, John Kieran, cartoonist Al Capp and Russel Crouse

Episode #465 **Broadcast of April 16, 1948.**
Panelists: Franklin P. Adams, John Kieran, Moss Hart and Clifton Webb

Episode #466 **Broadcast of April 23, 1948.**
Panelists: Franklin P. Adams, John Kieran, author/novelist Cleveland Amory and Francis Van Wyxk Mason. Mason, together with Helen Brawner, wrote, under a joint pseudonym, the Geoffrey Coffin mysteries.

Episode #467 **Broadcast of April 30, 1948.**
Panelists: Franklin P. Adams, John Kieran and author Robert Magidoff

Episode #468 **Broadcast of May 7, 1948.**
Panelists: Franklin P. Adams, John Kieran, studio publicist Howard Dietz and cartoonist Rube Goldberg

Episode #469 **Broadcast of May 14, 1948.**
Panelists: Franklin P. Adams, John Kieran, Russel Crouse and pianist Alec Templeton

Episode #470 **Broadcast of May 21, 1948.**
Panelists: Franklin P. Adams, John Kieran, Al Capp and Burgess Meredith

Episode #471 **Broadcast of May 28, 1948.**
Panelists: Franklin P. Adams, John Kieran, author James Michener and author Robert C. Ruark

Episode #472 **Broadcast of June 4, 1948.**
Panelists: Franklin P. Adams, John Kieran, Ray Milland and Raymond Massey

Episode #473 **Broadcast of June 11, 1948.**
Panelists: Franklin P. Adams, John Kieran, Ellis Arnall, former Governor of Georgia and lawyer Bartley Crum

Episode #474 **Broadcast of June 18, 1948.**
Panelists: Franklin P. Adams, John Kieran, James Michener and actor Dennis King

Episode #475 **Broadcast of August 9, 1950.**
Panelists: Franklin P. Adams, John Kieran, Fred Allen and Howard Lindsay

Episode #476 **Broadcast of August 16, 1950.**
Panelists: Franklin P. Adams, John Kieran, Captain Harold E. Stassen and Russell Crouse

Episode #477 **Broadcast of August 23, 1950.**
Panelists: Franklin P. Adams, John Kieran, Cornelia Otis Skinner and James Michener

Episode #478 **Broadcast of August 30, 1950.**
Panelists: Franklin P. Adams, John Kieran, author Richard Llewellyn and John Gunther

Episode #479 **Broadcast of September 10, 1950.**
Panelists: Franklin P. Adams, John Kieran, Russel Crouse and James Michener

Episode #480 **Broadcast of September 17, 1950.**
Panelists: Franklin P. Adams, John Kieran, Louise Hall Tharp and Richard Liewellyn, author of *How Green Was My Valley*

Episode #481 **Broadcast of September 24, 1950.**
Panelists: Franklin P. Adams, John Kieran, actor Boris Karloff and author Richard Liewellyn

Episode #482 **Broadcast of October 1, 1950.**
Panelists: Franklin P. Adams, John Kieran, sports commentator Red Barber and author James Michener

Episode #483 **Broadcast of October 8, 1950.**
Panelists: Franklin P. Adams, John Kieran, Senator Brian McMahon and Ellis Arnall

Episode #484 **Broadcast of October 15, 1950.**
Panelists: Franklin P. Adams and John Kieran. Guests unknown.

Episode #485 **Broadcast of October 22, 1950.**
Panelists: Franklin P. Adams, John Kieran, stage director Joshua Logan and stage designer Jo Mielziner

Episode #486 **Broadcast of October 29, 1950.**
Panelists: Franklin P. Adams, John Kieran, Sir Gladwyn Jebb, Ambassador to France and Lester B. Pearson, Minister-Counselor, Canadian Legation of Washington. Pearson would later become the 14th Prime Minister of Canada in 1963.

Episode #487 **Broadcast of November 5, 1950.**
Panelists: Franklin P. Adams, John Kieran, Russel Crouse and Joshua Logan

Episode #488 **Broadcast of November 12, 1950.**
Panelists: Franklin P. Adams, John Kieran, Howard Lindsay and author John Mason Brown

Episode #489 **Broadcast of November 19, 1950.**
Panelists: Franklin P. Adams, John Kieran, author Charles G. Bolte and journalist/broadcaster Alistair Cooke

Episode #490 **Broadcast of November 26, 1950.**
Panelists: Franklin P. Adams, John Kieran, Russel Crouse and actor/toastmaster George Jessel

Episode #491 **Broadcast of December 3, 1950.**
Panelists: Franklin P. Adams, John Kieran, actor Gene Lockhart and James Michener

Episode #492 **Broadcast of December 10, 1950.**
Panelists: Franklin P. Adams, John Kieran, singer Doc Rockwell and Fred Allen

Episode #493 **Broadcast of December 17, 1950.**
Panelists: Franklin P. Adams, John Kieran, Senator Charles W. Tobey and Senator John J. Sparkman

Episode #494 **Broadcast of December 24, 1950.**
Panelists: Franklin P. Adams, John Kieran, author Charles G. Bolte and Cornelia Otis Skinner

Episode #495 **Broadcast of December 31, 1950.**
Panelists: Franklin P. Adams, John Kieran, actor James Gleason and sports columnist Bill Corum. Gleason was originally scheduled as guest for the August 7, 1942 broadcast, but had to cancel out at the last moment. It wouldn't be until eight years later that Gleason finally appeared on the program.

Episode #496 **Broadcast of January 7, 1951.**
Panelists: Franklin P. Adams, John Kieran, Howard Lindsay and Russel Crouse

Episode #497 **Broadcast of January 14, 1951.**
Panelists: Franklin P. Adams, John Kieran, Raymond Massey and Alistair Cooke

Episode #498 **Broadcast of January 21, 1951.**
Panelists: Franklin P. Adams, John Kieran and John Mason Brown

Episode #499 **Broadcast of January 28, 1951.**
Panelists: Franklin P. Adams, John Kieran, John Gunther and author Charles G. Bolte

Episode #500 **Broadcast of February 4, 1951.**
Panelists: Franklin P. Adams, John Kieran, Howard Lindsay and Russel Crouse

Episode #501 **Broadcast of February 11, 1951.**
Panelists: Franklin P. Adams, John Kieran, Lawrence Tibbett and Cornelia Otis Skinner

Episode #502 **Broadcast of February 18, 1951.**
Panelists: Franklin P. Adams, John Kieran, baseball player Frank Frisch and baseball player Tommy Henrich

Episode #503 **Broadcast of February 25, 1951.**
Panelists: Franklin P. Adams, John Kieran, playwright Marc Connelly and Alistair Cooke

Episode #504 **Broadcast of March 4, 1951.**
Panelists: Franklin P. Adams, John Kieran, author Charles G. Bolte and mystery/suspense writer Vera Caspary

Episode #505 **Broadcast of March 11, 1951.**
Panelists: Franklin P. Adams, John Kieran, Russel Crouse and actor Richard Greene

Episode #506 **Broadcast of March 18, 1951.**
Panelists: Franklin P. Adams, John Kieran, Russel Crouse and Lawrence Tibbett

Episode #507 **Broadcast of April 1, 1951.**
Panelists: Franklin P. Adams, John Kieran, John Gunther and actor Richard Carlson. This broadcast was actually scheduled for March 25, 1951. Due to scheduling beyond Golenpaul's control, the program was unable to air over the Mutual Network. The panel went ahead as scheduled anyway, and a recording of that week's episode was rebroadcast for April 1, 1951.

Episode #508 **Broadcast of April 8, 1951.**
Panelists: Franklin P. Adams, John Kieran, Cornelia Otis Skinner and actor John Lund

Episode #509 **Broadcast of April 15, 1951.**
Panelists: Franklin P. Adams, John Kieran, John Mason Brown and Raymond Massey

Episode #510 **Broadcast of April 22, 1951.**
Panelists: Franklin P. Adams, John Kieran, Howard Lindsay and actress Dorothy Stickney

APPENDIX A: ABOUT THE GUEST EXPERT

On September 17, 1944, Richard Manney, a guest on the radio program, recalled his experience on the set in a newspaper column. That essay is now reprinted below:

"Contrary tremors ravage the cove invited to appear as a guest star in *Information, Please*. The bid to compete in wisdom and waggery with Fadiman, Adams and Kieran is so flattering that it reduces the candidate to a semi-swoon. The prospect of a triumph among the illuminati caresses the victim's ego until he purrs like a dynamo. In this early delirium he envisages a new life. Is he glib about the Peninsular and Punic campaigns, the author of a gay quip, does he beat Kieran to the punch when Beowulf comes up, then he will forever be the envy of his fellows, a man who can hold his head high in 21 or the Union Square subway station.

"Then doubt jostles his ecstatic speculations. What if for an agonizing half hour he remains mute and inglorious? As this suspicion grows his will is paralyzed. Shall he risk everything—his wife's esteem, the respect of his friends, the judgment of posterity—on a single cast of the encyclopedia? Successful, he will become one of the anointed overnight; failing, he may go clattering down the halls of time as one of the outstanding numskulls of the generation.

"While he is wincing under the impact of choice, Dan Golenpaul, creator of the double-domed program and its producer these many years, soothes the potential quizee with honeyed words. His nomination for the ordeal is a handsome tribute to his mental notoriety. After all, says Mr. Golenpaul, *Information, Please* does not woo ignoramuses. Many questions will be asked which lie within the intellectual scope of the aspirant. No one can answer all the questions. Didn't the learned Paul de Kruif fail to identify rubeola as a synonym for measles?

"Once he has pledged his appearance on NBC at 9:30 on the fateful Monday night, the terror of the competitor mounts. A thousand qualms rage round his ears. More than once he curses the day that he succumbed to the lure. In desperation he scurries to his warren, starts to prowl through Bartlett, the complete works of William Shakespeare, all of Audubon—there's sure to be something to bob up about a hybrid oriole—the Oxford Book of verse, the Encyclopedia and the World Almanac. What daffy impulse led him to perform his acquaintances of his impending folly? How can he escape the penalty? As he flagellates himself the entrant looks for a plausible exit. Can he plead illness, a newly acquired pestilence? Arrant cowardice! The doomed man sets his teeth and dives back into Bartlett.

"On the day of the test Mr. Golenpaul takes Spelvin into protective custody around 4 in the afternoon. He regales him with anecdotes, even a drink. It seems there was a motion picture star on *Information, Please* so befuddled that she couldn't identify the colossus she had just played in. Still another defier of the lightning answered never so much as a single question. Too late Golenpaul discovered that he was stone deaf.

"Soon Spelvin will be of that illustrious company: Russel Crouse, Christopher Morley, Deems Taylor, Cornelia Otis Skinner and Jan Struther—*Information, Please* veterans. Ann Golenpaul joins Golenpaul and the condemned man at dinner. The soup reeks of aloes. Was it Sterne or Smollett who wrote *Tristram Shandy*? The steak tastes like broiled beaver-board. There's vinegar in the ice. A double hooker of brandy? In that there's courage.

"Escorted to the platform on which Fadiman beams a welcome, and participating in a few preliminary Q's and A's, prior to taunting the ears of the unseen millions, Spelvin's courage rises. Perhaps it is the brandy. Perhaps it's because he has piped up with two replies, uttered in a hollow and unnatural voice quite unlike his own. The cock crows and Spelvin is on his own. Strangely enough he finds at once that the horrors of anticipation far outweigh those of participation. Once in the melee the lust for survival crowds out panic. More than one contestant, fearful lest the first question may be his last opportunity, lets fly with a speculation on Mr. Fadiman's first query. He finds to his great surprise and satisfaction that Fadiman coddles the haunted, that Adams and Kieran are not above yielding to the neophyte. Too late, to be sure, he thinks of a witticism that would have floored his listeners in Fargo, N.D.

"As a survivor of three of these cerebral ambushes I may only say that my most hair-raising moment came when, casting a furtive look at the studio audience, I caught the eye of Wolcott Gibbs, *The New Yorker*'s critic and bon vivant. Mr. Gibbs leered at me like a hyena from the front row, and whirled his forefinger about his ear in a circular movement. And I squirmed, too, for my fellow-guest on that awful evening was Mr. Frank Sullivan, the Saratoga sage. Just as the shambles was about to get under way Mr. Sullivan was handed a telegram. Expecting a reprieve he ripped it open. It read: 'You were great'."

APPENDIX B: CELEBRITY LETTERS RECEIVED BY THE STUMPERS

The following reprinted below are letters from Hollywood notables who submitted questions in an attempt to stump the experts. The letters/questions reprinted below were not accepted for use on the radio program.

Vincent Burns of the Log Cabin Studio in Palisade, N.J. submitted on August 8, 1938:

Dear Clifton Fadiman,
    Here's a few sticklers from the author of *I Am a Fugitive from a Chain Gang*:
1. When do we say a thing is "villous"?
2. When do we say a thing is "alate"?
3. Is "cauline" a kind of Irish lassie, or what?
4. Does "ament" have anything to do with religion?
5. According to its scientific or Latin name, what is another name for the pansy in English?

    Answers: 1. When it is hairy. 2. When it is winged. 3. Cauline means "belonging to the stem." 4. An ament is a catkin or scaly spike. 5. The "three-colored violet" since the Latin name is "Viola tricolor."

    Good luck in your program, it's a whiz!
    V. Burns

Harry Cohn, president of Columbia Pictures Corporation submitted on October 11, 1939:

Dear Mr. Fadiman:

The following is a question which I think will stump the experts, particularly Mr. Levant. "What are the first three songs which Irving Berlin wrote, and in what order were they written?" The answer is: 1. "Marie From Sunny Italy," 2. "The Best of Friends Must Part" and 3. "Queenie, My Own." The *Information, Please* program is very successful here on the coast, although we are a bit disappointed that we have to listen to a rebroadcast instead of hearing it direct.

Yours,
Harry Cohn

On October 2, 1939, actor James Gleason of Beverly Hills, California submitted a difficult series of questions about horses, the breeds, where they come from and what they are noted for.

On February 14, 1940, John Golden of the Saint James Theatre in New York City submitted the following:

Dear Clif:

Here's my entry and if you edit it—or cut—or revise—or add—or subtract—divide—multiply—or do anything else with it, except throw it out, I won't "worry about that." Oscar Levant, John Kieran, Frank Adams—all your experts know all about the composers, but I suspect that, like most other musically minded folk (and unmusical ones too), they've never been really interested in the poor forgotten man who wrote the words—as, for example, I wrote the words of "Goodbye Girls I'm Through" and "I Can Dance With Everybody But My Wife" and more—but does anybody know it?

All right—here's a dozen musical selections. They should name the composers as a matter of routine—but who wrote the words? That's the question. At least, ten must be answered correctly. Have your musicians play the first few bars of:

1. "Toreador Song" from *Carmen*.
2. "Sextette" from *Lucia*.

3. "Jewel Song" from *Faust*.
4. "Oh Promise Me" from *Robin Hood*.
5. "Kiss Me Again" from *Mademoiselle Modiste*.
6. "Follow On" from *Belle of New York*.
7. "The Bowery"
8. "I Don't Care What Teacher Says—I Can't Do That Sum"
9. "Poor Butterfly"
10. "Brown October Ale" from *Robin Hood*.
11. "I Dreamt I Dwelt in Marble Halls" from *The Bohemian Girl*.
12. "Celeste Aida" from *Aida*.

                        Yours, John Golden

P.S. If a dozen is too many, cut them to six and make them name at least five of the lyric writers. The answers are on the sheet attached—verified by the Metropolitan Opera Librarian and my friend, Max Dreyfus, head of Harms & Co.

Cyril Clemens, President of the International Mark Twain Society in Webster Groves, Missouri submitted the following on February 22, 1939:

What famous author was born with a planet and died at its return appearance? Halley's Comet appeared in 1835, Twain's birth year and did not appear again until his death year, 1910. Twain often remarked, "I came in with Halley's comet; I guess I'll go out with it."

On October 20, 1938, comedian Chico Marx submitted the following questions on MGM stationery:

Dear Mr. Fadiman:
    Here are some questions for your program:
1. Name the five presidents of the United States with names beginning with the letter H.
Answer: Wm. Henry Harrison, 1841; Rutherford B. Hayes 1877; Benjamin Harrison, 1889; Warren G. Harding, 1921; and Herbert Clark Hoover, 1929.
2. Name the fifth heavy-weight champion of the world, beginning with John L. Sullivan.
Answer: Tommy Burns

3. What is the fifth man in a bridge game called?
Answer: Kibitzer
4. What is the Fifth Commandment?
Answer: Honor thy father and thy mother that thy days may be long upon the land which the Lord thy God giveth thee.
5. What is the name of the fifth Marx brother?
Answer: Milton (Gummo) Marx

Yours, Chico Marx

On February 21, 1940, the three Marx Brothers submitted the following questions:

Dear Sirs:
1. Name five songs dealing with trains.
Answers: *When the Midnight Choo-Choo Leaves for Alabam', Wreck of the Old 99, Casey Jones, Shuffle Off to Buffalo, Honeymoon Express,* and *Train on the Roof.*
2. Name four motion pictures in which days of the week are mentioned in the title.
Answers: *One Sunday Afternoon, His Girl Friday, Saturday's Children,* and *The Man Who Was Thursday.* (We would have sent in six but Chico went to Santa Anita.)
3. Name five songs in which months of the year are mentioned in the title.
Answers: *June in January, Maytime, April Showers, April in Paris, Roses in December, September in the Rain, A Day at the Races, Horse Feathers, Cocoanuts,* and *A Night at the Opera.*

Wishing your experts more and better headaches over the above, (if any, please refer them to Dr. Hugo Quackenbush), and with Bromo-Seltzers to all, we are

Sincerely,
Groucho!!
Harpo ?????
Chico !!
The Marx Bros.

Author's note: Harpo signed his name on the submission with a doodle of a harp and nothing more. Groucho signed his name and also Chico's with the notation next to Chico's (by G).

On April 12, 1940, actor Adolphe Menjou in Hollywood, California submitted the following:

Dear Mr. Fadiman:
    As frantic fan of your program we submit the following questions. Name the characters whose likenesses are used on the following pieces of U.S. paper currency. $5.00 bill, Lincoln. $10.00 bill, Hamilton. $20.00 bill, Jackson, and $50.00 bill, Grant. Sinclair Lewis couldn't answer all correctly. Can F.P.A., Kieran or Levant? Continued good luck to the best half-hour on the air.
                    Adolphe Menjou and Vera Teasdale

On January 26, 1940, actor Burgess Meredith of New York City submitted the following:

Dear Clifton:
    Here is a question I will put in two ways. If you think it is worthy pick the way which will be most likely to earn me an *Encyclopedia Britannica* – for which I have great need. The following world important accomplishments were made by three men, all of whom were dentists. What were their names?
    1. A dentist from Brooklyn who wrote a thesis which changed the history of China.
    2. A dentist from Hartford, Conn. who discovered a chemical which changed the methods of operations.
    3. A dentist from Pennsylvania who influenced the history of football.
    Or perhaps the question should be put this way – The following three men were all dentists. They made contributions to science and to affairs of the world which completely revolutionized methods heretofore employed. What were their contributions?
    1. Dr. Maurice Williams

2. Dr. Horace Wells
3. Dr. Jock Sutherland

Sincerely yours,
Burgess Meredith

On March 29, 1939, James Truslow Adams of Southport, Conn. submitted the following:

Dear Mr. Fadman:
I am not a radio fan, and the only programs I listen to regularly are *Charlie McCarthy*, *Information, Please*, and *The Cavalcade of America*. I have noted that in *Information, Please* you have a lot of questions about sport, music, stage, etc. etc., but practically nothing on history. I send in a few from which five might be picked, although none may be suitable. I do not recall the address as given on the air so am sending this to the only one given for you in *Who's Who*. I am doing it just for fun and no harm is done if you cannot use them. One of these days I still hope our paths may cross, but I seldom get to town though only an hour away.

Sincerely yours,
James Truslow Adams

(Note: No questions were found with the letter during the course of research.)

Even radio celebrity Rudy Vallee of New York City submitted his own stumpers:

Gentlemen:
Here are some New York City questions that might stick the gentlemen of *Information, Please*:
1. Who is buried in Grant's Tomb?
Answer: The average person will say Grant and think you're being facetious, but actually, Grant's wife is also buried there. Her name was Julia Dent Grant.
2. Name four clubs in New York City whose names begin with the letter "U".
Answer: Union, Union League, University and the Uptown club.

The last one would stick them.
3. Who was the first elected mayor of New York City?
Answer: Mr. Kieran will probably say Thomas Willett, who was the first mayor of New York City in 1665 – but, the first elected mayor of this city was Peter Delanoy, who in 1689 was elected by the votes "of Protestant freemen." My authority is the 1937 World's Almanac, page 472.
Hope you can use these...

Sincerely,
W.L. Vallee

Others who submitted questions that never got featured on the program were Roy Post and Austin Ripley, collaborators of many articles in *Reader's Digest*; Raymond Griffith of Beverly Hills, California; Rollin Kirby of the *New York World-Telegram*; and Gelett Burgess, humorist and author of *Goops and How to Be Them* (1900) and the well-known poem "The Purple Cow."

Two days after Elmer Rice's appearance on the radio program of December 6, 1940, his wife Margaret Rice submitted questions to the board. On June 21, 1939 Harry Seymour Ross, president of Emerson College submitted questions dealing with the incunabula of American Literature. On the same date, June 21, 1939, John A. Schaeffer, president of Franklin and Marshall College in Lancaster, Pennsylvania submitted questions concerning practical science as a whole. On July 27th, 1939, James J. Lyons, president of the Borough of the Bronx, submitted questions about the past and present Presidents of the United States. Author Upton Sinclair submitted questions on June 8, 1939 asked by highly educated Englishmen, regarding their involvement with the United States.

APPENDIX C:
THE CONTRACTS

CLIFTON FADIMAN'S INITIAL CONTRACT

May 10, 1938
Mr. Clifton P. Fadiman, New York City.
Dear Mr. Fadiman:
   This letter and your acceptance represents our understanding which shall constitute a binding agreement between us.
   I have created and devised a radio program, the predominating idea of which is the submission of questions by the public to a board of persons, who will undertake to answer these questions to the best of their ability during the course of the broadcast. The program has been tentatively named *Information, Please* but I reserve the right to substitute any appropriate name, and our arrangement refers to a program of this general nature, regardless of the name applied to it.
   I agree to employ you as the Master of Ceremonies of this program, to collaborate and cooperate with the members of the board by asking them the questions submitted, commenting on their answers, and generally participating in the program as a Master of Ceremonies. You hereby agree to accept such employment. You further agree to present yourself at any designated broadcasting studio in New York City for each broadcast, in ample time to proceed with the program; to conform with the rules and regulations of the broadcasting company and of the producers and sponsors of the production; and in all other respects to give your cooperation in connection with the production.
   You further agree that I may use your name, photograph, or other

likeness for advertising and publicity purposes in connection with the broadcast.

The programs are to be broadcast once each week for thirty (30) minute periods. The particular day and time of the day are to be designated by me.

For your said services, I agree to pay you, and you agree to accept the following compensation:

(a) In the event that the programs are not commercially sponsored, the sum of One Hundred ($100.) Dollars per broadcast for the first eight (8) programs, and the sum of One Hundred Fifty ($150.) Dollars for each and every broadcast thereafter.

(b) In the event the programs are commercially sponsored, the sum of Two Hundred Fifty ($250.) Dollars per broadcast for the first thirteen (13) programs; in the event the same sponsor renews its sponsorship for an additional thirteen (13) week period, the sum of Four Hundred ($400.) Dollars per broadcast for the second thirteen (13) programs; and in the event the same sponsor exercises further renewals, the sum of Six Hundred ($600.) Dollars per broadcast thereafter. The foregoing rates shall apply with respect to each new commercial sponsor unless the new sponsor initially pays me a gross amount for the production which is at least equal to the gross amount paid by the old sponsor for the last thirteen (13) weeks of its sponsorship.

You agree to participate in each and every weekly program, except that if the production is not commercially sponsored, you shall have the right to absent yourself from not more than four (4) consecutive weekly programs while on your vacation, and from six (6) additional weekly programs (not more than two (2) of which shall be consecutive) during the remainder of any year.

My agreement to employ you is, of course, subject to my ability to have the production broadcast either as a sustaining or commercial program. However, so long as the production is broadcast, I agree to employ you for each of the weekly programs commencing Tuesday, May 17th, 1938.

This agreement shall commence as of the date of this letter, and shall continue so long as the production remains on the air. For purposes of this agreement, the production shall be deemed on the air so long as there are at least ten (10) weekly broadcasts for the remainder of 1938, and at least twenty-six (26) weekly broadcasts for each calendar year thereafter.

This agreement shall terminate as of the last day of any calendar year during which the number of broadcasts does not reach the above minimums. It may also terminate, at your option, at any time after the fifty-second (52nd) broadcast provided you give me two months' notice in writing of your intent to terminate. Such notice must be addressed to me at my last known address, and this agreement shall terminate at the expiration of two (2) months from the receipt of such notice.

It is understood and agreed that your services hereunder are special and unique and that during the term of the agreement, or after its termination if you elect to terminate after the fifty-second (52nd) broadcast as provided above, you will not become employed in connection with, or in any manner whatsoever participate in any radio programs similar to that described in the second paragraph of this letter. For purposes of our agreement, any program involving the asking and answering the questions, or any program featuring a quiz, or intelligence test or information test, shall be deemed similar to my program.

If the foregoing represents your understanding and is satisfactory to you, will you please so indicate at the place provided below for that purpose?

Very truly yours,

(signed) Dan Golenpaul

I have read the foregoing letter and the same represents my understanding, and is satisfactory to me.

(signed) Clifton Fadiman

CLIFTON FADIMAN'S REVISED CONTRACT

December 1, 1938

Dear Mr. Fadiman:

This letter and your acceptance thereof represents our understanding and shall constitute a binding agreement between us, modifying our existing agreement of May 10th, 1938, which covers your employment as Master of Ceremonies on the *Information, Please* radio program.

In lieu of the compensation which you are to receive as fixed in our said agreement of May 10th, 1938, I will pay you, and you agree to accept, the following compensation:

(a) In the event that programs are not commercially sponsored the sum of $150.00 for each and every broadcast.

(b) In the event that the programs are commercially sponsored:
(1) On gross payments to me from the sponsor of anything up to $3,000.00 per broadcast you are to receive $250.00 per broadcast plus 25% of the gross amount paid me by the sponsor between $2,500.00 and $3,000.00.
(2) On gross payments to me from the sponsor of $3,000.00 to $3,500.00 per broadcast you are to receive $500.00 per broadcast plus 25% of the gross amount paid me by the sponsor between $3,000.00 and $3,500.00.
(3) On gross payments to me from the sponsor of $3,500.00 to $4,400.00 per broadcast you are to receive $750.00 per broadcast plus 10% of the gross amount paid me by the sponsor between $3,500.00 and $4,400.00.
(4) On gross payments to me from the sponsor of $4,400.00 or over per broadcast you are to receive the flat figure of $850.00 per broadcast cast.

Further in connection with the above, it is understood that under my existing agreement with J.M. Mathes, Inc., representing Canada Dry Gingerale, Inc., based upon the foregoing that I obligate myself to pay to you in the event that the options to renew in said agreement are exercised:
(1) The first 13-week period under Canada Dry sponsorship – $250.
(2) The second 13-week period under Canada Dry sponsorship – $500.
(3) The third 13-week period under Canada Dry sponsorship – $750.
(4) The fourth and succeeding 13-week periods under Canada Dry sponsorship – $850.

It is further agreed that you hereby consent to the use of your name, portrait and likeness for the purpose of any proper advertising and publicity by Canada Dry or any other sponsor in connection with its sponsorship of the broadcasting of *Information, Please*, it being, however, distinctly understood that such use shall not be for the purpose of either directly or indirectly endorsing any commercial products.

You further agree that during the term of this agreement, in addition to the restrictions already contained in our agreement of May 10, 1938
(1) that you will not participate in any radio program sponsored by a competitor of Canada Dry Gingerale;
(2) that you will not participate in any radio program of whatsoever nature broadcast on the same day as *Information, Please* is broadcast;

(3) that you will not participate in more than one radio program per week in addition to your participation in the *Information, Please* program;

(4) that you will not at any time appear on any commercial radio program together with Franklin P. Adams and John Kieran.

Except as herein modified our agreement of May 10, 1938 shall remain in full force and effect. If the foregoing is satisfactory to you, will you please so indicate at the place provided below for that purpose.

            Very truly yours,
            (signed) Dan Golenpaul

            Accepted:
            Clifton Fadiman,
            by – (signed) Edwin Fadiman,
            Authorized Personal Representative
            (signed) Clifton Fadiman

On January 2, 1941, Clifton Fadiman signed another revised contract, in light of the new sponsorship, the American Tobacco Company. Just like the contract above for Canada Dry, the new contract listed the same terms and conditions with a few revisions. One, Fadiman agreed not to participate in any capacity, directly or indirectly, in any radio or television program whatsoever other than *Information, Please*, without permission from Golenpaul, and a limit of eight guest appearances. Second, Clifton Fadiman no longer permitted or consented to have his name, facsimile signature, picture or other likeness used by any person, firm or corporation which may be engaged in the sale or distribution or manufacture of tobacco products, nor give any testimonial or endorsement of the product of such firm or corporation. Lastly, compensation was revised as the following:

 On gross payments to Golenpaul from any Sponsor of $5,500, Fadiman received $950 per broadcast.

 On gross payments to Golenpaul from any Sponsor of $6,500, Fadiman received $1,050 per broadcast.

 On gross payments to Golenpaul from any Sponsor of $7,500, Fadiman received $1,200 per broadcast.

 On gross payments to Golenpaul from any Sponsor of $8,500, Fadiman received $1,500 per broadcast.

For purposes of record, Golenpaul did confirm that the new sponsor, the American Tobacco Company, was paying him the gross amount of $8,500 per broadcast!

On March 24, 1943, Edwin Fadiman sent Dan Golenpaul the signed agreement regarding transfer of the Heinz program of various restrictions on Clifton Fadiman. The two-page contract, dated March 18, 1943, offered the same terms as the last contract, with only one difference. All references to the American Tobacco Company were replaced with the H.J. Heinz Company.

In November of 1946, Fadiman signed a one-page contract renewal, again with the same terms and stipulations as the last, with the exception of Parker Pen Company replacing all references to the H.J. Heinz Company. There was one additional clause added, which was never listed in any previous contracts. Clause four stated: "I will not appear with either or both of Franklin P. Adams and John Kieran on any radio program without the written consent of the Parker Pen Company or its advertising agency first obtained."

JOHN KIERAN'S INITIAL CONTRACT

July 8, 1938
Mr. John Kieran, New York City.

Dear Mr. Kieran:
This letter and your acceptance represents our understanding and shall constitute a binding agreement between us.

I have created and devised a radio program, the predominating idea of which is the submission of questions by the public to a board of persons, who will undertake to answer these questions to the best of their ability during the course of the broadcast. The program has been tentatively named *Information, Please* but I reserve the right to substitute any appropriate name, and our arrangement refers to a program of this general nature, regardless of the name applied to it.

I agree to employ you as a member of the board to collaborate with the other members in answering, to the best of your ability, questions submitted, and you agree to accept such employment. You further agree to present yourself at any designated broadcasting studio in New York City for each weekly broadcast designated by me in ample time to proceed with the program; to conform with the rules and regulations of the broadcasting company and of the producers and sponsors of the production, and in all other respects to give your cooperation in connection with the production.

You further agree that I may use your name, photograph, or other likeness for advertising and publicity purposes in connection with the broadcast.

Programs are to be broadcast once each week for thirty (30) minute periods. The particular day and time of the day are to be designated by me.

For your said services, I agree to pay you, and you agree to accept the following compensation:

(a) In the event that the programs are not commercially sponsored, the sum of $50.00 per broadcast.

(b) In the event the programs are commercially sponsored, the sum of One Hundred Fifty ($150.) Dollars per broadcast for the first thirteen (13) programs; in the event the same sponsor renews its sponsorship for an additional thirteen (13) week period, the sum of Two Hundred ($200.) Dollars per broadcast for the second thirteen (13) programs; and in the event the same sponsor exercises further renewals, the sum of Two Hundred Fifty ($250.) Dollars per broadcast thereafter. The foregoing rates shall apply with respect to each new commercial sponsor unless the new sponsor initially pays me a gross amount for the production which is at least equal to the gross amount paid by the old sponsor for the last thirteen (13) weeks of its sponsorship.

My agreement to employ you is, of course, subject to my ability to have the production broadcast either as a sustaining or commercial program. However, so long as the production is broadcast, I agree to employ you in connection with at least ten (10) weekly broadcasts programs out of every thirteen (13).

This agreement shall commence as of the date of this letter, and shall continue so long as the production remains on the air. For purposes of this agreement, the production shall be deemed on the air so long as there are at least ten (10) weekly broadcasts in which you participate for the remainder of 1938, and at least twenty-six (26) weekly broadcasts in which you participate for each calendar year thereafter.

This agreement shall terminate as of the last day of any calendar year during which the number of broadcasts does not reach the above minimums.

It is understood and agreed that your services hereunder are special and unique and that during the term of the agreement, you will not become employed in connection with, or in any manner whatsoever participate in any radio programs similar to that described in the second paragraph of this letter. For purposes of our agreement, any program involving the asking and answering the questions, or any program featuring a quiz, or intelligence test or information test, shall be deemed similar to my program.

If the foregoing represents your understanding and is satisfactory to you, will you please so indicate at the place provided below for that purpose?

Very truly yours,

(signed) Dan Golenpaul

I have read the foregoing letter and the same represents my understanding, and is satisfactory to me.

(signed) John Kieran

On September 10, 1940, an amendment was drafted for John Kieran in light of Dan Golenpaul's agreement with the new sponsor, the American Tobacco Company. Kieran received a raise of $600.00 per broadcast.

On March 11, 1943, an amendment was drafted for John Kieran in light of Dan Golenpaul's agreement with the new sponsor, H.J. Heinz Company. The financial reimbursement for the weekly appearances remained the same. Reprinted below is the two-page contract.

March 11, 1943
Mr. John Kieran, New York, New York.

Dear Mr. Kieran:

This letter, and your acceptance at the place provided below for that purpose, represents our understanding and shall constitute a binding agreement between us, modifying our original agreement of July 8, 1938 as subsequently amended October 28, 1938 and September 10, 1940 agreement of July 8, 1938, as subsequently modified, including the within modification, shall constitute one single agreement. It is agreed as follows:

(a) During the term of the agreement between Dan Golenpaul Associates and H.J. Heinz Company, covering the commercial sponsorship for *Information, Please* or any renewal thereof, you will not participate in any other radio program sponsored by a competitor of H.J. Heinz Company.

(b) During the term of the said agreement, you will not participate in any radio program of whatsoever nature, broadcast on the same day as *Information, Please.*

(c) During the term of the said agreement, you will not permit or consent to be used your name, facsimile signature, picture or other likeness by any person, firm or corporation, engaged in the sale, distribution or manufacture of food products, other than the H.J. Heinz Company, nor in any testimonial or endorsement of such products for any such other company.

Except as herein provided, our original agreement of July 8, 1938, as modified, shall remain in full force and effect.

Very truly yours,
(signed) Dan Golenpaul

I have read the foregoing and the same is satisfactory to me,
(signed) John Kieran

One week later, Golenpaul revised the amendment because he had one date listed wrong, and again Kieran signed the revised amendment, with an attached note which read: "Mr. Dan'l Boone Golenpaul: Sure, I'll sign anything. I told you those contracts were no good. Neither are these, but if you want 'em signed, I'll sign 'em and as many more as you send as long as the ink holds out. Yours in part, John James Audubon Thoreau Kieran, 'tweet tweet'."

In October of 1946, an amendment was drafted for John Kieran in light of Dan Golenpaul's agreement with the new sponsor, the Parker Pen Company. The financial reimbursement for the weekly appearances still remained the same, with one additional clause added, which was never listed in any previous contracts. Clause four stated: "I will not appear with either or both of Clifton Fadiman and Franklin P. Adams on any radio program without the written consent of the Parker Pen Company or its advertising agency first obtained."

It should be noted that regardless of a clause in his contract, John Kieran did a large number of guest appearances on other radio programs including *The Family Theatre, Command Performance, The Bill Stern Colgate Sports Newsreel, The NBC University Theatre, The United Nations Today*, and *Millions for Defense*.

FRANKLIN P. ADAMS' INITIAL CONTRACT

Franklin P. Adams signed his contract on June 27, 1938. After carefully comparing the contracts for both Franklin P. Adams and John Kieran, the author can verify that the contracts for both men, including terms and financial reimbursement, were exactly the same. There was no difference between the two whatsoever.

On September 10, 1940, an amendment was drafted for John Kieran in light of Dan Golenpaul's agreement with the new sponsor, the American Tobacco Company. Kieran received a raise of $600.00 per broadcast.

Unlike the other members of the board, Adams' contract included one additional clause because of his involvement with another program:

Therefore this letter and your acceptance below represents our understanding and shall be binding upon both of us. You agree:

(1) That during the term of our agreement you will not appear in or in any manner, whether directly or indirectly, participate in any radio or television program other than *Information, Please*, with the single exception that you may participate in the radio program which has heretofore been auditioned and tentatively entitled *Let's Go*, provided that such program shall not be sponsored by any person, firm or corporation engaged in the manufacture, sale or distribution of tobacco products. I shall, when requested by you, from time to time, endeavor to secure from American Tobacco Company its consent that you make single guest appearances over the air.

This clause is interesting because it was during the Lucky Strike sponsorship that Franklin P. Adams made one of his rare radio appearances on another program, Fred Allen's *The Texaco Star Theatre*, on March 5, 1941. The radio program Adams had auditioned for, entitled *Let's Go*, wasn't a success and never made it to the prime-time airwaves.

On March 18, 1943, an amendment was drafted for Franklin P. Adams in light of Dan Golenpaul's agreement with the new sponsor, H.J. Heinz Company. The financial reimbursement for the weekly appearances remained the same. Comparing Adams' contract with that of Kieran's, except for the dates, the contract remained the same in every word.

OSCAR LEVANT'S INITIAL CONTRACT

Oscar Levant made a total of thirty appearances on *Information, Please* before he signed on permanently as a regular member of the board. Having proven that he could handle the toughies (especially questions pertaining to music), and because of the impressive amount of fan mail from listeners who expressed their pleasure in listening to Levant's charm and witty remarks, Golenpaul drafted a contract dated November 14, 1939. Reprinted below is Levant's initial contract:

Mr. Oscar Levant, New York City
Dear Mr. Levant:
     This letter and your acceptance represents our understanding and shall constitute a binding agreement between us.
     I agree to employ you in connection with my radio program, *Information, Please*, as a member of the Board of Experts, to collaborate with the other members in answering, to the best of your ability, questions submitted and generally to perform services similar to those heretofore performed by you as a member of the Board. You agree to accept such employment. You further agree to present yourself at any broadcasting studio which I may designate, in New York City, for each weekly broadcast on which you are to appear, in ample time to proceed with the program; to conform with the rules and regulations of the broadcasting company and of the producers and sponsors of the production, and in all respects to give your cooperation in connection with the program.
     You agree that I may use your name, photograph, or other likeness for advertising and publicity purposes in connection with the broadcast; and you likewise consent to the use of your name, portrait and likeness for the purpose of any proper advertising and publicity by Canada Dry Gingerale, Inc. in connection with its sponsorship of the broadcasting of *Information, Please*, it being distinctly understood that such use shall not be for the purpose, however, of either directly or indirectly endorsing the products of Canada Dry, Inc. Should there be any charge in sponsorship, you

agree that this consent shall apply to any other sponsor.

The programs are to be broadcast once each week for thirty (30) minute periods. The particular day and time of the day are to be designated by me.

For your said services, I agree to pay you $50.00 per broadcast when the programs are not commercially sponsored and the sum of $300.00 per broadcast when the programs are commercially sponsored.

This agreement shall commence as of November 14th, 1939 and shall continue for twenty-six (26) weeks, terminating May 7, 1940, unless I shall exercise my privilege to renew as hereinafter provided. During the term of this agreement, and any renewals, you agree to appear upon not less than six (6) and not more than seven (7) programs during each thirteen (13) week period, so that in the event you appear on seven (7) programs during any particular thirteen (13) week period, you shall appear on six (6) such programs during the next thirteen (13) week period, making a total of thirteen (13) programs during any consecutive twenty-six (26) week period. I agree on my part to employ you for such number of programs.

You agree that I shall have the following options in respect of the renewal of this agreement for successive thirteen (13) week periods, it being understood that my right to exercise any particular option (with the exception of the first) is conditioned upon my having exercised the option immediately preceding:

May 14, 1940 to August 6, 1940
August 13, 1940 to November 5, 1940
November 12, 1940 to February 4, 1941
February 11, 1941 to May 6, 1941
May 13, 1941 to August 5, 1941
August 12, 1941 to November 4, 1941

In the event I elect to exercise any one or more of the said options to renew, I agree to give you written notice of my election at least two weeks prior to the beginning of the particular renewal period covered by the notice.

All of the terms, conditions and provisions of this agreement shall apply to each renewal.

Should the program go off the air during the term thereof, or any renewal this agreement shall terminate forthwith on the date of the last broadcast.

It is understood and agreed that your services hereunder are special

and unique and that during the term of this agreement you will not
  (1) Participate in any radio programs of the same type and nature as *Information, Please*;
  (2) Participate in any radio program sponsored by a competitor of Canada Dry, Inc., or in the event of any future sponsor, by a competitor of such future sponsor;
  (3) Participate in any radio program of whatsoever nature, broadcast on the same day as *Information, Please*; and
  (4) Participate in more than one radio program per week in addition to *Information, Please*.

Any quiz program shall be deemed a program of the same type and nature as *Information, Please* for the purposes of this agreement and in addition programs through not technically of the quiz type shall be deemed of the same type and nature, if similar to *Information, Please* in that they feature a board or group of experts who participate with a master of ceremonies and deal with literary, musical, political and sports topics.

Finally you agree that in the event that I exercise all of the options as hereinabove provided, that you will not thereafter, so long as *Information, Please* remains on the air, become employed by or in connection with an similar program as herein defined.

If the foregoing represents your understanding and is satisfactory to you, will you please so indicate in the space provided below for that purpose?

Very truly yours,
(signed) Dan Golenpaul

I have read the foregoing letter and the same represents my understanding, and is satisfactory to me.

(signed) Oscar Levant

What makes the date of this contract interesting is that even though Levant had not signed until November of 1939, three months earlier in August, the National Broadcasting Company engaged the services of Oscar Levant for a an hour-long broadcast on August 28, 1939 by paying Dan Golenpaul the fee of $500.00 for permission to feature Oscar Levant on the program!

One can only imagine how much Golenpaul was paid to lend out Oscar Levant for other radio programs. Levant was guest on *The Texaco Star Theatre* (May 3, 1942), *The Pause that Refreshes* (September 20, 1942),

The Cresta Blanca Carnival (January 13, 1943), *The Jack Benny Program* (January 17, 1943), *Mail Call* (August 5, 1943), *The Telephone Hour* (February 28, 1944), *The Texaco Star Theatre* (April 23, 1944), and numerous other appearances on *Command Performance, The Telephone Hour, Mail Call, Concert Hall* and *The Fred Allen Show.*

On September 10, 1940, an amendment was drafted for Oscar Levant in light of Dan Golenpaul's agreement with the new sponsor, the American Tobacco Company. Levant, just like Kieran and Adams, received a raise of $600.00 per broadcast.

AGREEMENT BETWEEN PATHE NEWS, INC – and – DAN GOLENPAUL

Dated March 21, 1939, drafted by Charles F. Goldberg, Attorney-at-Law, No. 22 East 40th Street, NY, NY

AGREEMENT dated March 21, 1939, between Pathe News, Inc., having an office and principal place of business at 35 West 45th Street, New York, N.Y. (hereinafter called "Pathe") and Dan Golenpaul, an individual, residing at the Ansonia Hotel, Broadway and 73rd Street, New York, N.Y. (hereinafter called "Golenpaul").

WHEREAS, Golenpaul is the owner of a certain radio program entitled *Information, Please* which is being broadcast weekly, and Pathe desires to produce one or more one-reel motion pictures based upon and using the cast of the aforesaid radio program;

NOW, THEREFORE, in consideration of the premises and mutual promises and agreements herein contained, the parties hereto hereby agree as follows:

1. Golenpaul agrees to furnish to Pathe the script for each picture produced hereunder. As used herein, "script" shall mean the continuity of the master of ceremonies and a series of questions similar to those used on the *Information, Please* radio programs, adequate to sustain a motion picture show of approximately one half hour's duration. The script for the first picture shall be furnished within forty-five (45) days after the date of this agreement. Golenpaul agrees to furnish the entire cast of the aforesaid radio program to appear in each picture, which cast shall include Messrs. Fadiman, Kieran, Adams and Levant, and in addition one guest expert. If Messrs. Fadiman, Kieran, Adams

and Levant, or any of them, shall be unable to appear in any picture by reason of death or illness or for any other reason beyond Golenpaul's control, Golenpaul will furnish in their place another person or persons of equal talent and suitability. Golenpaul represents that he had entered into contracts with the said persons requiring their performance hereunder, copies of which agreements are annexed hereto as Exhibits A, B, C and D, respectively.

2. The selection of all literary material used in each script, and the selection of the guest expert shall be made solely by Golenpaul, who shall also have general supervision of the manner in which such material is presented in the filming of the picture or pictures.

3. Prior to the commencement of the actual filming of each picture, Golenpaul will obtain (and deliver to Pathe) from each person, including himself, who is to appear in such picture, the written consent for Pathe to use his or her name and photograph, and to reproduce his or her voice in such picture, and to use his or her name and photograph in any commercial advertising or publicity in connection with the picture, it being distinctly understood that in no event shall such use be for the purpose of advertising and endorsing any products, commodities or services. Pathe further agrees that it will not under any circumstances use, sell or in any other manner dispose of the said pictures or any of them in connection with any commercial tie-up with any other person persons, or corporation, and the said pictures will be used and distributed exclusively for exhibition purposes.

4. Pathe shall not be obligated to make any payment to any person furnished by Golenpaul in connection with the production or distribution of any picture hereunder, it being the intention of the parties hereto that Pathe shall not be required to make any payments to Golenpaul or to the members of his cast other than those mentioned in Article 18 hereof.

5. Pathe understands that the literary material to be furnished by Golenpaul consists of (1) questions submitted to him by the public; and/or (2) questions constructed by Golenpaul; and (3) the continuity of the master of ceremonies as hereinabove described. With respect to such material only, Golenpaul

warrants that he is the owner thereof and has the exclusive right to dispose of the same for moving and sound pictures.

6. Pathe agrees to film each picture provided for hereunder not later than twenty days after the receipt from Golenpaul of the script for such picture. Each picture produced hereunder shall be produced in the City of New York.

7. Golenpaul agrees to have himself and all other persons who are to appear in each picture available to Pathe in the City of New York at any reasonable time in connection with the production of each picture, provided however, that neither Golenpaul nor any other person shall be required to be available in connection with the filming of any single picture in excess of three (3) consecutive hours (except as provided below) and provided further that they will not be required to be available in connection with the filming of any picture at any time which will conflict with any radio broadcast of the radio program entitled, *Information, Please*, or their other regular occupations. Notwithstanding the foregoing, whenever Pathe shall deem it necessary, it may require Golenpaul and the cast for an additional two hours in connection with the production of the pictures, provided the additional two hours are on the same day as the three hours originally scheduled for the productions and consecutive therewith.

Pathe will give Golenpaul not less than ten (10) days' notice of the time when Golenpaul and the other persons are to appear for the commencement of the production of the respective pictures.

8. Within fourteen (14) days after the filming of the first picture hereunder, Pathe will screen such picture for Golenpaul. Within three (3) days thereafter, each party will notify the other whether or not such party considers the picture suitable for general release. If Golenpaul considers the picture unsuitable for general release, the same shall not be released and this agreement shall thereupon cease and terminate in all respects without any liability on the part of either party to the other. If Pathe considers the picture unsuitable for general release, the same shall not be released, and thereupon (a) Pathe shall pay Golenpaul the sum of Seven Hundred and Fifty ($750) Dollars for his services hereunder and (b) this agreement shall cease and come to an end without any further liability on the part of either party to the other.

Pathe agrees that in the event it be the party that considers the picture unsuitable for general release, it will turn over the negative of the picture to Golenpaul, to be his property unconditionally, and that it will destroy any and all other prints made therefrom.

If both parties shall consider the picture suitable for general release, Pathe will thereupon cause the picture to be distributed as hereinafter provided.

9. If both parties consider the first picture hereunder suitable for general release, Pathe and Golenpaul agree that six (6) additional pictures shall be made upon the same terms and conditions (excepting as to Cancellation as provided in Article 8) as apply with respect to the first picture hereunder, and the scripts for each such picture shall be furnished by Golenpaul to Pathe within forty-five (45) days after the submission to Pathe of the script for the preceding picture.

10. In the event that seven (7) pictures are completed hereunder, Pathe shall have the right to make six (6) more pictures thereafter upon the same terms and conditions as apply with respect to the last six (6) of the first seven (7) pictures hereunder.

If Pathe shall elect to exercise its right to make such six (6) pictures, it will notify Golenpaul of such election within fourteen (14) days after the completion of filming the seventh (7th) picture hereunder.

11. If the first picture shall be suitable for general release as hereinbefore provided, Pathe will distribute such picture and all other pictures made hereunder through RKO Radio Pictures, Inc.

12. Pathe shall have the right to cut and edit each picture hereunder in whatever manner and to whatever extent it may deem advisable.

13. Pathe shall have the right to cause each picture to be distributed and exhibited upon any size print.

14. Pathe shall have the right to use the title *Information, Please* in connection with each picture hereunder. Pathe shall credit Golenpaul and the members of the cast on the main or credit titles of each print of each picture made hereunder.

15. The negative of each picture produced hereunder and each lavender print and positive print made therefrom shall belong to and be the sole property of Pathe, and Golenpaul shall have no

interest whatsoever in such negative or prints, except as heretofore provided in Article 8.

16. Pathe agrees that it will cause each picture released hereunder to be distributed by RKO Radio Pictures, Inc. as widely as possible. If at any time Pathe shall consider that the further distribution of any picture hereunder is no longer profitable in any particular country, then and in such event Pathe shall have the right to terminate the distribution of such picture in such country.

17. Any picture hereunder may be licensed for exhibition or distribution in a group with any picture or pictures not distributed hereunder, provided however, that in all such cases an equitable part of the consideration received for the entire group shall be allocated to the picture being distributed hereunder, such consideration to be commensurate with the demand for and the quality of the picture.

17 (a). Pathe represents that it has obtained from RKO Radio Pictures, Inc., its distributor, an undertaking whereby the said distributor agrees that in selling the pictures provided for hereunder to the theaters of companies affiliated with it, it will not in any manner discriminate in prices in favor of such theaters. A copy of said undertaking is annexed hereto and marked Exhibit "E".

18. In the event of the release of the first picture hereunder Pathe will pay Golenpaul Three Thousand Five Hundred ($3,500) Dollars with respect to such picture twenty days after the filming thereof and in respect of the subsequent pictures provided for hereunder it will pay him a like amount for each and every such picture not later than seven (7) days after the respective filmings thereof. In addition to the foregoing payments, it will pay him at the times and in the manner hereinafter provided in Article 20, Fifteen (15%) percent of all amounts, if any, in excess of Fifteen Thousand ($15,000) Dollars and less than Twenty-Five Thousand ($25,000) Dollars, and Twenty (20%) percent of all amount, if any, in excess of Twenty-Five Thousand ($25,000) Dollars of the gross receipts from the distribution of each picture provided for hereunder.

19. The term "gross receipts" in the case of each picture is defined to mean:

(a) All monies paid by theatre exhibitors for a license to exhibit such picture in cases where such license is acquired directly from RKO Radio Pictures, Inc. or any corporation subsidiary to or affiliated therewith; and

(b) All sums actually paid to RKO Radio Pictures, Inc. or its subsidiary or affiliated corporations by subdistributors for distribution of or exhibition rights.

If any country or countries shall prohibit the withdraw of monies therefrom or the remittance of monies to parties not citizens or residents of such country, Pathe will cause all monies, if any, accruing to Golenpaul, from the distribution of the pictures hereunder in such country or countries to be deposited to the credit of Golenpaul in such bank or banks in such country or countries as Golenpaul may designate. Pathe will report to Golenpaul the sums so deposited at the time of making the reports of gross receipts hereinbefore provided for, and such deposits shall constitute due remittance of the sums due Golenpaul hereunder in respect to the distribution of the respective pictures in such country or countries.

Golenpaul's share, if any, of the gross receipts from the distribution of the respective pictures in foreign countries shall, in cases where the contracts for exhibition or distribution thereof for the end of the week in which they are earned at the published rate of exchange prevailing in such countries at the end of such week, except in cases where the laws or currency regulations of such countries prevent the withdraw of the same therefrom.

20. Pathe will keep correct books of account in connection with the distribution of each picture hereunder, showing the gross receipts from the distribution of each picture in each country or territory in which the same shall be distributed. Pathe will mail to Golenpaul regular reports showing the amount of the gross receipts from the distribution of each picture in each territory for the period covered by each such report. Such reports shall be sent to Golenpaul at intervals of not less than four (4) weeks nor more than five (5) weeks. At the time of the mailing of each such report, Pathe will remit to Golenpaul all sums which are shown on such report, if any.

21. The accounting by Pathe to Golenpaul shall be made separately with respect to each picture.

22. Golenpaul or his authorized representative shall have the right at any time within five (5) years after the general release of any picture hereunder, to inspect the books, records and accounts of Pathe with respect to the distribution of such picture.
23. This agreement shall be binding upon and inure to the benefit of the parties hereto, and the successors and assigns of Pathe, and the heirs, executors and administrators of Golenpaul.
24. Golenpaul shall not have the right to assign this agreement, except to the partnership of which he is a member, known as Dan Golenpaul Associates, which however shall in nowise relieve him personally of the personal services which he is obligated to perform hereunder.
25. All notices and reports required or desired to be given by either party to the other shall be sent by registered mail to the respective addresses set forth on the first page hereof.
26. This agreement constitutes the entire agreement between the parties and no promises or representations have been made by either party to the other except as set forth herein.

IN WITNESS WHEREOF, the corporate party hereto has caused this agreement to be executed by its duly authorized officer and its corporate seal to be hereto affixed, and the individual party hereto had hereunto affixed his hand and seal all as of the day and year first above written.

PATHE NEWS, INC.
(signed) Frederic Ullman, Jr., Vice-President

ATTEST:
(signed) A.J. MacPhail, Assistant Secretary

(signed) Dan Golenpaul

WITNESS:
(signed) Charles F. Goldberg

SPONSOR CONTRACT

For the most part, all of the sponsor contracts during the duration of radio's *Information, Please* remained the same, except for obvious changes such as the cost of productions, the on-air dates scheduled for broadcast, etc. For the sake of brevity, only one of these contracts is being reprinted in whole. The contract reprinted below is for the duration of the Parker Pen Company's sponsorship from October of 1946 to June of 1947.

J. WALTER THOMPSON COMPANY on behalf of PARKER PEN COMPANY—with—ANN GOLENPAUL and DAN GOLENPAUL, a co-partnership doing business under the name and style of DAN GOLENPAUL ASSOCIATES.

AGREEMENT dated October 2, 1946

AGREEMENT made and entered into this 2nd day of October, 1946, by and between DANIEL GOLENPAUL and ANN GOLENPAUL, doing business as DANIEL GOLENPAUL ASSOCIATES (hereinafter referred to as "Producers") and J. WALTER THOMPSON COMPANY (hereinafter referred to as "Agency") on behalf of its client PARKER PEN COMPANY (hereinafter referred to as "Sponsor").

FIRST: Agency hereby agrees Producers to produce and to cause to be performed a series of thirty-nine (39) consecutive weekly one-half (1/2) hour radio programs entitled *Information, Please* which program shall in all respects save those relating to Agency's selling efforts in behalf of Sponsor be similar to those heretofore produced and performed by the Producers. Said program shall be broadcast by and through the facilities of the coast to coast network of the Columbia Broadcasting System from its New York City studios, or elsewhere as may be determined by the Producers, on consecutive Wednesdays, beginning October 2, 1946 and ending June 25, 1947 from approximately 10:30 p.m. to approximately 11:00 p.m. New York time. It is understood that the program may be broadcast delayed over those stations on the network which shall not be available at the time of the live broadcast of the program. In the event that Agency deems it desirable to change the network, or the day or the time of the day of the broadcast, the Producers agree to render the aforementioned services on such other network or at such other days and time as may be mutually agreeable to Agency and Producers.

Producers grant Sponsor and Agency the right to broadcast said programs by transcriptions in Cuba, Panama, Puerto Rico, Alaska, Phillipines and Hawaii, provided however that no such broadcasts shall be made subsequent to thirty (30) days after the last "live" broadcast of the program hereunder; in the event, however, that Producers shall advise Agency in writing that the radio program *Information, Please* shall resume broadcast prior to the expiration of such thirty (30) day period, then Agency will take all practical measures to discontinue said transcription broadcasts prior to the resumption of broadcasting by the Producers.

SECOND: Agency agrees to pay Producers for all the rights and services hereunder, and the Producers agree to accept therefor, the sum of ($11,000.00) Dollars per program. Payment shall be made weekly, in New York funds, within one (1) week immediately following the broadcast of each program. Agency also agrees to furnish and provide the network facilities and arrangements for broadcasting the programs and the furnishing of commercial announcers and the commercial material.

THIRD: The Producers agree to render, with respect to said program, services similar to those heretofore rendered by them in connection with the *Information, Please* programs. Without limiting the generality of the foregoing, the Producers specifically agree:

(a) To furnish for said programs the services of Dan Golenpaul as producer and director.

(b) To furnish the services of Clifton Fadiman (hereinafter referred to as "Fadiman") as master of ceremonies.

(c) To furnish the services of John Kieran (hereinafter referred to as "Kieran") and Franklin P. Adams (hereinafter referred to as "Adams") as two of the four members of the Board of Experts.

(d) To furnish the services of two guest experts on each broadcast.

(e) To grant to Agency and/or Sponsor the exclusive right, privilege and license, for radio only, to the title *Information, Please*, the basic idea and formula of the program now known as *Information, Please*.

(f) To provide a list of questions to be propounded on such programs to the Board of Experts.

(g) To provide continuity and arrange all material for the entertainment portion of such programs.

(h) It is distinctly understood and agreed that all audience and fan mail relating to *Information, Please* shall be the property of the Producers.

(i) To pay and deliver prizes and prize money in connection with such programs by making payment direct to all prize winners or, in the discretion of Agency, by having Agency do so, the Producers to reimburse Agency therefor.
(j) To cooperate in fitting the commercials (as hereinafter defined) into the entertainment portion of the said programs.
(k) To furnish any and all props, musical instruments, talent and services which may be necessary to furnish a complete and finished radio show of the general type of *Information, Please*.

FOURTH: Agency agrees that the Producers shall have sole discretion and final judgement in selecting guest members of the Board; in selecting questions to be put to the Board during each program; in promulgating the rules which are to govern the asking and answering of the questions; the value of the prizes and in all other matters pertaining to the entertainment portions of the programs. For purposes of this agreement, the entire one-half (1/2) hour program shall be deemed the "entertainment portion of the program" with the exception of material advertising Sponsor's products and/or services (hereinafter referred to as commercials), said commercials to be fitted into the continuity after the fifth or sixth question and after the ninth or tenth question, plus whatever closing or sign-off statement Agency may desire to make.

Agency shall have complete control over the content and wording of the commercials, except the Producers shall have the right to disapprove any copy prepared by Agency, intended to be read by the Master of Ceremonies. It is understood and agreed however that the Master of Ceremonies may not be required to participate in delivering any commercial material to a greater extent or more often on the program than other commercial participation heretofore on *Information, Please*.

FIFTH: On all programs Daniel Golenpaul shall be entitled to a credit announcement as Producer of *Information, Please*.

SIXTH: Producers grant to Agency and/or Sponsor during the term hereof, the exclusive right to use *Information, Please* as the title of said programs and in connection with any publicity, advertising and sales promotion of Sponsor's products and/or services, and Producers further agree that they will not, during said term, grant such right to any other person, firm or corporation. Subject to the foregoing, any and all literary, motion picture, television and other property rights of whatsoever kinds and nature which may inhere in the said programs or any part thereof and in the title *Information, Please* shall be and remain the property of the Producers, it being the intent hereof that the rights herein granted to the Agency and/or Sponsor are limited to the radio broadcast of the program; provided, however, that during the term hereof, Producers shall not license such literary, motion picture, and other property rights for advertising and/or publicizing products and/or services competitive with those of the Sponsor and that with respect to television rights, they shall not license the same for any purpose whatsoever, and Producers represent that they have not granted any television rights for advertising or commercial purposes in the past.

Producers grant to Agency and/or Sponsor the right to use the names, portraits and likenesses of the Producers, Fadiman, Adams and Kieran and/or any substitute(s) therefor and/or the guests appearing on such programs, it being distinctly understood that such use shall not be for the purpose of endorsing the Sponsor's products and/or services.

SEVENTH:

(a) If any one of Fadiman, Kieran, Adams or a permanent substitute for any one of them as provided for in (b) below is not available for performance on any program, by reason of illness or other cause beyond Producers' reasonable control, Producer shall furnish a substitute therefor, it being understood that Producers' right of substitution shall be unrestricted and that the furnishing of any such substitute or substitutes satisfactory to Producers shall constitute full performance by Producers of their obligation to furnish talent under this agreement.

(b) If any one of Fadiman, Kieran or Adams or a permanent substitute for any one of them shall be unavailable for performance for more than six (6) consecutive broadcasts, then Producers shall furnish a permanent substitute therefor not later than the seventh (7) broadcast and shall notify Agency forthwith of such permanent substitution. If Agency shall not be satisfied with said permanent substitute, Agency shall so notify the Producers and shall have the right to terminate this agreement upon written notice to the Producers before the third (3) broadcast following Producers' first use of such permanent substitute, such termination to be effective no sooner than the conclusion of the twelfth (12) broadcast following the first broadcast cast on which Fadiman, Kieran or Adams or such permanent substitute shall have been unavailable for performance, unless the unavailable performer shall have returned to the program by the ninth (9) broadcast since his first absence.

(c) Except as provided in subdivision (d), if a permanent substitute shall have taken the place of any one of Fadiman, Kieran or Adams as provided in (b) above and subsequent to such substitution any one of the other two (2) named persons shall be unavailable for performance for more than six (6) consecutive broadcasts, then Producers shall furnish a permanent therefor as provided in (b) above, and, anything in 7 (b) above to the contrary notwithstanding, Agency shall have the right to terminate this agreement upon four (4) weeks prior written notice to Producers but the effective date of such cancellation shall not extend beyond the conclusion of the twelfth (12) broadcast following the first broadcast on which such unavailability occurred.

(d) It is specifically understood and agreed however that in the event Agency shall have exercised its option or options to renew this agreement as provided in Article Eleventh hereof, at a time when a permanent substitute or substitutes have already replaced one or more (as the case may be) of Fadiman, Kieran and Adams, then

(I) Agency shall be deemed to have approved the substitute or substitutes performing at the time of renewal, and

(II) the three (3) persons performing at such time shall be deemed permanent members of the cast and Producers' right of substitution thereafter shall be the same as if said three (3) persons had originally been named herein instead of Fadiman, Kieran and Adams.

EIGHTH: The Producers agree:

(a) That they will not, during the term of this agreement, direct or produce or in any other manner render services in connection with:

(1) Any radio and/or television programs for a commercial sponsor whose products and/or services are in competition with those of the Sponsor herein;

(2) Any radio and/or television programs of the same or similar title and/or type and nature as *Information, Please* and

(3) Any radio and/or television programs broadcast on the same day as *Information, Please.*

(b) That with respect to Messrs. Fadiman, Adams and Kieran and/or any permanent substitute(s) therefor, and each of them, that during the term of this agreement:

(1) They will not participate in any radio programs of the same type and nature as *Information, Please*;

(2) They will not participate in any radio programs the products and/or services of whose Sponsor are in competition with those of the Sponsor herein;

(3) They will not participate in any radio programs of whatsoever nature broadcast on the same day as *Information, Please*;

(4) No two (2) of them together shall appear collectively on any radio program without the written consent of the Sponsor first obtained. Producers agree to use their best efforts to obtain commitments from said persons providing for the same restrictions in respect of television as specified above in respect of radio.

NINTH: Producers agree to indemnify and hold harmless Sponsor and/or Agency against liability, claims, loss or damage, including attorneys' fees arising out of the broadcast and/or rebroadcast of any programs hereunder; provided, however, that the provisions hereof shall not be applicable with respect to any commercial announcements, and with respect to such commercial announcements Agency agrees similarly to indemnify Producers. In particular, and without limiting the foregoing, the Producers shall indemnify and save harmless the Sponsor and/or Agency from any and all claims, suits and actions of any nature whatsoever which may be asserted or brought against it, arising out of or incidental to the use of the words "Information Please," or any other words, slogans or identifying script used by the producers.

TENTH:

(a) It is understood and agreed that the Producers' services hereunder are extraordinary and unique and that there is no adequate remedy at law for a breach of this contract by Producers; in the event of such breach, Agency and/or Sponsor shall be entitled to equitable relief by way of injunction or otherwise.

(b) It is further understood and agreed that the services hereunder of Fadiman, Kieran and Adams and each of them, or any permanent substitute therefor, are unique and extraordinary and that Agency and/or Sponsor have no adequate remedy at law for a breach of this contract occasioned by the acts or failure of performance of any one of them; Producers represent that under their contracts with each of the said Fadiman, Kieran and Adams (or any permanent substitute therefor) whereby the latter are employed by Producers to perform the services each of them is to render hereunder, the unique and extraordinary character of their services and Producers' right of equitable relief by way of injunction or otherwise in the event of breach of such contract(s) with Producers is set forth, (or in the case of permanent substitute(s), will be set forth); Producers agree that in the event of breach or anticipated breach by any one of said named performers or permanent substitute(s) therefor, of such contract(s) with Producers, which in turn constitutes or would constitute a breach of this agreement, Producers will take any legal action necessary, by injunction of otherwise to prevent such breach or the continuation thereof.

ELEVENTH: The Producers hereby grant to Agency the following options to renew this agreement upon the same terms and conditions except as to the price specifically provided in option (b) hereunder:

(a) Thirty-nine (39) weeks from the date of commencement elected by Agency, such date to be no earlier than September 24, 1947 and no later than October 1, 1947, at Eleven Thousand ($11,000.00) Dollars per broadcast.

(b) Thirty-nine (39) weeks from the date of commencement elected by Agency, such date to be no earlier than September 22, 1948 and no later than September 29, 1948, at Thirteen Thousand, Five Hundred ($13,500.00) Dollars per broadcast.

If Agency intends to exercise option (a), Agency must so notify Producers in writing not later than April 25, 1947. If Agency intends to exercise option (b), having exercised option (a), Agency must so notify Producers in writing not later than sixty (60) days prior to the thirty-ninth (39) broadcast date contained in the option (a) period. It is specifically understood and agreed, with respect to the date fixing the commencement of the thirty-nine (39) week period contained in option (a) and option (b) hereof, that Agency must designate such commencement date at the time Agency elects to exercise the option.

TWELFTH: Producers shall have and exercise exclusive authoritative control over the means, methods, details and persons to be employed by Producers in performing the provisions of this agreement on Producers' part to be performed. Producers shall perform and discharge all obligations imposed upon Producers as employer under the rules of the American Federation of Radio Artists and the American Federation of Musicians, Workman's compensation, unemployment compensation or insurance, social security, withholding tax, and other federal and state laws and regulations including all orders and regulations dealing with restrictions and limitations upon salaries and wages; and without limiting the foregoing, Producers shall file all returns and reports and make all withholdings required of employers under the provisions of the foregoing and Producers shall pay all assessments, taxes, contributions or other sums imposed thereunder upon or with respect to the salaries or wages paid by Producers to the persons whose services Producers engage or furnish for these programs and all salaries and wages paid to all such persons shall be in accordance with all statutes, orders and regulations that may be in effect with respect to limiting and restricting salaries and wages. Producers accept exclusive liability for all such assessments, withholdings, taxes, contributions or other sums and the compliance with all the foregoing laws, orders and regulations and agree to indemnify and hold harmless Sponsor and/or Agency against and from all claims and demands arising under any of the foregoing laws, orders, rules and regulations with the respect to any of the money paid by Agency to Producers pursuant to this contract.

THIRTEENTH:

(a) In the event that during the term hereof, Ann Golenpaul shall die or for any reason whatsoever be permanently incapacitated so that she cannot perform her obligations hereunder, this agreement shall nevertheless remain in full force and effect.

(b) In the event that during the term hereof said Daniel Golenpaul shall die or for any reason whatsoever be permanently incapacitated so that he cannot perform his obligations hereunder, this agreement shall nevertheless remain I full force and effect for thirty (30) days after the happening of such event, during which period Ann Golenpaul shall act as producer and director. Agency shall have the option, exercisable within said thirty (30) days, either of

(1) accepting the services of Anne Golenpaul or such other person as shall be acceptable to both Agency and Producers, as pro-

ducer and director of the program for the balance of the term of this agreement; or

(2) canceling this agreement. If Agency elects to continue with the said Ann Golenpaul or such other mutually acceptable person as producer and director, this agreement shall remain in full force and effect.

FOURTEENTH:

(a) If for any reason such as strikes, boycotts, war, acts of God, labor troubles, riots, delays of commercial carriers, restraint by public authority, or for any other reason similar or dissimilar and beyond the Producers' control, including temporary incapacity of personnel, the Producers shall be unable to furnish a program in any particular week, the same shall not be deemed to be a breach of this agreement on the part of the Producer; but in such event the Producer shall not be entitled to any consideration for such omitted program.

(b) If for any reason such as strikes, boycotts, war, acts of God, labor troubles, riots, delays of commercial carriers, restraint by public authority, or for any other reason similar or dissimilar and beyond the Agency's control, Agency shall be unable to make available the facilities for broadcasting the program, the same shall not be deemed to be a breach of this agreement on the part of Agency.

FIFTEENTH: Producers grant Sponsor and/or Agency the right to make or authorize the making of off-the-line recordings of said broadcasts from which pressings can be made to give to the Army, Navy, Marine Corps, Coast Guard or other governmental agency for any use they elect to make of the and/or from which broadcasts may be made over short wave stations located in the United States for reception abroad.

SIXTEENTH: All notices hereunder shall be in writing and shall be sufficient if mailed to the party for whom the notice is intended at its last known address.

SEVENEENTH: Agency agrees in behalf of Sponsor that in the thirteen (13) week period next following the date of the expiration of this agreement, Sponsor shall not produce or cause to be produced at the same time as the *Information, Please* program was last broadcast hereunder, any quiz program or program similar in type to *Information, Please*; it being specifically understood and agreed however that this limitation shall not be or become operative in the event Agency shall terminate this agreement under the provisions of Article Seventh hereof.

EIGHTEENTH: This agreement shall be binding upon and shall ensure to the benefit of the parties hereto, their legal representatives, successors and assigns.

NINETEENTH: In making this agreement it is agreed that the undersigned "Agency," J. Walter Thompson Company, is acting as agent for and in behalf of "Sponsor," Parker Pen Company, principal, and, in exercising any and all rights hereunder, which it is agreed that said "Agency" may do, said corporation will be acting as said agent.

IN WITNESS WHEREOF, producers have caused this instrument to be executed by one of its partners and Agency has caused this instrument to be executed by an officer duly authorized and has caused its corporate seal to be hereunto affixed, all on the sate as above set forth.

SELECT BIBLIOGRAPHY

Books

Ashley, Sally, *The Life and Times of Franklin Pierce Adams*, Beaufort Books, 1986

Brooks, Tim and Marsh, Earle, *The Complete Directory to Prime Time Network and Cable TV Shows*, Ballantine, 1995

Dunning, John, *On the Air: The Encyclopedia of Old-Time Radio*, Oxford University Press, 1998

Grams, Jr., Martin, *Radio Drama: American Programs, 1932-1962*, McFarland & Company, Inc., 2000

Hickerson, Jay, *The 2nd Revised Ultimate History of Network Radio Programming*, Presto Print II, 2001

Levant, Oscar, *The Memoirs of an Amnesiac*, G.P. Putnam's Sons, 1965

Articles

Billboard, July 24, 1937

Bridgeport Life, January 1943 issue

Cleveland Plain Dealer, The, October 28, 1945

Cue, July 12, 1952

Esquire, January 1963 issue

Film Fan Monthly, June 1974

Harper, February 1942 issue

Life, August 29, 1938 and an undated 1939 issue

Milwaukee Journal, The, July 4, 1943

New York Herald-Tribune, The, March 4, 1948, May 15, 1948, January 11, 1951 and July 4, 1952

New York Post, The, September 13, 1938 and July 5, 1940

New York Post Daily Magazine, The, March 5, 1975

New York Sun, The, August 9, 1939 and October 4, 1940

New York Times, The, March 12, 1939, March 13, 1940, July 11, 1940, November 22,

1942, January 9, 1943, January 24, 1943, September 28, 1943, September 17,

1944, September 1, 1946, March 15, 1947, November 11, 1947, March 4, 1948,

May 15, 1948, January 9, 1949, May 5, 1969, March 5, 1989 and June 21, 1999

New York Times Book Review, The, February 22, 1948 and April 24, 1955

New York World-Telegram-Sun, The, December 23, 1937 and November 14, 1944

Newsweek, November 20, 1939, April 14, 1941 and December 11, 1944

P.M., February 16, 1943

Publisher's Weekly, April 6, 1940

Radio and Television Mirror, January 1941 issue

Radio Mirror, July 1939 issue

Reader's Club, The, June 1941 issue

Reader's Digest, January 1939 issue

Saturday Review of Literature, The, March 11, 1939 and April 6, 1940

T.W., October 26, 1952

Time, November 27, 1939

Variety, March 1, 1938, August 24, 1938, November 23, 1938, February 8, 1939, November 22, 1939, February 17, 1943, September 15, 1943, September 13, 1944, August 17, 1946, July 2, 1952 and June 28, 1999

Contracts and Memorandum of Agreements
(besides the ones reprinted in the book)

>The American Tobacco Company and Dan Golenpaul Associates, August 5, 1940.
>
>The American Tobacco Company and Dan Golenpaul Associates, October 25, 1940. (mem)
>
>The Pathe News, Inc. and Dan Golenpaul Associates, March 21, 1939. (mem)
>
>The Pathe News, Inc. and Dan Golenpaul Associates, April 16, 1940.
>
>The Socony-Vacuum Company and Dan Golenpaul Associates, November 21, 1944. (mem)
>
>The Socony-Vacuum Company and Dan Golenpaul Associates, February 10, 1945.
>
>The Parker Pen Company and Dan Golenpaul Associates, October 2, 1946.
>
>Franklin P. Adams and Dan Golenpaul Associates, May 1949.
>
>The General Electric Company and Dan Golenpaul Associates, March of 1952.

Other Sources

>Numerous editions of the *Information Please Almanac*.
>
>Listening to over 200 recordings of the *Information, Please* radio programs.
>
>Many scripts including *The Magazine of the Air* (January 17, 1934) and the 1942 audition; *Information, Please* (July 12, 1938, April 9, 1940 and January 22, 1943); *Raising Your Parents* (September 6, 1936, October 17, 1936, November 7, 1936, February 6, 1937, May 22, 1937, May 29, 1937, June 12, 1937, June 26, 1937, July 3, 1937, July 10, 1937, July 24, 1937, and October 2, 1937) and *The Education of Hyman Kaplan* (December 23, 1937).
>
>Consulted many official Associated Press Releases from 1939 to 1948.
>
>Numerous letters and correspondence between Dan Golenpaul and the people involved with *Information, Please*.

ABOUT THE AUTHOR

Martin Grams, Jr. is the author and co-author of numerous books including:

Suspense: Twenty Years of Thrills and Chills (1998)
The History of the Cavalcade of America (1998)
The CBS Radio Mystery Theater: An Episode Guide and Handbook (1999)
Radio Drama: An American Chronicle (1999)
The Have Gun – Will Travel Companion (2000)
The Alfred Hitchcock Presents Companion (2001)
The Sound of Detection: Ellery Queen's Adventures in Radio (2002)
Invitation to Learning (2002)
Inner Sanctum Mysteries: Behind the Creaking Door (2003)

He has also written magazine articles for *Filmfax, Scarlet Street, Old Time Radio Digest*, and SPERDVAC's *Radiogram*. He has contributed chapters and appendices for *Vincent Price: Midnight Marquee Actor Series* (1998) and *The Alfred Hitchcock Story* (1999). Martin has also contributed to BearManor Media's *It's That Time Again* (2002). Not only is he the recipient of the 1999 Ray Stanich Award for his writing, but he is presently completing two more books due for release within the next year—the official guide to Carlton E. Morse's *I Love a Mystery* and the history of the famous *Gangbusters* program. Martin lives in Delta, Pennsylvania.

INDEX

Ackerman, Carl W., 161
Adams, Franklin P., 1, 5, 15-16, 18, 20, 22-23, 26-29, 32-35, 39-40, 43, 51, 55, 60-62, 64, 66, 69-70, 74, 78, 81, 83-85, 90, 92-99, 106-107, 109-110, 112-113, 115-116, 129-136, 138-139, 146, 148, 151-199, 202, 212-213, 216-218, 221, 229, 231-234, 238, 240
Adler, Larry, 181, 188
Allen, Fred, 57, 61, 80, 94, 97-99, 163, 167, 173, 177, 181, 183, 185-190, 192, 194-195, 217, 221
Allen, Mel, 190
Allen, Frederick Lewis, 160, 170
Allen, Gracie, 30, 156
Allen, Robert, 62, 168, 191
Amory, Cleveland, 193
Andrews, Dr. Roy Chapman, 160
Arnall, Ellis, 95, 137, 182, 188, 190-191, 194
Ayres, Lew, 191
Baldwin, Faith, 166, 181
Baldwin, Hanson W., 172
Ball, Joseph H., 176
Barber, Red, 131, 176, 182-183, 194
Barkley, Alben W., 41, 179
Barrett, T.T., 169
Barrymore, Ethel, 157, 174
Bartholomew, Freddie, 186
Beardsley, James Wallace, 173

Beebe, William, 41, 157, 166, 176
Beecham, Sir Thomas, 36, 41, 167, 169, 175
Bellah, James Warner, 185
Benet, Stephen Vincent, 61, 167
Bennett, Augustus, 181
Bennett, James, 162
Benson, Sally, 166
Berg, Moe, 29, 32, 155, 158
Bernie, Ben, 153
Bernstein, Leonard, 179-180
Blandy, W.H., 193
Boehnel, William, 153
Boland, Mary, 166
Bolte, Charles G., 137-138, 185-186, 188-190, 195-196
Bottome, Phyllis, 186
Boyington, Gregory, 184
Brawner, Helen, 193
Bromfield, Louis, 117, 163, 167, 172, 177, 182
Broun, Heywood, 4, 155
Brown, John Mason, 5, 120, 124, 163, 169, 176, 181-182, 184, 186, 195-197
Brown, Louis, 176, 180
Brubaker, Howard, 152
Bryson, Dr. Lyman, 165-166
Burton, Harold, 179-180
Butterfield, Roger, 191
Caldwell, Erskine, 162

Calhern, Louis, 191
Canada Dry, 3, 24-26, 31-32, 42, 45-46, 54, 109-110, 149, 211-212, 218, 220
Caniff, Milt, 192
Capp, Al, 192-193
Capra, Frank, 188
Carey, Harry, 160
Carlson, Richard, 107, 197
Carradine, John, 55, 63, 117, 169
Carroll, Madeleine, 114, 170, 188
Caspary, Vera, 196
Chamberlain, John, 160
Chase, Ilka, 173
Chiang, T.F., 176
Childs, Marquis W., 183
Churchill, Randolph, 187
Clapper, Raymond, 170-171
Clement, Rufus, 189
Coburn, Charles, 173
Coffey, John M., 177
Cohan, George M., 29-30, 156
Connelly, Marc, 33, 42, 152, 162, 196
Cook, Alden, 152
Cooke, Alistair, 195-196
Corum, Bill, 195
Costain, Thomas B., 185-186
Craven, Thomas, 120, 124, 152
Cross, Wilbur L., 156
Crouse, Russel, 5, 27, 32, 107, 117, 138-139, 154-155, 157, 159-161, 167-169, 171, 176, 178-179, 181, 183, 185, 187, 189-191, 193-196, 199
Crum, Bartley, 194
Curran, Henry, 165
Davenport, Marcia, 81, 175-176, 182
Davidson, Jo, 164
Davies, Joseph E., 168
Davis, Jr., Benjamin, 185
Davis, Elmer, 116-117, 120, 124, 155, 187
Davis, Owen, 164
Davis, William H., 177
de Kruif, Paul, 19, 42, 151, 199
de Mille, Agnes, 178
Denny, Jr., George V., 167, 174
Deuel, Wallace R., 169-170
DeVoto, Bernard, 182
DeWitt, Jr., John H., 185
Dietz, Howard, 20, 152, 193

Dietz, Walter, 186
Digges, Dudley, 159
Doren, Carl Van, 158-159
Duffield, Marcus, 15, 19, 151-154, 157
Dunbar, Dr. Flanders, 193
Durant, Will, 40, 180
Durante, Jimmy, 161, 187, 191
Durante, Walter, 166
Eagan, Edward, 181, 183-184, 186, 191
Edmonds, Walter D., 163
Edmund, Irwin, 27, 154
Eldridge, Florence, 178
Elliot, Major George Fielding, 160, 179
Emerson, Faye, 186
Erksner, Frederick C., 170
Erskine, John, 27, 33, 105, 151, 162
Encyclopedia Brittanica, 3, 22, 31, 33, 41, 44, 53, 57, 62, 64, 67, 80-81, 88, 107, 120, 147, 175, 205
Esme, 180
Fadiman, Clifton, 1-234
Fairbanks, Jr., Douglas, 114, 184
Farley, James, 31, 41, 158
Ferber, Edna, 159, 168, 178
Field, Jr., Marshall, 183
Flanner, Janet, 169
Flynn, Edward J., 114, 190
Flynn, John T., 158
Forrester, C.S., 167, 171
Foss, Elizabeth, 155
Frick, Ford, 174, 182, 190
Frisch, Frank, 196
Fulbright, James William, 175
Funk, Wilfred, 157
Gallico, Paul, 168, 171, 188
Gannett, Lewis, 160
Gardiner, Reginald, 92, 179-180, 183, 188
Gish, Lillian, 19, 27, 32, 153, 157, 186
Gleason, James, 195, 202
Gogarty, Dr. Oliver St. John, 159-160
Goldberg, Rube, 193
Golenpaul, Dan, 1-2, 4-5, 11-16, 19, 22-23, 25, 29-33, 43, 46-48, 54, 57-61, 64-65, 67-78, 82, 86-88, 90-94, 96-108, 115-119, 121, 123-127, 129-130, 133-134, 136, 140-144, 146, 197-199, 210, 212-213, 215-218, 220-230, 235-236, 240
Gomez, Lefty, 167

Gordon, Ruth 114, 117, 159, 161
Gould, Morton, 183
Green, Theodore, 178
Greene, Richard, 196
Gunther, John, 18, 44, 62, 112, 117, 124, 152, 154-156, 161-162, 165-166, 168, 178, 181, 185-186, 188, 190-192, 194, 196-197
H.J. Heinz Company, 4, 77-81, 83, 85, 149, 213, 215-216, 218
Hacker, Louise, 151, 163
Hardwicke, Sir Cedric, 159
Hargrove, Marion, 178, 185-186
Hart, Moss, 84, 152, 155, 176, 179, 181, 183, 185, 192-193
Hayes, Arthur Garfield, 171
Hecht, Ben, 20, 152-153
Henderson, Leon, 39, 163, 170-174, 177
Henrich, Tommy, 196
Hill, Lester, 176
Hitchcock, Alfred, 166, 173, 193
Hobson, Laura Z., 189
Hooten, Ernest Albert, 163
Hope, Bob, 89, 187
Hough, Henry Beedle, 162
Howard, Leslie, 62, 168
Howe, Quincy, 152, 171, 176
Hussey, Ruth, 169
Huxley, Sir Julian S., 169
Ickes, Harold, 162
Information, Please Almanac, 2, 35, 41-42, 118-127, 141-142, 240
Ingersoll, Ralph, 161
Jackson, Charles, 185, 187, 189
Jacoby, Annalee, 187
Jacoby, Oswald, 153
Jaffe, Bernard, 31, 151-155, 180, 183
James, Marquis, 158
Janeway, Elizabeth, 177-178
Jebb, Sir Gladwyn, 137, 195
Jessel, George, 137, 195
Johnston, Alva, 162, 171
Johnson, General Hugh, 154
Johnson, Mrs. Martin, 161
Johnson, Nunnally, 159
Kaiser, Henry J., 179
Kaltenborn, H.V., 23, 156
Karloff, Boris, 63, 114, 117, 164, 169, 174, 180, 184, 192, 194

Kaufman., George S., 27, 33, 42, 132, 135, 152-154, 177, 179, 183, 188, 192
Kelland, Clarence Buddington, 112, 114-115, 117, 153, 156-157
Kellino, Pamela, 191-192
Kenny, George Churchill, 186
Kieran, James, 157
Kieran, John, 1, 17-21, 26, 28, 30, 32, 35, 39-41, 43, 51, 55, 61-63, 66, 69-70, 74, 78-81, 83-84, 90, 92-97, 99, 107, 109, 113, 115-116, 118-119, 124, 129-139, 141, 146, 151-199, 202, 205, 207, 212-213, 215-218, 221, 229, 231-234
Kilpatrick, John Reed, 191
Kimbrough, Emily, 83, 173, 180
King, Dennis, 186, 194
Knight, Eric, 170
Know, Alexander, 179
Krock, Arthur, 156
LaForge, Oliver, 160
LaGuardia, Fiorello, 167
Lanchester, Elsa, 165
Land, Emory S., 179
Landis, James M., 170
Laurence, William, 183
Lawes, Lewis E., 40, 163-164
Leach, Margaret, 167
Leinsdorf, Erich, 181-182
Lewis, Sinclair, 40, 174, 205
Levant, Oscar, 1, 18-21, 23, 26, 28-30, 32, 35-40, 51, 55, 58-59, 61, 63, 66, 69-72, 74, 77-78, 81-83, 87, 93-96, 99, 109-113, 115-116, 141, 144-146, 152-179, 186-190, 202, 205, 218, 221-222, 238
Leyden, Elmer F., 164
Lillie, Beatrice, 90, 183, 185
Lindsay, Howard, 107, 117, 138-139, 160, 181, 189-190, 192, 194-197
List, Eugene, 185
Litvinov, Madame Ivy, 169
Llewellyn, Richard, 194
Lockhart, Gene, 107, 139, 195
Lockridge, Richard, 176
Lodge, Jr., Major Henry Cabot, 171, 173
Loesser, Frank, 184
Logan, Joshua, 195
Longworth, Alice Roosevelt, 156

Louis, Wilmot, 57, 164
Luce, Clare Boothe, 162, 175
Lucky Strike, 54, 57, 72-75, 77, 80, 105, 149, 217
Ludwig, Emil, 169
Lukas, Paul, 165
Lund, John, 107, 197
Lynn, Diana, 83-84, 180, 183, 191
MacCracken, Henry Noble, 164, 166
MacDonald, Betty, 185
MacInnis, Helen, 171
MacPhail, Larry, 166
Magidoff, Robert, 193
Manney, Richard, 165, 170, 174, 198
Marble, Alice, 117, 157
March, Fredric, 178
Marquand, John P., 156, 177
Marshall, Herbert, 163
Marx, Groucho, 15, 68, 167
Marx, Harpo, 27, 46, 153
Mason, F. Van Wyke, 162, 193
Mason, James, 191-192
Massey, Raymond, 161, 188, 190, 193, 196-197
Mauldin, Bill, 184, 191
Maverick, Maurie, 157
Maximovich, Mrs. Maxim, 169
McAfee, Mildred, 171
McEvoy, J.P., 158
McGrath, J. Howard, 192
McMahon, Brian, 185, 194
McNutt, Paul V., 168
Melchior, Lauritz, 192
Menjou, Adolphe, 169, 205
Menuhin, Hephzibah, 189
Menuhin, Yehudi, 189
Merivale, Philip, 165
Michener, James, 129-132, 136, 139, 193-195
Mielziner, Jo, 136, 195
Milland, Ray, 160, 182, 185, 193
Miller, Douglas, 168
Montgomery, Robert, 98, 184, 187, 190-191
Moody, Helen Wills, 156
Moore, H. Napier, 157
Morley, Christopher, 27, 39, 112, 117, 120, 124, 157-164, 167, 169-170, 172-175, 177, 179-181, 183-184, 199

Murphy, Robert Cushman, 180-181, 190
Neagle, Dame Anna, 117, 161, 172
New York Post, The, 1, 5, 20, 22, 34, 239
New York Times, The, 1, 51-52, 67, 70, 75, 94, 96-98, 119, 129, 141, 144, 156, 162, 239
New Yorker, The, 1, 12, 15, 20, 33, 108, 200
Newell, Alice, 152
Niven, David, 184
Norris, Kathleen, 154
Nugent, Elliott, 187
O'Connor, Basil, 181
O'Donnell, Emmet, 184
O'Hara, John, 59, 164
Parker, Dorothy, 15, 155, 172
Parker Pen Company, 93, 96, 213, 216, 228, 237, 240
Pearlman, S.J., 164, 178
Pearson, Drew, 62, 168
Pearson, Lester B., 178, 195
Peattie, Donald Culross, 176, 179, 182
Pepper, Claude, 180
Perkins, Wilma Lord, 172
Phelps, William Lyon, 154
Philips, H.I., 156, 171
Piccard, Jean, 185
Pidgeon, Walter, 186
Pitkin, Walter, B., 159
Primrose, William, 184
Pringle, Henry, 159
Rathbone, Basil, 27, 153
Ratoff, Gregory, 64, 136-139, 171-176, 179-181, 185, 188-190
Rawlings, Marjorie Kinnan, 182
Reynolds, Quentin, 89, 178-179, 182, 184, 192
Rice, Elmer, 163, 207
Rice, Grantland, 120, 124, 170, 174
Rickard, Claude, 164
Robinson, Jackie, 96, 189
Rockwell, Doc, 195
Rogers, Jr., Will, 70, 173-174
Romulo, Carlos P., 174
Roosevelt, Elliot, 157, 186
Root, Waverly, 182
Roosevelt, Jr., Theodore, 154
Ruark, Robert C., 190, 193
Rubenstein, Artur, 176, 178, 180, 183-185, 192

Ryskind, Morrie, 155
Sandberg, Carl, 158, 172
Sanders, George, 189, 192
Saunders, Hillary St. George, 175
Schesinger, Jr., Arthur, 120, 124, 184, 186, 188
Schmitt, Gladys, 186
Schulman, Max, 186
Seldes, Gilbert, 4, 155
Sheehan, Vincent, 164
Shepard, Adeil, 188
Sherwood, Robert, 161
Shirer, William, 166, 173
Shulman, Max, 186, 189
Shuster, Dr. George N., 168
Simms, P. Cal, 158
Simpson, Kenneth, 161-162, 164
Skinner, Cornelia Otis, 41, 44, 83, 117, 137-138, 154, 165, 168, 170, 172-174, 182, 184-187, 190, 194-197, 199
Slater, Bill, 183
Smith, Betty, 176, 182
Smith, T.V., 159
Snow, Carmel, 20, 152
Spaeth, Sigmund, 4, 153
Spalding, Albert, 159, 190
Sparkman, John J., 195
Sparks, Ned, 63, 171
Spewak, Bella, 156, 160
Spewak, Sam, 160
St. John, Robert, 172
Stassen, Harold E., 120, 184, 187, 191, 193-194
Stern, Bill, 176, 217
Stewart, Donald Ogden, 165
Stewart, James, 114, 188
Stewart, Jesse, 177
Stickney, Dorothy, 197
Stokes, Thomas, 185
Stout, Rex, 27, 40, 111, 117, 155-156, 158, 161, 165
Struther, Jan, 44, 57, 83, 117, 162-165, 167-171, 173-175, 177-179, 181, 187-188, 199
Stuart, Gloria, 42, 159
Sullivan, Frank, 155, 165, 200
Swing, Raymond Graham, 157
Swope, Herbert Bayard, 21, 163

Taft, Charles, 192
Taylor, Deems, 5, 27, 31, 33, 61, 81, 117, 120, 155-156, 158-161, 163-168, 170-172, 175, 177-181, 183-184, 186-189, 191, 199
Templeton, Alec, 180, 184, 188, 193
Teyte, Maggie, 192
Tharp, Louise Hall, 194
Thompson, Mildred, C., 158, 175, 183
Thompson, Dorothy, 153
Thompson, Hugh, 181
Thurber, James, 158
Tibbett, Lawrence, 182, 191, 196
Tilden, Bill 166
Tobey, Charles W., 189, 191, 195
Tolischus, Otto D., 162
Tone, Franchot, 177
Traubel, Helen, 192
Tunney, Gene, 48, 111-112, 115, 117, 153, 165
Ullman, James Ramsey, 183, 185
Untermeyer, Louis, 31, 158, 172
Van Loon, Hendrik Willem, 154
Walker, Mickey, 186
Walker, Stanley, 156
Wallace, Henry A., 71, 175
Wallace, Judge James G., 164, 166, 181
Wallace, Myron, 28
Wanger, Walter, 162
Waxman, Percy, 152-153
Webb, Clifton, 180-183, 193
Webster, Margaret, 170
Welles, Orson, 64, 113, 172
Wescott, Glenway, 182
West, Rebecca Dame, 190
White, Theodore, 143, 187
Wilkie, Wendell, 82, 95, 114, 117, 160, 174, 177
Wolfert, Ira, 182
Woodward, W.E., 153
Woollcott, Alexander, 62-63, 154, 164, 168, 172
Woolley, Monte, 32, 161
Yost, Walter, 175
Young, Roland, 165, 170, 188

www.ingramcontent.com/pod-product-compliance
Lightning Source LLC
Chambersburg PA
CBHW070939230426
43666CB00011B/2497